The Classic British Novel

The Classic British Novel

EDITED BY
HOWARD M. HARPER JR.
AND CHARLES EDGE

THE UNIVERSITY OF GEORGIA PRESS
ATHENS

Library of Congress Catalog Card Number:
70–158000
International Standard Book Number:
0–8203–0281–3

The University of Georgia Press, Athens 30601

for H. K. Russell

He quietly asserts his rights in the affairs of every day;
he maintains his principles against the Cyclops in his cave
if the dignity of man is challenged; he suffers humiliation
and renews his hope; of his virtues the greatest is charity.

Table of Contents

[vi]

Preface

The epigraph to this book is from an article by H. K. Russell.* His words about Leopold Bloom, rather heretical in 1958, are now widely accepted. We chose them, however, not for their pioneering quality, but for the way in which they reveal Professor Russell himself. Much of what we get out of art is a product of what we bring to it, and it was therefore altogether fitting that Harry Russell should explore the sacramental dimension of *Ulysses*.

During his forty years in the English department at Chapel Hill he became its leading student and teacher of British fiction. In honor of that career we invited his colleagues at Chapel Hill to write essays on classic British novels. The thirteen original essays in this book are the result.

The essays move from the beginning of the English novel as a genre in the mid-eighteenth century to its fullest development in the early twentieth, the range of H. K. Russell's special interest. They deal with most of the major novelists and illustrate many critical approaches. The wide range of approaches is itself a tribute to Professor Russell's critical sophistication and to his role in creating a climate in which freedom and diversity are encouraged.

*"The Incarnation in *Ulysses*," *Modern Fiction Studies,* IV (1958), 53–61.

Introduction

Like the long and varied history of England and its great colonial empire, the history of the British novel is the record of rich and diverse human experience. And it too inevitably comes down to the study and appreciation of individual human beings and their acts. These novelists and their books are concerned, to be sure, with shared human experiences and with universal truths; and the basic ability of fiction to communicate these elements obviously depends upon a common language and, to some extent, at least, upon certain assumptions, values, experiences, and expectations which are shared by the author and his audience. Ultimately, however, our interest in a novel, as in any work of art, is not so much in how it is like other works as in how it is different from them, how it is special, distinctive, unique. We may begin to read Joyce because he is an important figure in "literary history," but we read *Ulysses* over and over again because of the special qualities and great dimensions of its artistic achievement. It contains universal truths and experiences, but their fascination is in the particular and distinctive shape which Joyce gives them. As Henry James said in his famous preface to *The Portrait of a Lady,* the house of fiction has innumerable windows, all of which view the human scene; but what makes a particular window interesting is the consciousness which shapes it and, through it, experiences and records a unique artistic vision of that human scene.

All the essays in this collection are concerned in some way with this unique vision, with the way in which an artist's consciousness has made a novel the particular and distinctive thing that it is. In a novelist of the stature of Fielding or Austen or Joyce, the dimensions of that consciousness and of its creation are huge. Our appreciation and understanding of them will always be partial, and our critical approaches to them always more limited than the work itself. But the critic's sharper focus and narrower field of view can clarify and enlarge our perceptions of the artist's vision.

In this collection a number of critical perspectives are brought to bear on particular British novels. These perspectives are not easy to classify. Most of the essays are eclectic; they combine various critical approaches. But certain dominant critical concerns can be identified.

Several of the essays are concerned primarily with a novelist's response to the intellectual climate of his times, and with the ways in which those responses are reflected in his work. Louis Rubin, in his essay on *Tristram Shandy,* discusses Sterne's views of the epistemological assumptions of his time, and shows, incidentally, why *Tristram Shandy* seems so relevant to many readers today. In his study of *David Copperfield* Sam Barnes shows that Dickens, inspired by the writings of Carlyle to assume the role of heroic man of letters, had already begun to move beyond that rather theatrical posture toward a fuller humanitarianism. Fred Thomson discusses the somewhat conservative political and social attitudes revealed in *Felix Holt,* and their origins in George Eliot's simultaneous attractions toward idealism and realism.

Other forms of historical criticism also appear in the collection. Hugh Holman discusses *The Fortunes of Nigel* as a paradigm of both the Waverley novels and Scott's literary method. The essay by J. O. Bailey on *Jude the Obscure* reveals for the first time details from Hardy's own background which influenced that tragic story. In his essay on *Mrs. Dalloway* Howard Harper sees the development of that novel as an objectification of Virginia Woolf's own psychic conflicts.

Several of the essays are concerned primarily with technique. The study of *Emma* by Charles Edge deals with Jane Austen's use of technique to define characters and themes, especially with the way in which she establishes comparisons and contrasts through the use of specific groups of metaphors. The piece by Dougald McMillan discusses Conrad's use of Christian parallels to reinforce the meaning and structural unity of *Nostromo.* Tom Stumpf's analysis of *Tom Jones* is focused on Fielding's technique of characterization, but it could also be called "epistemological," since it is concerned with Fielding's view of how a character may be known.

Two of the essays could be classified as generic studies. The analysis of *The Monk* by Richard Harter Fogle shows that "Monk" Lewis's archetypal Gothic novel is an earnest effort—much too earnest, in fact—to achieve Aristotelian tragedy. William West's defense of *The Last Chronicle of Barset* argues that Trollope's novel must be judged according to the standards and conventions of comedy.

And, finally, two of the essays seem to be concerned primarily with language. The study of *A Portrait of the Artist as a Young Man* by Weldon Thornton deals with the ways in which Joyce's view of language is related to his epistemology and to his view of the role of the artist. Howard Harper's essay on Lawrence uses the symbolic language of *Fantasia of the Unconscious* as a key to the symbolic action of *Women in Love*.

Despite the diversity of these essays, they are all involved, as we said earlier, with the artist's creative vision and with the ways in which that vision has shaped his work. The novel has many potential dimensions: formal, aesthetic, emotional, ideological, philosophical, religious, ethical, political, historical, sociological, linguistic, symbolic, mythic, psychological, and so on. In reviewing these essays, however, we decided that if one dimension predominates, it is the epistemological: each of the essays is importantly concerned with the problem of knowing, or of learning.

All but two or three of the essays deal rather directly with this problem of how we know: how we learn about reality, about people, about ourselves. In the first essay in the collection Stumpf's central concern is Fielding's epistemology as the basis for his novelistic technique: Tom Jones and the others are seen from the outside because that is the way that we learn about people and know them—not by their thoughts, which we don't know; nor their words, which may be deceiving; but by their acts, by what they do and what they are. This same concern appears in Louis Rubin's essay on *Tristram Shandy,* in Hugh Holman's on *The Fortunes of Nigel,* and to a lesser extent in almost all the other essays.

The novel often serves as a way of learning and knowing for the artist himself, as a vehicle for his attempts to explore, explain, or accept his own nature and experience. We see this aspect emphasized in the essays by Barnes on Dickens, by Bailey on Hardy, by Thornton on Joyce, and by Harper on Virginia Woolf.

Inseparable from epistemology is ontology: questions about knowing and learning are also questions about *being*, the ultimate subject of all literature. Since the possible dimensions of the novel—both in range and in flexibility—are greater than those of any other literary form, it is the form best suited, D. H. Lawrence said, to describe "the whole man alive." The novel is, in his words, "the one bright book of life."

The essays in this collection do not—and could not—tell definitively the story of the one bright book of life. But if they are read together, they can illuminate each other, and sometimes the history of the novel, in interesting and occasionally unexpected ways. Because they are arranged in the order of publication of the novels, they suggest some of the major directions in which the British novel has moved.

The English novel began in earnest with Richardson's *Pamela* (1740), and Fielding's career as a novelist began as a reaction to that book. Over the years most critics have awarded the victory to Fielding, but Richardson, as Dr. Johnson perceived, had more insight into the human heart. And after being overshadowed for a century and a half by the major tradition which comes from Fielding, the psychological concerns of the tradition of Richardson have become ascendant. Most of the controlling values which Fielding advocates—reason, order, justice, charity, decency, straightforwardness, common sense—seem much less relevant to the subjective explorations of modern fiction than they did in novels of the eighteenth and nineteenth centuries.

The modern novel has become overwhelmingly self-conscious. The world of Fielding and the rationalists, in which psychology was seen as sentimental, self-indulgent, imprecise, unreliable, has given way to the world of Joyce, Lawrence, Virginia Woolf, and their heirs, a world in which the ultimate realities are psychological. The Great Chain of Being has been broken, and man is condemned to freedom, condemned to improvise, somehow, a creation from nothing. In such a world the artist himself becomes the creator, and in an ironic fulfillment of the creation according to St. John, the word becomes god. The archetypal modern novel is about a novelist writing a novel.

This regressive self-consciousness is apparent also in the modern developments in novelistic craftsmanship, carried to its extreme in the work of Joyce. The preoccupation with craftsmanship is due in part to the modern epistemological concerns we mentioned earlier: there is now a heightened awareness of method as meaning, a realization that the way in which a novel is told is part of what it is about.

In the typical modern novel the major conflicts are internal and relativistic; in the earlier novel they arise when characters depart too far from generally accepted norms. The norms in the modern novel are discovered or created: the typical twentieth-century plot is about the discovery or creation of meaning. The prominence of symbolic, mythic, and purely linguistic dimensions in the modern novel also reflects this search for meaning.

The creation of meaning is also, of course, the creation of order. The novelist gains satisfaction from creating forms of order; the reader, from perceiving them. Traditionally the novel has been concerned with the social order. Recently the tendency has been to question the basic premises of social order, rather than to criticize behavioral deviations from accepted social norms. A similar development is evident with respect to moral order. The novel's traditional moral concern has become much more radical, so that the modern novel goes beyond the problem of social morality to explore, as William Golding and others do, the question of man's innate depravity. Beneath all of these concerns, of course, is the modern questioning of the cosmic order, a form of order which novelists had taken pretty much for granted until the time of Hardy. A prominent theme of the modern British novel, in fact, is the creation of a satisfying aesthetic order as a substitute for external and traditional forms of order which seem to have lost their validity.

Since the deaths of Joyce and Virginia Woolf in 1941, the British novel has moved in darker directions and into narrower channels. The promising Angry Young Men who emerged just after the war are no longer very young, very angry, or very promising. Not surprisingly, no new novelist of the stature of Joyce or Lawrence has appeared. The one who looms largest in the eyes of contemporary critics is a friend and early disciple of Joyce. It seems somehow fitting that Beckett should now receive the homage of the audience which Joyce created, and that the artist who stretched English prose to its outermost limits should have inspired the one who has shrunk prose to its innermost.

Beckett's is not the only impressive achievement, of course, in the contemporary British novel: Golding, Greene, Durrell, Burgess, Lessing, Powell, and others have written some very fine novels. The historical limits of the present collection of essays are admittedly arbitrary: we chose them because we preferred to deal with novels and novelists already well established as classics.

The Classic British Novel

Tom Jones
from the Outside

THOMAS A. STUMPF

For readers weary of claustrophobic analyses of the human heart in the Richardson tradition, the work of Fielding will always be refreshing, an open window to "England's green and pleasant land." It is all too easy, however, to invest his work with a stagy heartiness, a rude vigor, and roast-beef-of-Olde-England bluntness which are as false to the book as they are to life. *Tom Jones* is not that kind of book, and Fielding is not merely clearing the stale atmosphere of Richardsonian psychology with great gusts of country air. If he prefers to "busy himself out of doors" rather than to crawl about the dark corners of the psyche, it is not merely that he is simple-minded or obsessed with mental hygiene. Like Richardson he is concerned with the problem of *fides fronti,* the problem of trusting appearances. But unlike Richardson he denies that the seeing mind is truer or more important than the world it sees. His attitude, an unwillingness to enter the minds of his characters or to reveal there a very rich inner life, could be called anti-psychologism. Fielding, as he constantly reminds us, is writing a history, writing about the world of real phenomena in which we all must live and act as moral agents. As historian he sees things from the outside, with a painful sense of how inaccessible the "inner realities" really are.

When we speak of "anti-psychologism" in *Tom Jones,* we are, of course, speaking of a relative tendency. Though Fielding does occasionally take us into the minds of his characters, he does so only twice at any length, whereas Richardson, by means of the epistolary form, has us there constantly.[1] Moreover, Fielding takes some pains to explain his unwillingness to enter the minds of his characters. John Coolidge says that "Fielding can supply the 'character' of each person from his omniscient point of view and he almost invariably does so on the person's first appearance."[2] But this is not quite true. We may indeed get an accurate assessment of a character early in his career, but not because Fielding boldly enters his mind and describes everything there. His treatment, in the following passage, of Blifil's reaction to Sophia's preference for Tom is characteristic: "As he did not, however, outwardly express any such disgust, it would be an ill office in us to pay a visit to the inmost recesses of his mind, as some scandalous people search into the most secret affairs of their friends, and often pry into their closets and cupboards, only to discover their poverty and meanness to the world."[3]

In the same way, early in the book, Fielding explicitly declines to enter the minds of Doctor and Captain Blifil, Partridge, Honour, Square, and, indeed, Sophia herself; and when he does enter someone's mind, it is frequently with a parenthesis which indicates that his knowledge is by no means certain. So he says of Tom, who is hastening to return to the declining Allworthy: "nor did the idea of Sophia, I believe, once occur to him on the way" (v, vii, 188). To be sure, his very demurrals usually communicate something about the character. So the mention of "poverty and meanness" in the passage on Blifil pretty well tells us what we would be likely to find if we did enter Blifil's mind. Nevertheless, the refusal to *overtly* do so is significant and involves more than just a well-bred author's sense of decorum.

Fielding's anti-psychologism has been almost universally noted by the critics and has caused some lovers of *Tom Jones,* especially those who associate novelistic excellence with profound exploration of assorted psyches, some rather uneasy moments. In an otherwise appreciative essay, we find the assertion that "scenes take place which do not arise inevitably from character and motive. And the characters themselves are not, in the fullest sense, people. They are almost all 'flat' characters in the tradition of the comedy of humours, that useful but unsubtle theory based on the crude physiological psychology of the Middle Ages."[4] And even Mr. McKillop sounds a trifle defensive on this subject: "We may say that Fielding's treatment of characters eschews detailed psychology and leans heavily on typical patterns of behavior, on a fixed scheme of social relationships, and on the workings of fortune. But to say this is very different from experiencing the effects of the synthesis made by the author."[5]

There have been several explanations, or perhaps defenses, of Fielding's treatment of characters; but it has been most commonly assumed that type-characters, "flat characters," are one of the exigencies of comedy, and that thereby Fielding, "the master of the comic, preserves his own status, and that of the reader, as an observer."[6] Ian Watt, discussing the same problem, agrees that "Fielding's comic purpose itself required an external approach,"[7] because this effectively prevents the sort of sympathetic identification that would be prejudicial to comedy. Watt assigns yet another reason for "Fielding's predominantly external approach to character."[8] His "taxonomic" approach requires him to be interested "only in those features of the individual which are necessary to assign him to his moral and social species."[9] All this is very true; but it is also true that Fielding's anti-psychologism is of a piece with his distrust of contemplation and particularly self-contemplation, and with his notion that too much self-consciousness, or for that matter, motive-mongering, tends finally to divorce one from the real world, from what exists outside of the mind, and is therefore not only dangerous but delusive.

The Man of the Hill is, of course, the perfect example. "Thinking too precisely on th' event" has given him wisdom without social virtue, a spurious wisdom after all. In a world which demands participation, he, in Pope's words, "finds virtue local" (*Dunciad,* iv, 479). George Sherburn and others have shown clearly enough that "good works are the sure manifestation" of good nature,[10] and that "man is naturally and fundamentally a social animal."[11] Virtue must be then, for Fielding, excursive. It must embody a "movement out of the self into right action in the world."[12] Anything, therefore, which minimizes the importance of the outside world (e.g., the doctrine of faith without works, excessive contemplation) is pernicious.

Fielding uses an interesting image to describe the kind of mental narcissism which excludes the outside world altogether.[13] He speaks ironically of "that noble firmness of mind which rolls a man, as it were, within himself, and, like a polished bowl, enables him to run through the world without being once stopped by the calamities which happen to others" (xiv, vi, 668). The image is Horatian and is, interestingly enough, first used by the Man of the Hill, who quotes it in the original:

> Fortis et in seipso totus teres atque rotundus
> Externi ne quid valeat per laeve morari
> In quem manca ruit semper Fortuna.

Immediately after hearing the passage, "Jones smiled at some conceit which intruded itself into his imagination. . . ." Though Fielding characteristically tells us nothing more about this "conceit," we can assume that Jones finds this self-contained insusceptibility to anything external—so obviously achieved by the Man of the Hill—less desirable than Horace makes it out to be. The image recurs in *The Covent-Garden Journal* a few years later, in a letter from the unambiguously named Iago. "Horace, who was a sensible writer, and knew the World, advises every Man to roll himself up in himself, as a polished Bowl which admits of no Rubs from without."[14]

To "make the mind its own place" and to admit "no Rubs from without," while it may be wisdom of a sort, is, for Fielding, a very dubious achievement. An interesting corollary to this is Fielding's relative depreciation of virtues of temperance and continence which are, as it were, the result of the mind working on itself, virtues which do not correspond to what H. K. Miller calls "Fielding's fundamentally social criterion."[15] Temperance and continence are, in fact, what might be called reflexive virtues, and if Fielding undervalued them, it was probably because they smacked too much of self-containment, of a mind that doesn't heed or value the world or even its own body, in short, of the polished bowl. Clarissa is perhaps the object lesson of the way in which a narcissistic chastity admits "no Rubs from without." Fielding's virtue, then, is the virtue of a realist, one who concentrates upon the object perceived rather than the mind perceiving, upon the world rather than the psyche; and this unwillingness to give the mind more importance than he thought it deserved accounts at least in part for his unwillingness to make the minds of his characters the focal point of the novel.

Fielding's anti-psychologism does not only manifest itself in his reluctance to enter the minds of his characters, however. One of the most interesting and certainly one of the most characteristic devices in *Tom Jones* is the narrator's deliberate suggestion of false motives for his characters. This assumption of plausible but not at all correct motives is employed by Fielding in dealing with most of the characters in the book, with the conspicuous exceptions of Allworthy and Tom himself. One of the earliest, and one of the nicest, examples of this is the reaction of Mrs. Wilkins upon hearing of Allworthy's decision to disregard her advice and adopt the abandoned bastard: "Such was the discernment of Mrs. Wilkins, and such the respect she bore her master, under whom she enjoyed a most excellent place, that her scruples gave way to his peremptory commands; and she took the child under her arms without any apparent disgust at the illegality of its birth; and declaring it was a sweet little infant, walked off with it to her own chamber" (I, iii, 8). That deadly parenthesis, "under whom she enjoyed a most excellent place," makes it clear enough to the reader that Mrs. Deborah's "discernment" is a discernment of her own interests and that the word "apparent" is used with deliberate irony. The principle is the same, however. Remove the parenthetical asides and we are presented with what might be at least plausible motives for such an action.

Blifil is a frequent object for this exercise of Fielding's irony. When he tattles on Black George, altering the circumstances to make the gamekeeper's crime seem more heinous, the narrator attributes it to love of justice: "Master Blifil fell very short of his companion in the amiable quality of mercy; but he as greatly exceeded him in one of a much higher kind, namely, in justice" (III, x, 103). And much later, when Blifil has been brutally repulsed in his wooing of Sophia, the narrator comments that "the philosophy which he had acquired from Square, and the religion infused into him by Thwackum, together with somewhat else, taught him to bear" the affront (x, viii, 479). By this time, of course, we are aware that Blifil's devotion to either philosophy or religion is largely a sham, and we more than suspect that the "somewhat else," which the narrator seems to drop almost by accident, is the selfish coldness of Blifil's nature. The reader is not deceived here, but Fielding retains his almost maidenish coyness about ever plainly assigning true motives. Sometimes he does this to the point of absurdity, as when Bridget Allworthy's eavesdropping is described as becoming "acquainted with her brother's inclinations without giving him the trouble of repeating them to her" (I, vii, 21).

Fielding's narrator has almost assumed for ironic purposes the role of a rather simple-minded *naif,* relating the facts and anxious to put the best construction on them he can imagine, leaving the reader, with his own rather more sophisticated knowledge of the world, to make more accurate judgments. It is, moreover, a technique Fielding applies to more amiable characters than the redoubtable Bridget or the odious Blifil. The much berated Jenny Jones is finally assaulted by a woman who allows that " 'The man must have a good stomach who would give silk gowns for such sort of trumpery!' Jenny replied to this with a bitterness which might have surprised a judicious person who had observed the tranquility with which she bore all the affronts to her chastity; but her patience was perhaps tired out . . ." (I, vi, 16). The reader, who is not as innocent as the narrator appears to be, will probably conclude that, as Jenny values beauty more than chastity, so she can more easily see the latter disparaged than the former. In like manner, when the bare-breasted Mrs. Waters refuses Jones's offer of a coat, we can guess the reason why, though the narrator solemnly assures us that *he* doesn't know. But then he also supposes that Mrs. Waters was "awakened from her sleep" to find "two men fighting in her bedchamber" (x, ii, 450). He even credits Sophia with more modest reserve than, in fact, she has: "Jones, who had hitherto held this lovely burthen in his arms, now relinquished his hold; but gave her at the same instant a tender caress, which, had her senses been then perfectly restored, could not have escaped her observation. As she expressed, therefore, no displeasure at this freedom, we suppose she was not sufficiently recovered from her swoon at the time" (v, xii, 210). The reader will suppose otherwise; but by being forced so consistently to see motives less noble than those suggested by the narrator, the reader may find, to his annoyance, that he is providing a faintly cynical knowledge of the world while the narrator escapes with his innocence. And should he know Fielding very well, he may wonder, though only fleetingly, if he isn't subjecting himself to the condemnation reserved for those who judge ill of the world because of the flaws of their own hearts.

Much of this, of course, is simply a matter of Fielding fondly indulging his sense of irony, but Ronald Paulson suggests a more intriguing reason. "As a satirist he is overwhelmingly interested in actions, and his aim is to distinguish the good from the evil; but as he learns how misleading not only words but even actions and consequences can be, he finds it increasingly difficult to judge them except in terms of motives. . . . Through the ironic complexity of *Tom*

Jones he seems to say that motive is so difficult to assign that only much later, by surprise, by accident, can we see behavior as good or evil." [16] If Paulson is right, we might conclude that Fielding's reluctance to assign precise "causes" to the actions he depicts is the result of a despair of ever being able to assess motives accurately. By the same token, moreover, the narrator's consistent misjudgment of motives, which we noticed above, could simply be ironic evidence of the fact that motives are "so difficult to assign." This is a clear and attractive theory but not, I think, an entirely satisfying one.

One reason is that it assumes the importance of motive-hunting and thereby fails to take into account Fielding's distrust of mere psychology, of that which tends to exalt the mind above the world outside it where actions take place. Another reason, perhaps connected with the first, is that it ignores the author's sense of himself as a mere reporter, too humble to speculate about such theoretical niceties as motives or causes, content only to record and observe the facts:

> . . . for it is our province to relate facts, and we shall leave causes to persons of much higher genius. (ii, iv, 49)

> I shall set forth the plain matter of fact, and leave the whole to the reader's determination. (iv, vi, 126)

> We would have these gentlemen know we can see what is odd in characters as well as themselves, but it is our business to relate facts as they are; which, when we have done, it is the part of the learned and sagacious reader to consult that original book of nature. . . . (vii, xii, 314)

One example (and there are many) of this scrupulous, almost judicial avoidance of the tendentious occurs when the narrator admits that Mrs. Waters had an assignation with Ensign Northerton and yet adds gallantly "with what view and for what purpose must be left to the reader's divination; for though we are obliged to relate facts, we are not obliged to do violence to our nature by any comments to the disadvantage of the loveliest part of the creation" (ix, vii, 443).

In each of these cases Fielding's confidence in his own role of a simple recorder of facts depends upon an equally unshakeable confidence in the ability of the "facts," the events and episodes of the novel, to speak for themselves. The presumption is that judicious observation is finally more important than psychological speculation, that indeed, as the Mrs. Waters-Ensign Northerton assignation makes perfectly clear, there is no need to go into the characters' minds if one attends carefully enough to what they *do*. In the same way, the narrator's consistently wrongheaded attributions of motive provide an almost burlesque *monitum* to those who believe that actions tell us nothing unless we are privy to the motives of the agents. In short, Fielding is a realist who finds that he must go for truth not to that mare's nest, the human mind, but to what is obvious, external, and present to the senses—human actions.

The idea of letting the facts speak for themselves requires some qualification and defense. This is a novel, after all, built around imposition, deceit, and affectation, a novel in which the facts sometimes seem strangely reluctant to speak for themselves, a novel in which characters and reader and narrative *persona* are often duped, or at least surprised. Finally, it is a novel in which, it would seem, the constant ironic undercutting of the narrator effectively prevents the facts from speaking for themselves.[17] This last objection has particular force since it is true that the narrator, despite or because of his persistent misapplication of motives, in effect indicates motives through a kind of *via negativa*. Even here, however, we are seldom told all. In some cases, as in Bridget's love for the infant Jones, the motives assigned by the narrator do not imply the true motives, and the reader is left to guess as best he may. In other cases, the "facts," the scenes or actions presented by Fielding, provide a necessary context for assessing the narrator's irony. Thus the true nature of Mrs. Deborah's "respect" and "discernment" becomes evident when we see her browbeating her social inferiors in the village. And finally there are characters like Tom himself about whom the narrator *says* relatively little but whom he *shows* in innumerable small actions which effectively define his character.

But what about the affectation and deceit which pervade the novel? Are they not indicative of the *inability* of the facts to speak for themselves, the necessity of knowing motives, and therefore the greater importance of knowing what goes on in the mind? We have already noted Fielding's distrust of contemplation, particularly self-contemplation, and his disapproval of anyone who is imprisoned within his own mind. As Morris Golden says, "Preoccupation with the self causes, and manifests itself in, limited ways of knowing";[18] and this certainly accounts for a good deal of the misjudgment in the book, particularly on the part of those characters who tend to posit selfish and interested motives for all human actions. As Fielding writes in *The Champion,* "those who deduce actions, apparently good, from evil causes can trace them only through the windings of their own hearts."[19] And in an oft-quoted passage from *Tom Jones,* Fielding speaks harshly of "the truth-finder," who, "having raked out that jakes, his own mind, and being there capable of tracing no ray of divinity, nor anything virtuous or good, or lovely, or loving, very fairly, honestly, and logically concludes that no such things exist in the whole creation" (vi, i, 215).

Though these are generalizations, the novel is full of instances of people who judge unworthily because of the unworthiness of their own minds. Captain Blifil, for example, is convinced that Allworthy, "notwithstanding his disinterested professions . . . , would . . . refuse his consent to a match so disadvantageous, in point of interest, to his sister" (i, xi, 33). Partridge is also unconvinced by Allworthy's apparent goodness and cannot believe that his pension is not due to some ulterior motive. Mrs. Western, of course, overreaches herself as regularly as Polonius, but most especially when she has to judge someone as artless as Sophia: "To sum the whole, no species of disguise or affectation had escaped her notice; but as to the plain simple workings of honest nature, as she had never seen any such, she could know but little of them" (vi, ii, 218). All these are good examples of characters preoccupied with the machinations of their own minds and unwilling to accept anything as simple and straightforward as the appearances of things, characters who are, as a result of continually hunting for hidden motives, continually deceived. But Squire Allworthy, than whom none can be more candid and open-hearted, is also continually deceived and, it would seem, for much the same reason. As George Sherburn writes, "The Good Man cannot, for example, be suspicious, since he is innocent of any knowledge of evil."[20] Accurate character judgment, then, would seem to be largely a matter of chance: "the good mistake the motives of the evil, and the evil mistake those of the good,"[21] in which case, to get back to our original problem, the facts of a given case in no sense speak for themselves since, by the very nature of his psychology, the good man will understand other good men and misunderstand the wicked, regardless of what they may do.

If this is the case, there is no reason to trust to an accurate observation of the facts, since we will know only by kindred sympathy and, finally, will know only variants of ourselves. I think the novel makes it fairly clear, however, that this kind of knowledge is neither desirable nor inevitable. First of all, Allworthy subjects himself to censure as surely as does Mrs. Western. Like her he judges the world by what exists in his own mind, and Fielding condemns this on general principles: "Doth the man who recognises in his own heart no traces of avarice or ambition, conclude, therefore, that there are no such passions in human nature? Why will we not modestly observe the same rule in judging of the good as well as the evil of others? Or why in any case, will we, as Shakespeare phrases it, 'put the world in our own person'" (vi, i, 216). Fielding may be directing his remarks primarily at those of the Mandevillian persuasion, but the shoe fits Allworthy well enough. Allworthy is flawed because the state of his own mind prevents him from seeing the world as it really is, as it presents itself before his eyes.

If it is argued, as Sherburn or Golden would seem to argue, that this is an inevitable occupational hazard of being good, we might first of all reply that Fielding is hardly likely to condemn what cannot be amended; and secondly, and more convincingly, we might point to the examples of Tom and Sophia. Both of them, especially Sophia, are remarkably accurate judges of character, while remaining at the same time innocent and admirable.

Though Fielding does not call attention to it, the difference between Sophia's sagacity (the evidence of her name is surely not accidental) and Allworthy's gullibility is great enough to require some sort of explanation. "Sophia, when very young, discerned that Tom, though an idle, thoughtless, rattling rascal, was nobody's enemy but his own; and that Master Blifil, though a prudent, discreet, sober young gentleman, was at the same time strongly attached to the interest only of one single person. . . . She honoured Tom Jones and scorned Master Blifil, almost as soon as she knew the meaning of those two words" (iv, v, 118). In fact, the early part of the novel is full of examples of Sophia's discernment. She draws perfectly accurate conclusions about Blifil and Jones from the former's release of her bird and the latter's rescue of her person, and she is, moreover, able to guess the truth of the Jones-Seagrim affair with fairly little trouble. It may be objected that Sophia is not simply letting facts speak for themselves here, that she has a strong emotional interest in these matters which both colors and assists her judgment. But no such objection can be made in the case of Mrs. Fitzpatrick. Neither Sophia nor the reader has had access to Mrs. Fitzpatrick's private thoughts, and we know only what that lady has told us; yet the reader agrees with Sophia when she conceives "an opinion that her cousin was really not better than she should be" (xi, x, 534).

Now since Fielding, as we have seen, has frequently asserted that it is the wicked mind that most easily smells out wickedness, he obviously has some explaining to do. What he says about Sophia's shrewdness here seems to me of the utmost importance in assessing his general anti-psychologism and his profession to give only the facts, with the attendant implication that the facts will speak for themselves. Fielding decides to provide

> a word or two to our reader touching suspicion in general.
> Of this there have always appeared to me to be two degrees. The first of these I choose to derive from the heart, as the extreme velocity of its discernment seems to denote some previous inward impulse, and the rather as this superlative degree often forms its own objects—sees what is not, and always more than really exists. This is that quick-sighted penetration whose hawk's eyes no symptom of evil can escape . . . and, as it proceeds from the heart of the observer, so it dives into the heart of the observed, and there espies evil, as it were, in the first embryo—nay, sometimes before it can be said to have been conceived.
> A second degree of this quality seems to arise from the head. This is, indeed, no other than the faculty of seeing what is before your eyes, and of drawing conclusions from what you see. . . . From this degree of suspicion she had, in fact, conceived an opinion that her cousin was really not better than she should be. (xi, x, 533–534)

The mode of character judgment which Fielding finds most important, therefore, is not a kind of unnatural sagacity in which mind penetrates mind but an ability to see, objectively and comprehensively, the facts, the external phenomena which are placed before us.

To the reader of Fielding's *Miscellanies,* this will come as no surprise.[22] The phrase "seeing what is before our own eyes" is constantly used by Fielding to express the most perfect kind of character judgment. A number of the *Covent-Garden Journal* approvingly quotes Cardinal de Retz: "Custom blinds us with a Kind of Glare to those objects before our Eyes, and I have often doubted whether we should have been as much surprised at Caligula, when he made his horse a Consul, as we are apt to imagine we should have been."[23] Perhaps we might view Mrs. Western's preoccupation with the manners of the town in this light. In the important "Essay on the Knowledge of the Characters of Men," Fielding writes: "I have often thought mankind would be little liable to deceit (at least much less than they are) if they would believe their own eyes, and judge of men by what they actually see them perform towards those with whom they are most closely connected . . . " (xiv, 301). One can be blinded by one's own interest, as in the case of the landlady at Upton who, scenting profit from the gentlefolk, tries to persuade the chambermaid Susan that the bedroom farce she witnessed did not take place at all. " 'Well,' says Susan, 'then I must not believe my own eyes.'—'No, indeed, must you not always,' answered her mistress . . . " (x, iii, 454).

An even greater danger is an overnice inquiry into motives. In the "Essay on the . . . Characters of Men," Fielding says plainly that we should not trouble ourselves about possible changes of heart but simply proceed with the awareness that "as the actions of men are the best index to their thoughts . . . they do, if well attended to and understood, with the utmost certainty demonstrate the character" (xiv, 302). Though Fielding admits that motive can be important, it is more important from the point of view of character judgment to note what we can see than to imagine what we cannot: "Actions are their own best expositors; and though crimes may admit of alleviating circumstances . . . from the motive for instance, as necessity may lessen the crime of robbery . . . yet the crime is still robbery, and the person who commits it is a robber; though he should pretend to have done it with a good design, or the world should concur in calling him an honest man" (xiv, 290–291). In short, then, "the actions of men seem to be the justest interpreters of their thoughts, and the truest standards by which we may judge them" (xiv, 289). The facts will, therefore, more often than not speak for themselves if we look at them clearly, not blinded by custom or interest and, even more important, not obsessed with the kind of motive-mongering that, as we have seen, so consistently marks Fielding's gullible narrator and many of the characters, from Captain Blifil to Partridge, in *Tom Jones.*

Sometimes, indeed, Fielding reinforces these beliefs even when he is being most ironic about them. At one point he implies that while facts observed may speak for themselves, facts related are another matter. When Jones relates his life history to Partridge, Fielding concludes:

> . . . for let a man be never so honest, the account of his own conduct will, in spite of himself, be so very favourable, that his vices will come purified through his lips, and, like foul liquors well strained, will leave all their foulness behind. For though the facts themselves may appear, yet so different will be the motives, circumstances, and consequences, when a man tells his own story, and when his enemy tells it, that we scarce can recognize the facts to be one and the same. (vii, v, 352)

But there is a double irony here, for indeed Jones has no vices, no foulness, and almost all the facts known to the reader, almost all of Jones's *actions,* simply reinforce our impression of his innocence and goodness, so that regardless of who tells the story, the facts themselves *do* give an accurate impression. When young Blifil reports to his uncle on the bloody nose he has received from Tom, he must, to get a favorable hearing, not only color the facts but materially alter them.

On the other hand, actions might be deliberately performed to mislead or deceive, and in such a case would not reveal the man. Fielding recognizes this in an interesting passage in "The Champion," but at the same time, with characteristic irony, he refuses us the comfortable conclusion that actions are therefore no index of character: "By this virtue, which is generally called charity itself . . . is not meant the ostentatious giving a penny to a beggar in the street (an ostentation of which I do not accuse the clergy, having to my knowledge never seen one guilty of it . . .)" (xv, 270). It is possible, Fielding implies, that one who publicly gives alms is ostentatious, but it is certain that one who does not is niggardly; and we suspect that to do good deeds, even for bad motives, is a bit better than doing no good deeds at all. It is an almost constant maxim with Fielding, therefore, that actions are the best, perhaps the only way to reveal character, that excursions into the psyche are in real life dangerously delusive and set a bad example in fiction. It is only proper then that in the novel the "actions," the events of the plot, should be allowed to speak for themselves. For all the narrator may posit ridiculous motives, hint at genuine ones, posture, and roll his eyes, he must remain outside, never telling us what we could not have guessed and frequently much less. Empson puts it with admirable succinctness: "I take it he refused to believe that the inside of a person's mind (as given by Richardson in a letter, perhaps) is much use for telling you the real source of his motives. You learn that from what he does, and therefore a novelist ought to devise an illustrative plot."[24]

It is not quite enough to show, as R. S. Crane has shown, that the plot of *Tom Jones* is not just a mechanical marvel, like Locke's "famous clock at Strasbourg,"[25] ticking its merry, intricate way while lively but shallow characters scurry about like mice, occasionally getting caught in the works. The actions of the plot not only arise from the nature of the characters, they reveal those characters to us. It is simply not true that Fielding provides each of his figures with a kind of Theophrastian character as he is introduced. We learn about Jones, for instance, from what he does. We see him refusing to peach on Black George and enduring his punishment with courage. We are also told about his boyish pranks—all this before Fielding's narrator comments, almost reluctantly, "that Tommy Jones was an inoffensive lad amidst all his roguery" (III, iv, 86). By the same token, we are told of Blifil's prattling piety, we hear him call Tom a beggarly bastard, we see him lose the fight and run weeping to Allworthy with a convenient lie. All this is perfectly illustrative. There needs no narrator to tell us of the relative merits of the boys or to take us on a circumstantial tour of their minds. Our opinion of Jones is built up episodically: his generous attempt to recapture Sophy's bird, his rescue of Sophia herself, his attempts to relieve the Seagrims through the sale of his horse and Bible, his cherishing the muff, his rescue of the Man of the Hill, his forgiveness of the highwayman, his good offices for Nightingale, even his various amours—all these are things which *show* us Tom's good nature. Wayne Booth is a bit off the mark when he opines that "Tom's conduct frequently becomes so imprudent that most readers, unaided by the narrator, might find it difficult to remember the real virtue that prompts his actions."[26] The most questionable thing that Tom does is to allow himself to be kept by Lady Bellaston, but by this point we have already *seen* him do so many good things that our good opinion is really in no danger.

It would be incorrect, of course, to try to maintain that Fielding always and exclusively reveals characters through action, and it is interesting that the most conspicuous exception is Allworthy. It is unnecessary for Fielding to tell us constantly about Blifil's malice, Tom's good nature, Sophia's charm, or Squire Western's oafish brutality. But he does remind us again and again of Allworthy's excellence. The result is that Allworthy is the least alive of any of the characters, and the reason, it seems to me, is that Allworthy doesn't *do* anything. He is the one character who is not continually revealed by the actions of the plot. Fielding does have to tell us about him, and to reiterate the message rather frequently and nervously, since the reader who "sees what is before his eyes" recognizes only a well-intentioned, faintly pompous gull—however many pensions may be distributed offstage.

If the reader of the novel learns about the characters by a discerning observation of the facts placed before his eyes, the same is true of the characters in their relationships with each other. We have already commented on Sophia's ability to judge character, and the same is true, for the most part, about Tom. One scene, especially, illustrates Fielding's conviction that even small and insignificant facts can speak as effectively as volumes of confessional correspondence. Maurice Johnson has written of the importance of Sophia's muff;[27] and we might here call attention to Sophia's harpsichord playing. The squire, brawlingly grateful to Tom for having rescued Sophia from a refractory horse, offers him that very horse as a reward.

> " . . . She cost me fifty guineas, and comes six years old this grass."—"If she had cost me a thousand," cries Jones passionately, "I would have given her to the dogs."—"Pooh! pooh!" answered Western; "what! because she broke thy arm?"
> . . . The countenance of Sophia had undergone more than one change during the foregoing speeches; and probably she imputed the passionate resentment which Jones had expressed against the mare to a different motive from that from which her father had derived it. Her spirits were at this time in a visible flutter; and she played so intolerably ill, that had not Western soon fallen asleep he must have remarked it. Jones, however, who was sufficiently awake, and was not without an ear any more than without eyes, made some observations. . . . (v, ii, 166–167)

What is interesting here, I think, is the almost complete externalization of emotion—the way Fielding, in a few words and a single event, literally embodies the emotions of his characters. Jones's romantically ridiculous statement, passionately cried, Sophia's poor playing and visible flutter—all exemplify Fielding's notion that what goes on before our eyes is pregnant with meaning, whether or not the narrator calls attention to it, if we will be but a bit more observant than Squire Western.

It will be remembered that it is not only Sophia's bad playing but her "visible flutter" that reveals her to Tom in the passage quoted above, and this introduces yet another problem. If what happens on the outside, in the world of appearances, is more revealing and finally more important than the tortuous shadings of the human mind, then everything which is external is significant—not just actions but physical appearance, countenance, complexion, gesture. We are up against the problem of physiognomy. Fielding is by no means perfectly clear in his attitude toward physiognomy; but he is intrigued by it, and the phrase that keeps recurring to his mind is Juvenal's *nulla fides fronti*. Partridge uses it in *Tom Jones*, though in very ironic circumstances,[28] and Fielding devotes a whole section of the "Essay on the Knowledge of the Characters of Men" to a proper understanding of the phrase. He insists that it must be taken in context, and that Juvenal simply meant to say "that an austere countenance is no token of purity of heart" (xiv, 284). He goes on to say, "I conceive the passions of men do commonly imprint sufficient marks on the countenance. . . ." This is as clear a statement of principle as one could desire, but Fielding allows later that although "nature doth really imprint sufficient marks in the countenance to inform an accurate and discerning eye," this "discerning eye" is a rare phenomenon, "the property of few" (xiv, 288–289). For those who have it, however, this is yet another way in which the characters of men become apparent to the human eye, without the necessity of entering the recesses of the heart.

Of course Fielding cannot in *Tom Jones* present an illustrative countenance as easily as he can present an illustrative action, but the book is, nevertheless, full of physiognomical observations. Sophia is beautiful, and Fielding tells us, "Such was the outside of Sophia; nor was this beautiful frame disgraced by an inhabitant unworthy of it" (iv, ii, 111). Molly Seagrim is florid and healthy, and Fielding tells us, "Nor was her mind more effeminate than her person. As this was tall and robust, so was that bold and forward" (iv, vi, 126). Lady Bellaston, as Squire Western sees her, is a "fat-assed b--ch," and, mutatis mutandis, even this pithy description might enable us to draw a few accurate conclusions about her mind. In situations throughout the novel the face frequently reveals the mind. Thus Tom is able to deduce something of Sophia's love from her countenance: "for love may again be likened to a disease in this, that when it is denied a vent in one part, it will certainly break out in another. What her lips, therefore, concealed, her eyes, her blushes, and many little involuntary actions, betrayed" (v, ii, 166). Thwackum and Square, upon hearing Allworthy's will, tell us and the narrator a great deal by means of "the discontent which appeared in their countenances" (v, viii, 193). And even the infamous Blifil, that master of deceit and disguise, is smoked out by the sort of sudden question which, as Fielding comments, "causes frequently such an alteration in the countenance, that the man is obliged to give evidence against himself" (xviii, v, 835–836). Though Allworthy remains as perfectly obtuse as ever, it is as if Fielding were crying to the other characters in the book and indeed to the reader, "he who has eyes to see, let him see."

Though it is always dangerous, even for the "discerning eye," to read a character by physiognomy alone, sometimes appearances are so persuasive that they force conclusions; and this is clearly the case with Tom himself. The novel contains an incredible parade of characters, not all of them wise or sophisticated—the Quaker, Partridge, Mrs. Whitefield, the Man of the Hill, Mrs. Miller, et. al.—who are forced by Tom's appearance to recognize not only his good nature but his gentility as well. Certainly the frail Mrs. Waters was not proof against a face which, "besides being the picture of health, had in it the most apparent marks of sweetness and good-nature" (ix, v, 433). Like so many of the characters, and indeed like the reader, she sees Tom Jones from the outside—what he looks like, what he does—and, like the reader, she requires no more.

We spoke at the beginning of the essay about Fielding's adherence to the kind of realism that places true knowledge in the proper appraisal of the objects outside us rather than in a delicate—I am tempted to say neurasthenic—self-consciousness. We spoke of his distrust of those who are wrapped up in their own minds, or whose minds provide a distorting filter which prevents them from seeing what lies before their eyes. We noted his unwillingness to "psychologize" his characters and his conviction that actions, and even countenances, if properly observed, will tell us more than all the subtle tracking of motives in the secret places of the heart. If we had to place some sort of generalization, some philosophical conviction, behind or beneath this complexus of attitudes, we could best do so, I think in the following passage from *Tom Jones*. "The truth is, as the sagacious Sir

Roger L'Estrange observes, in his deep reflections, that 'if we shut Nature out at the door, she will come in at the window . . . ' " (xII, ii, 541). It is a sentiment which Fielding echoes frequently when his characters are trying to conceal themselves. It is, in short, the nature of nature, like the nature of God, to reveal itself, to communicate itself. We can detect here, perhaps, some of the eighteenth century's distrust of the arcane, the hidden. Nature will out, and it is thus that we can see the happy ending of *Tom Jones* as not simply ingenious but inevitable. It is the nature of nature to reveal itself, to make appearance a genuine indication of reality, and therefore affectation is profoundly unnatural; and, as Mrs. Miller says, "time will show all matters in their true and natural colours" (xvII, vii, 804). What happens at the end of the book (as at the end of all high comedy) is that nature reasserts itself, and we are reassured that, to us and to the characters of the book, things are once again what they appear to be —what we can see is what there is to know.

Notes

1. See the treatment of Allworthy throughout, especially in I, ii and iv, and also the treatment of Blifil in xvIII, xi.

2. "Fielding and the 'Conservation of Character,' " *MP*, LVII (1960), 246.

3. *Tom Jones* (New York, 1950), p. 112 (IV, iii). Subsequent references will be included in the text and will cite book and chapter numbers as well as the page numbers of the easily accessible Modern Library edition.

4. Arnold Kettle, *"Tom Jones,"* in *Fielding: A Collection of Critical Essays*, ed. Ronald Paulson (Englewood Cliffs, 1962), p. 85.

5. A. D. McKillop, "Some Present Views of *Tom Jones*," *College English*, xxI (1959), 20.

6. A. P. Humphreys, "Fielding's Irony: Its Method and Effects," *RES*, xvIII (1942), 188.

7. *The Rise of the Novel* (Berkeley, 1959), p. 265.

8. Ibid., p. 272.

9. Ibid.

10. "Fielding's Social Outlook," *PQ*, xxxv (1956), 8.

11. Henry Knight Miller, *Essays on Fielding's "Miscellanies": A Commentary on Volume One* (Princeton, 1961), p. 185.

12. Morris Golden, *Fielding's Moral Psychology* (Amherst, Mass., 1964), p. 128.

13. This subject is treated extensively in Morris Golden's book (note 12) in a chapter entitled "Self-Enclosure in the Novels," though Golden, surprisingly enough, does not mention the "polished bowl" metaphor.

14. *The Covent Garden Journal,* ed. G. E. Jensen (New Haven, 1915), I, 260. All subsequent references to this work are taken from this edition.

15. Miller, p. 79.

16. Paulson, *Fielding,* p. 9. See also Irvin Ehrenpreis, *Fielding: Tom Jones* (London, 1963), p. 49: "Through his very style of 'externalised' narrator, Fielding implies that nobody can see into another man's heart."

17. This idea runs throughout Eleanor N. Hutchen's *Irony in Tom Jones* (University, Ala., 1965).

18. *Fielding's Moral Psychology,* p. 42.

19. Henry Fielding, *Works,* ed. W. E. Henley (New York, 1967), xv, 94. Subsequent references to *The Champion* and the "Essay on the Knowledge of the Characters of Men" will be to volume and page of this edition.

20. *Tom Jones* (New York, 1950), p. x.

21. Golden, p. 66.

22. Those who have written on the "Essay on the Knowledge of the Characters of Men" have, of course, noted what Fielding says there about judging others from their actions. (See especially Miller, pp. 189–228, and Golden, pp. 31–32, 67.) To the best of my knowledge, however, none have connected this with Fielding's anti-psychologism, or even applied it very closely to his practice in *Tom Jones.* The recurrence of the phrase "believing one's own eyes" has, as far as I know, gone unnoticed.

23. I, 239.

24. William Empson, "Tom Jones," in Paulson, p. 135.

25. John Locke, *Essay Concerning Human Understanding,* ed. Alexander Fraser (New York, 1959), II, 58.

26. "The Self-Conscious Narrator in Comic Fiction before *Tristram Shandy,*" *PMLA,* LXVII (1952), 178.

27. *Fielding's Art of Fiction* (Philadelphia, 1961), pp. 129–138.

28. XVI, v, 759. Partridge uses it to describe his own hilarious reaction to a performance of *Hamlet.*

The White Bear

LOUIS D. RUBIN JR.

In all the nine books of *Tristram Shandy* there is no more fetching passage than that which concludes the fifth volume. Walter Shandy is explaining to Yorick, his brother Toby, and Corporal Trim the salient features of the *Tristrapoedia,* the system of education which is to preserve the young Tristram from the misfortune that by his fifth year has already threatened to mar all his future days. There is, declares Mr. Shandy, a "North-west passage to the intellectual world," whereby the mind of a youth may be guided toward its mastery. It consists of a thorough education in the auxiliary verbs, by which one may "in a few lessons . . . teach a young gentleman to discourse with plausibility upon any subject, *pro* and *con,* and to say and write all that could be spoken or written concerning it, without blotting a word, to the admiration of all who beheld him." Properly used, the auxiliaries could "set the soul a going by herself upon the materials as they are brought her; and by the versatility of this great engine, round which they are twisted, to open new tracks of enquiry, and make every idea engender millions."[1]

Yorick's curiosity is greatly aroused; Uncle Toby does not understand at all. Corporal Trim thinks Mr. Shandy is talking about military auxiliaries, and specifically the Danes who were on the left at the siege of Limerick. "And very good ones, said my uncle *Toby.*—— But the auxiliaries, *Trim,* my brother is talking about,—I conceive to be different things——" (v, 406).

As indeed they are, for after Mr. Shandy has taken a turn across the room, he explains. "The verbs auxiliary we are concerned with here," he continues, "are, *am; was; have; had; do; did; make; made; suffer; shall; should; will; would; can; could; owe; ought; used;* or *is wont.*——And these varied with tenses, *present, past, future,* and conjugated with the verb *see,*——or with these questions added to them;——*Is it? Was it? 'Will it be? Would it be? May it be? Might it be?* And these again put negatively, *Is it not? Was it not? Ought it not?*—Or affirmatively—*It is; It was; It ought to be.* Or chronologically,——*Has it been always? Lately? How long ago?*——Or hypothetically,——*If it was; if it was not?* What would follow?——If the *French* should beat the *English?* If the *Sun* go out of the *Zodiac?*" (v, 406).

The auxiliary verbs thus constitute an infallible system for organizing and mastering all knowledge, for they are the vehicle whereby, through analogy, metaphor, and comparison, all ideas and concepts, no matter how seemingly remote or recondite, may be grasped and understood. With them at his disposal, the young Tristram will be prepared for whatever varieties of experience may lie ahead; no matter what he encounters, he will possess the cerebral tools for handling and shaping it to size. "Now, by the right use and application of these, continued my father, in which a child's memory should be exercised, there is no one idea can enter his brain how barren soever, but a magazine of conceptions and conclusions may be drawn forth from it" (v, 406).

Whereupon, without a moment's break in his discourse, to prove his hypothesis and to drive home his point by an example that even so singularly literal a mind as Corporal Trim's can comprehend, he offers a magnificent illustration: "——Did'st thou ever see a white bear? cried my father, turning his head round to *Trim,* who stood at the back of his chair . . ." (v, 406).

It is the incongruity that does it—the sudden concreteness of the example, coming after the splendidly abstract disquisition, pronounces the absurdity. It is a mixture, or an abrupt change rather, in levels of discourse, resulting in a thundering anti-climax. But it is more than that. It is a masterly dramatic stroke on the author's part, a marvelous device of characterization. The breathlessness with which the inquiry is made, terminating as it does an impassioned philosophical exposition by the redoubtable Mr. Shandy, not only demonstrates his intensity, but is emblematic of the mad ingenuity whereby Mr. Shandy contrives to bring his brilliantly bizarre theorizings down to earth, thus bravely adapting his cosmological systematizing to the imperfect everyday world he must inhabit, peopled by intellects so regrettably inferior to his own. "Did'st thou ever see a white bear?" You may not, that is, know what an auxiliary verb is, Trim and Toby, but you know what white is, and what a bear is, and you can imagine a white bear even though your eyes have never gazed upon one.

But even if one *can* imagine a white bear, what of it? That is the implied moral of the passage. As Tristram observes, "Did my father, mother, uncle, aunt, brothers or sisters, ever see a white bear? What would they give? How would they behave? How would the white bear have behaved? Is he wild? Tame? Terrible? Rough? Smooth?—Is the white bear worth seeing?—Is there no sin in it?—Is it better than a BLACK ONE?" (v, 407). How different, in short, the reality of the white bear from the theory of the concept. And how much more formidable, more believable, in its very concreteness, the image of the white bear than the systems of knowledge and schemes of epistemological grouping. How vast the gap between explanation and experience, and how insubstantial Mr. Shandy's hypothesis before the actual example itself. So that, if at first it is the descent in level of discourse that seems to be amusing, it turns out that the example is really more noteworthy than the theory. Not the absurdity of the illustrative example, but the inadequacy of the philosophical system to regulate the image drawn from the recalcitrant world of things, is where the humor—and the pathos—lie.

What the white bear passage finally produces, then, is a quite definite deflation of systematizing, done through humorous irony, and to that extent it is a deflation of a method of thinking characteristic of its time. Much of the fascination of *Tristram Shandy* lies in the fact that it is not only so very much an eighteenth-century kind of book, but also one which ironically satirizes the eighteenth century for what it was. The whole of the novel is in one sense a wryly comic delineation of the times, by a discerning contemporary who was able to perceive so much of the incongruity and contradiction in what was being thought, said, and done all around him.

Laurence Sterne could perceive it, one might add, a good deal more sharply than did that astute citizen of eighteenth-century England, Samuel Johnson. For if Dr. Johnson is, all things considered, a more appealing man than Laurence Sterne, and if his mind was considerably more rigorous and his intellect more formidable, he was so much *of* his time, so exemplary of much of the best in his time, that he was not always willing to admit to its contradictions. He was not *detached,* in the way that Laurence Sterne was. How could he have been? Beliefs, principles, morality *mattered* to him in a way that they did to few other men of the age. The hard-won consistency of his life and ideas was not to be endangered by easy skepticism. By no means was Samuel Johnson complacent about his own worth—the picture of him standing penitently in Uttoxeter Market, head bared to the rain, is unforgettable; yet his faults, as he saw them, arose from his failure to be what he had determined he *ought* to be. Laurence Sterne, who did not worry often enough, perhaps, over what he should be, saw only too well how inadequate any view he might take of his own proper conduct would be when it came to making consistent sense out of his own experience. There is in Sterne a detached skepticism about many of the values of his own time that we do not find in Johnson. Ursa Major did not draw back at the thought of white bears.

Despite ill health that exceeded even Johnson's, Sterne enjoyed himself, and enjoyed being himself, and he found death, that "son of a whore," not terrible as Johnson did, but merely despicable. Though no unbeliever, the Reverend Laurence Sterne seems to have conceived of his Divinity along characteristically eighteenth-century lines, as a Supreme Being who functioned from afar. Though it will not do to interpret Uncle Toby's simple faith in God merely as a device of characterization, neither ought we to assume that Walter Shandy's lack of piety was foreign to Sterne's makeup. The truth is that, as Scott Fitzgerald was to say about first-class intellectuals, Sterne could harbor two seemingly contradictory attitudes toward God and Providence within his mind without giving any evidence of undue perturbation. He did not need to grapple with his faith, as Johnson clearly did; his religious concerns did not dominate his thought to such an extent that he found it necessary to test every idea that came into his mind against the tenets of his faith, and to agonize over an apparent contradiction.

Another word for this kind of mind is Secular, and many have used it to describe Sterne's cast of thought. It is not that Sterne was an unbeliever, but rather that religious faith did not significantly affect his thinking. In part this is why Sterne was able to perceive so well many of the incongruities of eighteenth-century thought and belief, and to recognize so much of the contradiction and confusion attendant upon them. Samuel Johnson, whose mind was so thoroughly permeated by his religious belief, was challenged by the secularity of his time; he sought to square his experience as an Englishman of the eighteenth century with what he believed, and when the two could not be harmonized (as they probably could have been during the seventeenth century), he was tortured by doubt and filled with gloom. His response, when the awareness of contradiction was inevitable, was characteristically a fervent assertion of religious orthodoxy, and a desperate refusal to think further on the matter.

A great deal of Johnson's celebrated "common sense" was a manifestation of this kind of response. His famous "refutation" of Berkelean idealism, for example, was not the expression of a sensible man's refusal to occupy his mind with abstruse philosophical theorizing, so much as an insistence upon keeping a theologically-troubling notion out of his thought. It is difficult to believe that the intellect of Samuel Johnson was so completely unable to grasp the implications of what Berkeley meant, as the episode would indicate; it is rather that he would not *allow* himself to consider it. If we examine Johnson's famous book of prayers, a volume in many ways more appropriate to the previous century than to Johnson's times, we get a sense, I believe, not so much of an abiding faith in an Anglican God, as of a desperate insistence upon finding religious meaning for his experience.

If Laurence Sterne ever felt such a compulsion, it is absent from his writings. The *Sermons of Mr. Yorick,* whatever they may be, were not conceived in spiritual agony, and are not emblematic of spiritual travail. They are a thoughtful, somewhat ingenious group of set pieces, with little sense of their author's experiencing any difficulty in making his religious belief cover the problems of his existence as a man. In one of his best-known sermons, "The House of Feasting and the House of Mourning," it is difficult to think of the house of mourning, with its deathbed scene, as being very much other than an occasion for the tender effusion of sentimental pathos, not importantly different from that accompanying the death of Le Fever in *Tristram Shandy.*

Ideas, whether Berkelean, Lockean, or whatever, did not threaten to destroy Sterne's equilibrium, because he seems never to have thought of them as being anything more than just that: ideas; and he was always convinced of the limitations of ideas. This was not because he could not think, or did not think, nor yet that he thought only haphazardly. Rather it was a matter of his being convinced that his thoughts were only one aspect of his experience, not the sum total of it, and that the experience was larger than the thinking about it, so that to give over his mind to ideas at the expense of the complexities of life itself would represent an impoverishment of the totality of his existence as a man. He regarded elaborate philosophical systems as in the nature of hobby-horses; and he perceived a great deal of humor in attempts to order and to codify the bewildering richness and variety of human life.

Even his beloved John Locke he found amusing in this respect. If *Tristram Shandy* is a demonstration of associational psychology, done along Lockean lines, it is also true that Sterne was thoroughly aware of the elements of absurdity inherent in the attempt, and of the limitations of Locke, so that the book is also very clearly and enjoyably a spoof on Lockean associationalism. This is so not simply in the obvious way of using the doctrine of the association of ideas for comic effect—"Pray, my dear, have you not forgot to wind up the clock?"—but in a more pervasive sense. For Sterne was highly skeptical of the capacity of humans, however well intentioned, ever to arrive at those "clear and self evident" ideas that Locke believed constituted true wisdom. Locke's assumption that the human mind can, if properly instructed and sufficiently clear-headed, attain moral and social truth through the use of reason, and that human beings, by reasoning upon sensations, can achieve understanding, seemed foolishly naive to Sterne. Empirical reasoning was, for him, an inadequate explanation of the process of human cognition; what he knew of men, including himself, told him that the Lockean belief in the possibility of clear, empirically-based judgment, devoid of emotion, was not merely beyond the capacity of humans, but was only a partial approach to the nature of knowledge. He refused to accept Locke's divorcement of wit from judgment, with its implied premise that "your men of least *wit* are reported to be men of most *judgment.*" Devoid of wit themselves, "your graver gentry . . . ," he declared, "raised such a *hue* and *cry*" against wit, and in favor of judgment, that even ". . . the great *Locke,* who was seldom outwitted by false sounds,—was nevertheless bubbled here" (iii, 201–202). A just assessment of human intellect, he believed, involved a "proper balance" between wit and judgment. The function of reason was in part to "govern and subject to reason" what he declared was "the springtide of our blood and humours," a very different matter from seeking to ignore such matters and remove them from consideration (III, 197).

It is precisely this attitude on Sterne's part that is responsible for much of the humor in the characterization of Walter Shandy. For Mr. Shandy thinks of himself as a Lockean philosopher, an exponent of that faultless system of epistemology, "the succession of our ideas," able, through his power of perception and reason, to form what Locke called those "clear and determinate" ideas upon which all knowledge rests. Yet it is hilariously evident that Walter Shandy's supposedly reasoning judgment is powerfully affected by what Locke would have termed his "enthusiasm," his wildly impassioned imagination—in Locke's words, "the ungrounded fancies of man's own brain"—and one result is those magnificently comic theories that render Tristram's father the delightful man he is. The doctrine of names, of foot-first child delivery, of noses, of "the due contention for mastery betwixt the radical heat and the radical moisture," of the *Tristrapoedia* itself are, for Walter Shandy, "clear and determinate" ideas, apprehended, he thinks, through unclouded, dispassionate empirical reasoning. What Sterne knows is that Walter Shandy's intellect is composed of at least as much "wit"—which is to say, passion, imagination, intuition—as "judgment." There is not a character in all of *Tristram Shandy*, least of all Walter Shandy, who is able to conduct his life solely on the basis of dispassionate judgment. If we fail to recognize in the characterization of Walter Shandy a magnificent representation of the limitations of systematic philosophy, we ignore one of the most delightful dimensions of *Tristram Shandy*.

Sterne's distrust of reason, or rather, his awareness of the limitations of reason in encompassing and interpreting the breadth of human experience, made him highly skeptical of the ideas and systems of ideas that characterize one phase of eighteenth-century thought. *Tristram Shandy* thus is a perceptive critique of its time and place. Sterne was hardly the only citizen of his time to espy the limitations of the Age of Reason—indeed, with almost as much appropriateness, one could make a case for calling the century the Age of Skepticism. As D. W. Jefferson has pointed out, the eighteenth century still contained a large measure of the old medieval, pre-Enlightenment heritage of belief in a harmonious system of knowledge "between things and their meanings, between concrete particulars and the intellectual patterns into which they fit."[2] Descartes, Newton, and Locke may have gravely damaged the theological underpinnings for such a heritage, but the habit of thought persisted, and the new science and the psychology of associationism were thrust into the role formerly played by religious orthodoxy. The result was widespread systematizing and theorizing, with Reason, man's ability to solve his problems through thought, seized upon by many as the new key to human happiness. But along with empiricism and science necessarily went the observation of nature, and it soon became all too evident that no such easy systematizing and harmonizing were in fact possible. The empirical method was quick to produce extensive evidence of the shortcomings of empiricism itself; the use of reason soon made the limitations of reason abundantly clear. Thus the thought of the century is filled with contradictory insights, with splendid systematizing and witty skepticism existing side by side. To a man such as Sterne, with his open mind and his taste for incongruities, the spectacle was delicious to behold. However fascinated he was with the system of ideas, and however much he believed that John Locke had been able "to free the world from the lumber of a thousand vulgar errors," he was by temperament so conscious of the frailty of the intellect that he could never surrender himself for long to the praise of the unaided reason. And in the great tradition of British comedy, he wrote his book in part to portray the discrepancy between the conflicting beliefs of his age and the behavior of his fellow Englishmen.

The most fundamental example of this is the contrasting characterization of the two Shandy brothers. Uncle Toby, the old soldier, is Sterne's embodiment of sweetness and natural benevolence. The man who would not harm a fly because "the world surely is wide enough to hold both thee and me," whose simple goodness of heart seems at times to serve as so effective a counterpart to his brother's complex cerebrations, who, when told by Dr. Slop that the devil "is cursed, and damn'd already, to all eternity," says simply that "I am sorry for it," is a wonderfully admirable character. His defects are those of naivete alone; his intentions and his actions are always of the best. Yet with supremely conscious irony, Sterne makes him a professional soldier (similar to his own father) whose ruling passion is war, and who together with his servant Corporal Trim spends the major part of his energies in digging fortifications and· re-enacting the campaigns of Marlborough. Thus when the Peace of Utrecht in 1713 brought an end to the war for a time, and therefore to Uncle Toby's building of fortifications, he was so distraught that "to the end of his life he never could hear *Utrecht* mentioned upon any account whatever,—or so much as read an article of news extracted out of the *Utrecht Gazette,* without fetching a sigh, as if his heart would break in twain" (vi, 458).

Walter Shandy, for all his love of his brother, cannot restrain himself from pointing this out: "Never mind, brother *Toby,* he would say, —by God's blessings we shall have another war break out again some of these days . . ." (vi, 458). Uncle Toby's response, an eloquent defense of his profession, is that " 'Tis one thing, brother *Shandy,* for a soldier to hazard his own life—to leap first down into the trenches, where he is sure to be cut in pieces," to fight bravely and well on all occasions, and " 'tis another to reflect on the miseries of war;— to view the desolation of whole countries. . . ." But in war, he continues, all depends on why it is being fought: for a war, "when fought as ours has been, upon principles of *liberty,* and upon principles of *honour*—what is it but the getting together of quiet and harmless people, with their swords in their hands, to keep the ambitious and the turbulent within bounds? And heaven is my witness, brother *Shandy,* that the pleasure I have taken in these things,—and that infinite delight, in particular, which has attended my sieges in my bowling green, has arose within me, and I hope in the corporal too, from the consciousness we both has, that in carrying them on, we were answering the great ends of our creation" (vi, 461–462).

But if this is sufficient for Toby's defense, it will not do for Sterne, for all his admiring presentation of Toby Shandy's sweetness and gentleness. Sterne sees Toby's point, but knows that there is more to it than that. For in the very last chapter of *Tristram Shandy* he returns to the matter when he has Walter Shandy discourse ironically on warfare:

> —The act of killing and destroying a man, continued my father raising his voice, and turning to my uncle *Toby*—you see, is glorious—and the weapons by which we do it are honorable—We march with them upon our shoulders—We strut with them by our sides—We gild them—We carve them—We in-lay them— We enrich them—Nay, if it be but a *scoundril* cannon, we cast an ornament upon the breach of it.—(ix, 645)

The point is not that Uncle Toby was being hypocritical. It is rather that he is not, and, given the nature of human limitations, cannot be aware of such radical and total inconsistency. The harmless fortifications and armed towns that he and Trim so zealously construct and then destroy represent what in real life are frightful carnage, hideous suffering, untold misery. But for Toby Shandy and Corporal Trim they are a delightful game, full of purpose and excitement—and (what is even more appalling) one which, for all their individual generosity, kindness, and love of their fellowmen, they had engaged in while campaigning before Namur, just as on Uncle Toby's bowling green. That Toby should regret the Peace of Utrecht because it makes his game impossible to play any more is as ironic, and as astute, an observation upon the limitations of human compassion as has ever been made.[3]

Yet of the two Shandy brothers, it is Walter, the civilian, the man of peace, who is infinitely more bellicose in his opinions and attitudes, and infinitely less tolerant of other people's ideas. He does not hesitate to rage against Uncle Toby's harmless preoccupation with his fortifications, Mrs. Shandy's inability to comprehend his ideas, and the shortcomings of the world in general, even while totally failing to recognize his own deficiencies. It never occurs to My Father to examine his own peculiarities. Yet if Uncle Toby is obsessed with fortifications, so is Walter Shandy with noses; if Uncle Toby collects every book he can find on the science of fortification, so does Walter Shandy collect "every book and treatise which had been systematically wrote upon noses, with as much care as my honest uncle *Toby* had done those upon military architecture.——'Tis true, a much less table would have held them,——but that was not thy transgression, my dear uncle——" (III, 224). Walter Shandy flies off in passion, rails against the limitations of the flesh and spirit, and is otherwise a man of extravagant gesture and combative extremes of temperament. The man of peace is thus a much less peaceable soul than his brother who is dedicated to the profession of arms.

Sterne, it must be insisted, does not himself pass judgment upon either party. *He* is not constructing a hypothesis; *Tristram Shandy* is no philosophical treatise. It is not Sterne's (or Tristram's) business to postulate what should be, but to describe what is. And this, in a century filled with many heroic and many, absurd postulations of what should be, itself constituted perforce something of a critique. "It is the nature of an hypothesis," Tristram declares in a memorable passage, "when once a man has conceived it, that it assimilates every thing to itself as proper nourishment; and from the first moment of your begetting it, it generally grows the stronger by every thing you see, hear, read, or understand" (II, 151). A shrewd observation to make, surely, during the Golden Age of British Empiricism.

The gross physicality of much of *Tristram Shandy,* which so angered Samuel Johnson and disgusted Thackeray and the Victorians, also constitutes, it seems to me, a discerning observation about the times. I refer here not only to the ribaldry and the double-entendre, but to the general surfeit of corporeality throughout. There is an absolute absence of aethereality; man is of the flesh, and cannot be separated from his body. The very starting point of life, the "homunculus" itself, as we are reminded early in the novel, "consists, as we do, of skin, hair, fat, flesh, veins, arteries, ligaments, nerves, cartilages, bones, marrow, brains, glands, genitals, humors, and articulations . . ." (I, 5). And Walter Shandy's wonderfully despairing meditation upon the indignity of sexual desire at the close of the novel points out the pathos of the matter eloquently:

> —That provision should be made for continuing the race of so great, so exalted and godlike a Being as man—I am far from denying—But philosophy speaks freely of every thing; and therefore I still think and do maintain it to be a pity, that it should be done by means of a passion which bends down the faculties, and turns all the wisdom, contemplations, and operations of the soul backwards —a passion, my dear, continued my father, addressing himself to my mother, which couples and equals wise men with fools, and makes us come out of caverns and hiding places more like satyrs and four-footed beasts than men. (IX, 644–645)

As befits a novel composed by one whose lungs might at any moment hemorrhage and cause him to bleed to death, and who had from his youth onward lived in wretched health, *Tristram Shandy* is filled with sickness, disease, wounds, stretching all the way from Walter Shandy's affliction of sciatica in the second chapter, which prevented Tristram from being begotten earlier than he was, through the wound in Toby Shandy's groin which so perturbs the Widow Wadman, in the final episode, that she spoils her chances of remarriage by her insistence upon finding out the facts. Jonathan Swift himself was scarcely more obsessed with carnality than Sterne. Groin wounds, knee wounds, asthma, caesarian deliveries, farting and hiccupping, obstetrics, sutures, flattened noses, injuries to a male organ when a window sash falls upon it while Tristram is making water out of the window, purges, salt-peter, enemas, blisters, poultices, calomel, tooth-aches, coughs, clap—scarcely a chapter in the novel but has its urgent reminder of the physicality of human experience. Well might Walter Shandy lament the cruel handicaps placed by nature upon the race of men. Nowhere is the contrast between the human condition as it daily manifested itself, and the splendid generalizations of some of the century's most honored philosophers, more clearly confronted than in the pages of *Tristram Shandy*. It is a novel in which abstruse philosophical theories and crude physical facts exist side by side, in telling irony, and written about an age in which, in Peter Quennell's words, "with the urbanity of its civilization went an appalling physical harshness. The hand holding a calf-bound volume had been twisted and knobbed by gout; the face under the candlelight was scarred by smallpox. Child after child died before it left its cradle; women struggled resignedly from one childbirth to the next; the young and hopeful dropped off overnight, a prey to mysterious disorders that the contemporary physician could neither diagnose nor remedy."[4]

Sterne composed his critical commentary on the time and place, of course, not in the role of judge, or even as satirist—*Tristram Shandy* differs importantly from, for example, *Candide,* in this respect, in that the French work was written primarily to ridicule the shallow philosophical optimism of the period, while the English author was out primarily for fun and for pathos. Sterne lacks the engagement of the satirist, which is to say, the belief in an implied norm against which the errors under attack are measurable. He shows the discrepancies between his century's situation and its ideals and beliefs not because he is savagely indignant over the vast distance between them, but because he is amused and made melancholy at the spectacle. For in his judgment, much of the discrepancy lies not in remediable shortcomings, but in the very nature of the human condition. Walter Shandy may be the caricature of a Lockean-style philosopher, but more importantly he is every earnest man who, possessed of only human intellect, tries to make systematic sense out of human experience and to regulate his behavior in accordance with his conclusions. Sterne is not a reformer; he is a skeptic, which is another matter entirely.

As a writer, says Ian Watt, Sterne was so great a master of realistic presentation that had he worked toward the usual goals of the novel, he would "probably have been the supreme figure among Eighteenth-Century novelists."[5] But, of course, *Tristram Shandy,* so far as its author was concerned, rests on no such negative grounds as that. To be sure, in part it is a parody of what eighteenth-century novelists were doing, but it is also and much more significantly an attempt at the representation of reality, that imagic ordering of experience that any novelist seeks, and which Sterne obviously felt was inadequately handled in the fiction of the day. Were *Tristram Shandy* anything less, it would not have survived its time.

The eclipse of Sterne in the nineteenth century, and his reemergence in our own time, have been explained on the grounds that his radical system for the depiction of time, which to the Victorians appeared as an absence of any system or order at all, became highly relevant to twentieth-century writers who began finding conventional chronological narrative inadequate for their purposes. Sterne is thus the forerunner of Bergson, and the precursor of Proust, Joyce, Virginia Woolf, and others. This likewise is true enough, provided that we remember that it is not Sterne's narrative technique, nor his method of representing temporality, that gives him his importance, but the artistic fruits of that technique and method. *Tristram Shandy* is not a textbook in literary structure; it is a tremendously appealing description of the Shandy family and their friends and acquaintances, told by Tristram, who interprets them—and himself—for us. What goes on at Shandy Hall is very much a critique of the author's eighteenth-century English world, with its oddities, attitudes, and attainments displayed for view by one who knew it incredibly well, loved it, but refused to be taken in by its pretensions. And what makes and keeps it so appealing is that in Sterne's depiction of his times, we can recognize our own as well: the eighteenth-century Shandean universe is only a little more naive, a little more optimistic, a little less complicated than ours.

The point is that Sterne himself saw the incongruities. Writing from the edge of death, he did not fail to recognize the precarious nature of what both in his time and ours passed for "knowledge" and "reality," nor did he fail to perceive the joys and triumphs. Who can say that, for our own time, we have come very much closer than Tristram Shandy's father in fitting our empirical knowledge, and our systems for codifying and applying it, to the brute fact of the white bear?

Notes

1. *The Life and Opinions of Tristram Shandy, Gentleman,* ed. James Aiken Work (New York, 1940), v, 404–405. Hereafter citations will be made to this edition, with volume and page numbers given parenthetically.

2. *"Tristram Shandy* and Its Tradition" in *From Dryden to Johnson,* ed. Boris Ford, No. 4 in the Pelican Guide to English Literature (Harmondsworth, Middlesex, 1957), p. 339.

3. Sterne scholars might well object that in insisting upon Sterne's irony here, I am giving a twentieth-century motivation to an eighteenth-century author, when the truth is that Sterne's view of the matter is essentially that expressed through Uncle Toby in his apologia. But I cannot believe so ironic a juxtaposition is a mere accident. Sterne does not condemn Toby Shandy; it is merely an instance, for him, of the vastly contradictory nature of human experience. It does not trouble Uncle Toby that his profession is a hideous refutation of all that he believes.

4. *The Profane Virtues: Four Studies of the Eighteenth Century* (New York, 1945), p. 3.

5. *The Rise of the Novel* (Berkeley, 1957), p. 291.

The Passions
of Ambrosio

RICHARD HARTER FOGLE

John Crowe Ransom has remarked that Milton succeeded in *Lycidas* in including every motif in the tradition of the pastoral elegy. Lewis surely came close to the same achievement with the Gothic novel in *The Monk,* although Montague Summers notes with some regret that despite his fondness for graveyard scenes he is wholly lacking in vampirism.[1] At the least he provides vigorous, expansive, full-blooded melodrama, with a wicked monk who sells himself to the devil, a fair fiend who betrays him, burial alive, incest, parricide, the Wandering Jew, a Bleeding Nun, the Spanish Inquisition, a haunted castle in Germany, intricate love-intrigues, spectacles, some highly competent balladry, and an ending that must be as daring as any in the history of fiction.

Coleridge summarized and judged the work with great precision:

> Ambrosio, a monk, surnamed the Man of Holiness, proud of his own undeviating rectitude, and severe to the faults of others, is successfully assailed by the tempter of mankind, and seduced to the perpetration of rape and murder, and finally precipitated into a contract in which he consigns his soul to everlasting perdition.
>
> The larger part of the three volumes is occupied by the underplot, which, however, is skillfully and closely connected with the main story and is subservient to its development. The tale of the bleeding nun is truly terrific; and we could not easily recollect a bolder or more happy conception than that of the burning cross on the forehead of the wandering Jew. . . . But the character of Matilda, the chief agent in the seduction of Ambrosio, appears to

us to be the author's master-piece. It is, indeed, exquisitely imagined, and as exquisitely supported. The whole work is distinguished by the variety and impressiveness of its incidents; and the author everywhere discovers an imagination rich, powerful, and fervid.[2]

This famous review is by no means as favorable in its totality as in the excerpt I have quoted. In fact, the following sentence reads, "Such are the excellences;—the errors and defects are more numerous, and (we are sorry to add) of greater importance." The most important of these defects is immorality: "Not without reluctance then, but in full conviction that we are performing a duty, we declare it to be our opinion, that *The Monk* is a romance, which if a parent saw in the hands of a son or daughter, he might reasonably turn pale."

I am concerned here, however, primarily with Coleridge's praises of *The Monk,* and above all with his admiration of its plot structure. Critics have almost invariably been struck with Lewis's conception of his chief character Ambrosio, but have been less impressed by the novel as a whole. Coleridge is in fact too generous to the "underplot"; this is an amiable foible, however, and also most suggestive. Both the Ambrosio story and the underplot are conducted with care and skill, and as Coleridge says the two are very nicely connected. Nevertheless, there is simply too much of the latter; it is an intrigue-plot, ingenious rather than imaginative, a masterly job of carpentry by a master joiner.

Ambrosio himself can fairly be considered an Aristotelian tragic hero. (Inevitably, I am more interested in finding resemblances than differences, although I shall try to preserve due discriminations.) In the first place, he is like Oedipus a foundling, a circumstance that involves eventually the plot elements of reversal and recognition. His is the tragedy of a family or "house," which Aristotle says is the best kind because of its potentiality for interesting complications. Ambrosio's ignorance of his identity leads him, like Oedipus, unwittingly into incest and parricide. One has to add here the element of Elizabethan villainy and positive evil: Ambrosio knows perfectly well that he is committing murder and rape, although he is unaware that the victims, Elvira and Antonia, are his mother and sister. Lewis arranges his plot with great care, from the first mention of the circumstances in Leonella's story (p. 40) to the fiend's ultimate revelation at the end (p. 418).[3]

Ambrosio is a man of outstanding talents, and as abbot and preacher a leader in his society of Catholic Madrid, as is the Reverend Mr. Dimmesdale in the theocracy of Puritan Salem. As Coleridge mentions, he is generally called the Man of Holiness.

> He was a man of noble port and commanding presence. His stature was lofty, and his features uncommonly handsome. His nose was aquiline, his eyes large, black and sparkling, and his dark brows almost joined together. His complexion was of a deep but clear brown; study and watching had entirely deprived his cheek of colour. Tranquillity reigned upon his smooth unwrinkled forehead; and content, expressed upon every feature, seemed to announce the man equally unacquainted with cares and crimes. He bowed himself with humility to the audience. Still there was a certain severity in his look and manner that inspired universal awe, and few could sustain the glance of his eye, at once fiery and penetrating. Such was Ambrosio, abbot of the Capuchins, and surnamed "The Man of Holiness." (p. 45)

Apparently the ideal representative of his society, Ambrosio is of course too good to be true. His humility is false, and his disastrous fault is pride. Yet he is at the beginning truly unaware of his own defects. He genuinely aspires to goodness, and is thus a true tragic character.

The fullest account of him comes later, when he is deeply involved in evil and danger. It is important enough to quote at length, since in discussing him Lewis conveys the central theme of *The Monk,* what corresponds in it to the Aristotelian element of "thought."

> It was by no means his nature to be timid: but his education had impressed his mind with fear so strongly, that apprehension was now become part of his character. Had his youth been passed in the world, he would have shown himself possessed of many brilliant and manly qualities. He was naturally enterprizing, firm, and fearless: he had a warrior's heart, and he might have shone with splendour at the head of an army. There was no want of generosity in his nature: the wretched never failed to find in him a compassionate auditor: his abilities were quick and shining, and his judgment vast, solid, and decisive. (pp. 237–238)

Unfortunately, however, he has been relegated to a monastery.

> Instead of universal benevolence, he adopted a selfish partiality for his own particular establishment: he was taught to consider com-

passion for the errors of others as a crime of the blackest dye: the noble frankness of his temper was exchanged for servile humility; and in order to break his natural spirit, the monks terrified his young mind, by placing before him all the horrors with which superstition could furnish them: they painted to him the torments of the damned in colors the most dark, terrible and fantastic, and threatened him at the slightest fault with eternal perdition. . . . While the monks were busied in rooting out his virtues, and narrowing his sentiments, they allowed every vice which had fallen to his share to arrive at full perfection. (p. 238)

With this education, he arrives at manhood full of contradictions.

Still in spite of the pains taken to pervert them, his natural good qualities would occasionally burst through the gloom cast over them so carefully. At such times the contest for superiority between his real and his acquired character was striking and unaccountable to those unacquainted with his original disposition. He pronounced the most severe sentences upon offenders, which the moment after compassion induced him to mitigate: he undertook the most daring enterprizes, which the fear of their consequences soon obliged him to abandon: his inborn genius darted a brilliant light upon subjects the most obscure; and almost instantaneously his superstition replunged them in darkness more profound than that from which they had been rescued. . . . The fact was, that the different sentiments with which education and nature had inspired him, were combating in his bosom: it remained for his passions, which as yet no opportunity had called into play, to decide the victory. Unfortunately his passions were the very worst judges to whom he could possibly have applied. (p. 239)

The "thought" or message of *The Monk* is sincere and sustained, though not particularly impressive. It is simply that repression of the natural man is wrong, and the anti-Catholicism, anti-monasticism, and hereditary hatred and fear of Spanish institutions that Lewis could expect of his English audience would make this message easy to swallow, like an artfully sweetened pill. "Superstition" and repression are objects of attack throughout the novel. Yet deeper, however, is the agency and the tragedy of the passions, principally sexual, by which all action in *The Monk* is motivated, and from which all misfortune arises.

Thus the unfortunate Marguerite is led into villainy, though eventually redeemed: " 'A villain made himself master of my affections, and to follow him I quitted my father's house. Yet, though my passions overpowered my virtue, I sunk not into that degeneracy of vice but too commonly the lot of women who made the first false step. I loved my seducer. . . . Even at this moment I lament his loss, though 'tis to him that I owe all the miseries of my existence' " (p. 137). " 'My nature was licentious and warm, but not cruel . . .' " (p. 139). The baroness Lindenberg, who exercises a malign influence upon the love affair of Agnes and Raymond, is far from wholly bad, but she is passion's slave. "Her understanding was strong and excellent when not obscured by prejudice, which unluckily was but seldom the case. Her passions were violent: she spared no pains to gratify them, and pursued with unremitting vengeance those who opposed themselves to her wishes. The warmest of friends, the most inveterate of enemies, such was the baroness Lindenberg" (p. 147).

Agnes, who commits the indiscretion of pregnancy while under the laws of the nunnery of St. Clare, pleads mere love, with the excuse that she has been unwillingly forced into taking the veil. " 'Tax me not with impurity, nor think that I have erred from the warmth of temperament. Long before I took the veil, Raymond was master of my heart: he inspired me with the purest, the most irreproachable passion, and was on the point of becoming my lawful husband.' " They are separated, but " 'Accident again united us; I could not refuse myself the melancholy pleasure of mingling my tears with his. We met nightly in the gardens of St. Clare, and in an unguarded moment I violated my vows of chastity. I shall soon become a mother.' " At this discovery her relentless superior the prioress is enraged: "the domina's countenance grew inflamed with passion" (p. 72). She is "a woman of violent and revengeful character, capable of proceeding to the greatest extremities" (p. 197). Since she entombs Agnes alive, with her child unborn, this description of her is not exaggerated.

Passion in *The Monk,* then, has something of the dignity of fate, an element not to be repressed or avoided. And in the conduct of Ambrosio's downfall the movement of his passions is realized with great artfulness and symmetry. Despite the large problem that Lewis gives himself of conveying significant emphasis in a book where all is emphatic, the relentless downward course of Ambrosio has life, development, and progression. Each episode is consistent with his "thought" about Ambrosio, as I have quoted it, but with enough flexibility to maintain the interest. The monk is always offered a moral choice, he always hesitates, then chooses wrong—and we always sympathize and understand his erring. At worst, Lewis is an amazingly successful *advocatus Diaboli*. John Berryman complains that he tells us too much at the beginning: "We probably resent the secret of his character's having been delivered up to us at once in the initial epigraph given by Lewis, which is about Angelo's apparent character in *Measure for Measure*. In Chapter Two, when we come upon him [Ambrosio] alone, the note of spiritual pride is struck so emphatically that his hypocrisy seems almost laughable."[4] The objection has force, and in any event it occurs in an appreciative and profitable discussion of Lewis's skill as a novelist. It is, however, unrealistic, as regards the possibility of any writer of fiction of the English eighteenth or nineteenth century, including Richardson, Fielding, Smollett, Scott, Dickens, Thackeray, George Eliot, and Trollope, either achieving or in any way desiring the twentieth-century art of gradual revelation of character. Their forte was to establish it firmly. Ambrosio is thus from the beginning boldly outlined, though the outline is not the complete picture.

His characteristic movement is inevitably downward, but rather oscillating than rigidly linear. Thus he finally yields to Matilda's seductions, influenced by love and gratitude as well as sexual passion. "The burst of transport was past: Ambrosio's lust was satisfied" (p. 226). Incidentally, if one yields to lawless speculation, this transport has lasted 118 pages. It was commenced on page 109 (" 'Thine, ever thine,' murmured the friar, and sunk upon her bosom"), and has been suspended during the entire interim, consisting mainly of the "History of Don Raymond, Marquis de las Cisternas." Ambrosio suffers a violent reaction, and reproaches his seductress and himself: " 'What atonement can purchase the pardon of my crime? Wretched Matilda, you have destroyed my quiet forever!' " He is, however, won over by her arguments: " 'Unnatural were your vows of celibacy; man was not created for such a state: and were love a crime, God never would have made it so sweet, so irresistible! Then banish those clouds from your brow, my Ambrosio.' "

One further instance of this basic movement, more complex and horrific, may stand for the rest. Ambrosio, now almost at the end of his progress toward damnation, has ravished the angelic Antonia in the gloomy vaults of St. Clare. Considering its content *The Monk* is remarkably free of perversity, but in this instance "even the gloom of the vault, the surrounding silence, and the resistance which he expected from her, seemed to give a fresh edge to his fierce and unbridled desires" (p. 365). The act accomplished, Ambrosio feels revulsion and self-disgust, "aversion and rage" (p. 368). This gives way to pity: "As his gloomy rage abated, in proportion did his compassion augment for Antonia. He stopped, and would have spoken to her words of comfort; but he knew not from whence to draw them. . . . What could he do for her" (p. 370). He is inclined to release her, despite the danger of exposure: "However well-founded were these apprehensions, compassion, and a sincere wish to repair his fault as much as possible, solicited his complying with the prayers of his suppliant" (p. 372). But Matilda appears, and is too strong for him; at her persuasion he consults his own safety by murdering his victim—who unknown to him is his sister.

Coleridge condemns the supernatural machinery of *The Monk:* "where the order of nature may be changed whenever the author's purposes demand it. . . . No address is requisite to the accomplishment of any design. . . . The writer may make us wonder, but he cannot surprise us."

> For the same reasons a romance is incapable of exemplifying a moral truth. No proud man, for instance, will be made less proud by being told that Lucifer once seduced a presumptuous monk. *Incredulus odit.* Or even if, believing the story, he should deem his virtue less secure, he would yet acquire no lessons of prudence, no feelings of humility. Human prudence can oppose no sufficient shield to the power and cunning of supernatural beings; and the privilege of being proud might be fairly conceded to him who could rise superior to all earthly temptations, and whom the strength of the spiritual world alone would be adequate to overwhelm. So falling, he would fall with glory, and might reasonably welcome his defeat with the haughty emotions of a conqueror.[5]

Coleridge is so thoroughly exercised by the problems of *The Monk* that he goes on with a statement that Raysor judiciously characterizes as one of his "best achievements in criticism." It is very relevant indeed to the issues that are here being ventilated.

> The romance-writer possesses an unlimited power over situations; but he must scrupulously make his characters act in congruity with them. Let him work *physical* wonders only, and we will be content to *dream* with him for a while; but the first *moral* miracle which he attempts, he disgusts and awakens us. Thus our judgment remains unoffended, when, announced by thunders and earthquakes, the

spirit appears to Ambrosio involved in blue fires that increase the cold of the cavern; and we acquiesce in the power of the silver myrtle which made gates and doors fly open at its touch, and charmed every eye into sleep. But when a mortal, fresh from the impression of that terrible appearance, and in the act of evincing for the first time the witching force of this myrtle, is represented as being at the same moment agitated by so fleeting an appetite as that of lust, our own feelings convince us that this is not improbable, but impossible, not preternatural, but contrary to nature. The extent of the powers that may exist, we can never ascertain; and therefore we feel no great difficulty in yielding a temporary belief to any, the strangest, situation of *things*. But that situation once conceived, how beings like ourselves would feel and act in it, our own feelings sufficiently instruct us; and we instantly reject the clumsy fiction that does not harmonize with them.[6]

Now to the fundamental questions raised by this great critic about Lewis's use of the supernatural: one would first concede that Lewis cannot compare with Coleridge himself in *The Ancient Mariner* and *Christabel;* his spiritual beings are relatively superficial, merely material and spectacular. But, as John Berryman well says, "the point is to conduct a remarkable man utterly to damnation. It is surprising, after all, how *long* it takes—how *difficult* it is—to be certain of damnation. This was Lewis's main insight, fully embodied in his narrative . . ." (Introduction, p. 13). There is great fascination in the entrapment itself, and its progress is managed by Lewis with marvellous ingenuity and resourcefulness. I have attempted to demonstrate something of the detail of this in two of the episodes of Ambrosio's fall. Further, once he has selected his terms, Lewis carries them out with the utmost boldness and consistency. He sticks to his guns: Ambrosio is to be damned, and damned he is; correspondingly, having elected the supernatural, he does not betray it with naturalistic explanations, like Mrs. Radcliffe, or Charles Brockden Brown, or John Dickson Carr, the modern inheritor of English Gothic. In this he is both courageous and sure-footed, with exceptions which I will later note. The fantastic conclusion of *The Monk* is a triumph of sheer pertinacity. Driven to the last extremity, Ambrosio tries to pray. At this the devil, "darting his talons into the monk's shaven. crown," flies away with him.

The caves and mountains rang with Ambrosio's shrieks. The daemon continued to soar aloft, till reaching a dreadful height, he released the sufferer. Headlong fell the monk through the airy waste; the sharp point of a rock received him; and he rolled from precipice to precipice, till, bruised and mangled, he rested on the river's banks. Life still existed in his miserable frame: he attempted in vain to raise himself; his broken and dislocated limbs refused to perform their office, nor was he able to quit the spot where he had first fallen. The sun now rose above the horizon; its scorching beams darted full upon the head of the expiring sinner. Myriads of insects were called forth by the warmth; they drank the blood which trickled from Ambrosio's wounds; he had no power to drive them from him, and they fastened upon his sores, darted their stings into his body, covered him with their multitudes, and inflicted on him tortures the most exquisite and insupportable. The eagles of the rock tore his flesh piecemeal, and dug out his eye-balls with their crooked beaks. A burning thirst tormented him; he heard the river's murmur as it rolled beside him, but strove in vain to drag himself towards the sound. Blind, maimed, helpless, and despairing, venting his rage in blasphemy and curses, execrating his existence, yet dreading the arrival of death destined to yield him up to greater torments, six miserable days did the villain languish. On the seventh a violent storm arose: the winds in fury rent up rocks and forests: the sky was now black with clouds, now sheeted with fire: the rain fell in torrents; it swelled the stream; the waves overflowed their banks; they reached the spot where Ambrosio lay; and when they abated, carried with them into the river the corse of the despairing monk. (pp. 419–420)

Lewis all but carries Ambrosio to Hell himself.

He manages a genuinely tragic dilemma by holding to the notion of an omnipotent deity, in Ambrosio's imagination both vengeful and loving. Ambrosio holds to his faith in God's infinite mercy almost to the end—to make him utterly despair is the devil's final triumph. Coleridge, condemning Lewis's psychology, at the same time testifies to his success. "Now, in addition to constitutional warmth and irresistible opportunity, the monk is impelled to incontinence by friendship, by compassion, by gratitude, by all that is amiable, and all that is estimable; yet in a few weeks after his first frailty, the man . . . degenerates into an uglier fiend than the gloomy imagination of Dante would have ventured to picture."[7] Ambrosio, however, is a fiend only at the end, and Coleridge has failed to perceive the many regular steps that bring him to damnation.

As regards Coleridge's chief contention—that *The Monk* falsifies human nature by motivating Ambrosio with "lust"—plainly few moderns would agree with him. This, however, is not the point, which is that Lewis clearly felt otherwise about the matter, and that *The Monk* is consistently a tragedy of passion, sexual and otherwise. One would argue, too, for the dramatic appropriateness of Ambrosio's desires. He is a *monk,* sworn to chastity, and he places great weight on the sin of breaking his vow. It symbolizes the defeat of the spirit by the flesh. Rationally, repression of the natural man brings great and dreadful consequences. Further, as Coleridge himself implicitly acknowledges, what Ambrosio feels is a good deal more complicated than lust. He is led into his disastrous connection with Matilda by affection and gratitude, and his unhallowed longings for the unhappy Antonia are mingled with reverence for her archetypal innocence.

Indeed, Ambrosio's disastrous mixture of sacred and profane love has extremely interesting effects. He worships a picture of the Madonna, which turns out to be a portrait of Matilda, whose face he has never seen till she reveals herself by apparent accident. "The suddenness of her movement made her cowl fall back from her head; her features became visible to the monk's enquiring eye. What was his amazement at beholding the exact resemblance of his admired Madonna! The same exquisite proportion of features, the same profusion of golden hair, the same rosy lips, heavenly eyes, and majesty of countenance adorned Matilda!" (p. 101).

Again, his feelings about Antonia are complex, and so are Antonia's feelings about Ambrosio. The unobtrusive resemblance of their names is a nice touch. At first sight she is instinctively attracted to him. Hearing him preach, " 'till this moment I had no idea of the powers of eloquence. But when he spoke, his voice inspired me with such interest, such esteem, I might almost say such affection for him, that I am myself astonished at the acuteness of my feelings' " (p. 47). Later, Elvira and Antonia both remark a strange familiarity in his voice.

> "His fine and full-toned voice struck me particularly; but surely, Antonia, I have heard it before. It seemed perfectly familiar to my ear; either I must have known the abbot in former times, or his voice bears a wonderful resemblance to that of some other, to whom I have often listened. There were certain tones which touched my very heart, and made me feel sensations so singular, that I strive in vain to account for them."

> "My dearest mother it produced the same effect upon me; yet
> certainly neither of us ever heard his voice till we came to Madrid.
> . . . I know not why, but I feel more at ease while conversing with
> him, than I usually do with people who are unknown to me." (p.
> 250)

The possibility exists, then, that Antonia's instinctive affinity for her
brother Ambrosio is sexual and incestuous. It is only a possibility, an
overtone—if it were more it would wreck the plot—but as a mere suggestion it enlivens the design appreciably.

Returning for the moment to *The Monk's* resemblance to Aristotelian tragedy, one would have to relegate it to Aristotle's second and
inferior class, the double action with poetic justice, where the wicked
are punished and the virtuous are—at long last—rewarded. The good
receive a due measure of happiness in the penultimate Chapter XI,
leaving the conclusion to fix Ambrosio in eternal misery. The terms
of happiness are significant beyond the characters they concern:

> The remaining years of Raymond and Agnes, of Lorenzo and Vir-
> ginia, were happy as can be those allotted to mortals, born to be
> the prey of grief, and sport of disappointment. The exquisite sorrows
> with which they had been afflicted, made them think lightly of
> every succeeding woe. They had felt the sharpest darts in misfor-
> tune's quiver. Those which remained, appeared blunt in compari-
> son. Having weathered fate's heaviest storms, they looked calmly
> upon its terrors: or, if ever they felt affliction's casual gales, they
> seemed to them gentle as zephyrs which breathe over summer-seas.
> (p. 400)

This too is the tragedy of passion, with something of the settled resig-
nation of a Greek ending. Poor Antonia, the beloved of Lorenzo, has
of course perished, and the beautiful Virginia de Villa-Franca is a
moderately satisfactory substitute for her.

This subplot of Raymond-Agnes and Lorenzo-Antonia-Virginia
functions as a mask and as counterpoint for the Ambrosio story. It is
expansive, leisurely, and varied, whereas the latter is concentrated,
swift, and direct, but is enveloped and half-concealed within the larger
narrative. As was remarked by Coleridge, the longer subplot is skil-
fully joined to the Ambrosio story, and perhaps its effect in turning
us back to Ambrosio is premeditated. We have noticed, for instance,
that the crucial seduction of Ambrosio by Matilda is broken off at its

climax by the expansive and retrospective "History of Don Raymond de las Cisternas," and returns 118 pages later exactly where it left off. The subplot is worked out with commendable care and skill. Lewis leaves no loose ends among the many strands of story and motif that he has set himself to weave together, and he prepares his grounds admirably in his opening chapter. It is in the subplot, for the most part, that his virtuosity in handling the largest possible number of Gothic elements chiefly appears. Nevertheless, in relative terms this plot is not finally an artistic and imaginative success.

Despite Lewis's conscientiousness he has given himself and his reader too much to keep up with. The story reads as if he had prepared an extremely careful and elaborate outline, then found that he had notwithstanding to fill in with afterthoughts. Singularly bold in his conduct of the supernatural, he is unhappily fussy about detail, like the wicked who flee where no man pursueth. Thus, in Raymond's "History," the hero overhears outlaws plotting against him outside his window. Now, it is a bitterly cold night, as is mentioned on several occasions, so it is carefully specified that "I drew near the window, which, as the room had been long shut up, was left open in spite of the cold" (p. 124). When we find out a few moments later that "He spoke in a low voice; but as he was just below my window, I had no difficulty to distinguish his words" (p. 125), our response is likely to be, "Oh, yeah?" Further on, Raymond instantaneously overpowers one of the brigands. "I sprang from my seat, darted suddenly upon Baptiste, and, clasping my hands round his throat, pressed it so forcibly as to prevent his uttering a single cry." This is a considerable feat, and so the author evidently finds it, for Raymond immediately explains, "You may remember, that I was remarkable at Salamanca for the power of my arm" (p. 133). Later, the same Don Raymond finds it necessary to masquerade as a gardener, "Disguised in a common habit, and a black patch covering one of my eyes. . . ." He is obliged to carry out his role: "I immediately entered upon my employment. Botany having been a favorite study with me, I was by no means at a loss in my new station" (p. 190). Part of the science-requirement at Salamanca, no doubt. With some difficulty he is able to arrange an assignation with Agnes, the reason for his masquerade. "She told me, that to grant my request at that moment was impossible: but she engaged to be in the same spot at eleven that night, and to converse with me for the last time." Lewis now worries about the probability of the lovers finding privacy in the convent garden, but he has his solution. "The chillness of the night was in my favour, since it kept the other nuns confined to their cells. Agnes alone was insensible of the inclemency of the air . . ." (p. 191). On a number of occasions characters are prevented from encountering each other, or from knowing some important circumstance, by protracted illness, or by coincidence. Thus Ambrosio is able to reach Antonia secretly because her garrulous aunt Leonella is suddenly put out of the way. Indeed, the absence of Leonella is essential to the plot, for Ambrosio is about to pursue his fatal designs upon Elvira and Antonia.

> It was here that he ran the greatest risque of a discovery. Had Leonella been at home, she would have recognized him directly. Her communicative disposition would never have permitted her to rest, till all Madrid was informed that Ambrosio had ventured out of the abbey, and visited her sister. Fortune here stood the monk's friend. On Leonella's return home, she found a letter instructing her, that a cousin was just dead, who had left what little he possessed between herself and Elvira. To secure this bequest she was obliged to set out for Cordova without losing a moment. Amidst all her foibles, her heart was truly warm and affectionate, and she was unwilling to quit her sister in so dangerous a state. [Elvira is ill and confined to her room, another aid to Ambrosio in getting at Antonia.] But Elvira insisted upon her taking the journey, conscious that in her daughter's forlorn situation, no increase of fortune, however trifling, ought to be neglected. (p. 245)

Leonella is unwilling to leave Madrid for another reason: she is in love with Don Christoval, who in his turn is barely aware of her existence. She hesitates, but eventually departs, swearing

> that nothing could make her forget the perfidious Don Christoval. In this point she was fortunately mistaken. An honest youth of Cordova, journeyman to an apothecary, found that her fortune would be sufficient to set him up in a genteel shop of his own. In consequence of his reflection he avowed himself her admirer. Leonella was not inflexible: the ardour of his sighs melted her heart, and she soon consented to make him the happiest of mankind. She wrote to inform her sister of her marriage; but, *for reasons which will be explained hereafter* [italics mine], Elvira never answered her letter. (p. 246)

Lewis threads his way admirably through all this circumstance, but his methods could hardly be called economical. Further, Leonella is almost a full-fledged comic character, who was developed at length in the opening chapter. She belongs in the tradition of the comic waiting-woman, shrewd, vain, and ridiculous—Fielding's Mistress Honour would be an instance. Structurally she is a foil and serves as comic relief, and in herself she is a respectable creation, treated with more decorum and much less cruelty than is the lot of most of her sisterhood. But there is certainly too much of her for the general weal of *The Monk,* unless we frame a theory of structure to account for her that would not be truly applicable to the book.

It is nothing if not profuse. The "History of Don Raymond" contains within it the interpolated stories of Marguerite, the Bleeding Nun, and, more briefly, the Wandering Jew; and there are ten songs and ballads in *The Monk,* extremely competent in versification and in their time much admired. Lewis's talents were many, and tended to jostle. His episodes are frequently constructed like theatrical scenes, to achieve a single striking effect, or a series of effects, both visual and oral. The main plot of Ambrosio usually subsumes these in its intensity, but not always. Thus Antonia, grieving for the death of Elvira and in general filled with thoroughly justified unease, picks up for diversion "a volume of old Spanish ballads" and reads "Alonzo the Brave and Fair Imogine," which is reproduced in its entirety. In its horrendous climax Alonzo comes back from the dead to claim the faithless Imogine, at her wedding to "A Baron all covered with jewels and gold."

> The lady is silent: the stranger complies.
>   His vizor he slowly unclosed:
> Oh! God! what a sight met Fair Imogine's eyes!
> What words can express her dismay and surprise,
>   When a skeleton's head was exposed!
> All present then uttered a terrified shout,
>   All turned with disgust from the scene.
> The worms they crept in, and the worms they crept out,
> And sported his eyes and his temples about,
>   While the spectre addressed Imogine.

It is remarked that "The perusal of this story was ill calculated to dispel Antonia's melancholy" (pp. 307–308), which is highly understandable. With us, however, the case is different; as Oscar Wilde said in a similar situation, "One must have a heart of stone to read the death of Little Nell without laughing."

Notes

1. "It is a puzzle indeed if we ask how it was that such writers as Monk Lewis, 'Apollo's sexton,' who would fain 'make Parnassus a churchyard' [Byron, *English Bards and Scotch Reviewers*]; and Charles Robert Maturin who, as he himself confessed, loved bells rung by viewless hands, daggers encrusted with long shed blood, treacherous doors behind still more treacherous tapestry, mad nuns, apparitions, *et hoc genus omne;* the two lords of macabre romance, should neither of them have sent some hideous vampire ghost ravening through their sepulchral pages" (Montague Summers, *The Vampire: His Kith and Kin,* New Hyde Park, N. Y., 1960, p. 277).

2. Quoted from T. M. Raysor, ed., *Coleridge's Miscellaneous Criticism* (Cambridge, Mass., 1936), pp. 370–371.

3. Page references are drawn from the First Evergreen edition, ed. L. F. Peck (New York: Grove Press, 1959). This is edited from Lewis's first and unexpurgated edition of 1796, "with variant readings" from the later editions.

4. Ibid., Introduction, p. 12.

5. *Coleridge's Miscellaneous Criticism,* p. 371.

6. Ibid., p. 373.

7. Ibid., p. 372.

Emma: A Technique
of Characterization

CHARLES EDGE

Emma Woodhouse, the heroine of Jane Austen's *Emma,* is a charming, lively, intelligent person. She is also vain, proud, and deficient in self-knowledge and tenderness of heart. In the course of the novel she attempts to make a match between Harriet Smith and Mr. Elton, flirts with Frank Churchill, discovers that she loves Mr. Knightley (though she fears that she has lost him to Harriet), and finally marries him. More important, she progresses "from self-deception and vanity to perception and humility"[1] and "learns how to commit herself fully and properly in the moral and social act of marriage, an act whose validity she has begun by denying and with which she begins her mature life."[2]

One of the most striking features of *Emma* is Jane Austen's use of three curious sets of comparisons and contrasts as a means of presenting her subject. In a sense the novel concerns teachers and students, rulers and their subjects, good health and bad health. Jane Austen invites us to apply each of these terms to her heroine. Furthermore, she surrounds Emma with teachers and students, rulers and subjects, and characters whose health is a matter for comment. Her emphasis on the resulting relationships is sufficient to make us aware of the complex possibilities for comparison and contrast.

I

In the background of the novel is Mrs. Goddard's school, "a real, honest, old-fashioned boarding-school"[3] and a prominent institution in Highbury; the three teachers, Miss Nash, Miss Price, and Miss

Richardson, figure in the conversation of Harriet Smith, a parlor boarder there. The novel also contains two governesses—or, more precisely, Mrs. Weston, who has served in that capacity, and Jane Fairfax, who is preparing to seek her first position and enduring meanwhile the presumptuous advice of Mrs. Elton, whose "manners . . . had been formed in a bad school" (p. 272).

Not all the teachers, however, are professionals. Though the Campbells never appear on the scene, they are important, partly at least because of their role in Jane Fairfax's education. Mr. Knightley has served as a teacher of sorts for years, and soon after the novel opens, Emma, his student, decides that she will "improve" Harriet, "form her opinions and her manners" (pp. 23–24).

But teachers are also rulers; a governess not only shapes and molds her pupil but also governs. And *Emma* is very much a novel about rulers. On this subject Mr. Elton's charade is emphatic with its references to "the wealth and pomp of kings," "Lords of the earth," and "the monarch of the seas," and its gallant compliment to "woman, lovely woman" who "reigns alone" (p. 71).

Before Frank Churchill arrives in Highbury, Emma's "idea" of him, she tells Mr. Knightley, is that he is a "universally agreeable" person. Mr. Knightley responds: "What! at three-and-twenty to be the king of his company—the great man—the practised politician, who is to read every body's character, and make every body's talents conduce to the display of his own superiority . . ." (p. 150). Mr. Knightley intends no compliment. Miss Bates does when she refers to Mrs. Elton as "queen of the evening" (p. 329) at the ball at the Crown Inn.

Though not distinguished by titles, Emma and her father are also rulers. The Woodhouses are "first in consequence" in Highbury. "All looked up to them" (p. 7). Wherever Emma is, she "presides" (p. 369), Frank Churchill says with great irony; and Mr. Woodhouse, who is "fond of society in his own way," can "command the visits of his own little circle" (p. 20).

Mr. Knightley, "a sort of general friend and adviser" (p. 59) with "a downright, decided, commanding sort of manner" (p. 34), offers a number of particulars about Emma as a ruler. Ever since she was twelve, he tells Mrs. Weston, she has been "mistress" of Hartfield and "of you all" (p. 37). He continues: "You might not give Emma such a complete education as your powers would seem to promise; but you were receiving a very good education from *her,* on the very material matrimonial point of submitting your own will, and doing as you were bid . . ." (p. 38).

Mr. Knightley's comment raises the question of rule in marriage, a subject noticed frequently in the novel. Mrs. Elton, for example, says to her husband: "Very pretty, sir, upon my word; to send me on here to be an encumbrance to my friends, so long before you vouchsafe to come!—But you knew what a dutiful creature you had to deal with. You knew I should not stir till my lord and master appeared.—Here have I been sitting this hour, giving these young ladies a sample of true conjugal obedience . . ." (p. 457). And we hear that Mrs. Churchill, the almost legendary ruler at Enscombe, "governed her husband" (p. 17).

Mrs. Churchill is significant in still another respect. This powerful figure suffers from ill health; and sickness and good health, as well as teachers and students, rulers and their subjects, are of importance in *Emma.*

Mr. Woodhouse and Isabella discuss matters of health with apprehension and fearful pleasure. She "was not a woman of strong understanding or any quickness; and with this resemblance of her father, she inherited also much of his constitution; was delicate in her own health, over-careful of that of her children, had many fears and many nerves, and was as fond of her own Mr. Wingfield in town as her father could be of Mr. Perry" (p. 92). Their conversation touches on sea-bathing, sore throats, the prevalence of colds, the good (and bad) air of London, the good air of Hartfield, and their apothecaries, Mr. Perry and Mr. Wingfield. Mr. Perry is "pretty well; but not quite well," says Mr. Woodhouse. "Poor Perry is bilious, and he has not time to take care of himself—he tells me he has not time to take care of himself—which is very sad—but he is always wanted all round the country. I suppose there is not a man in such practice any where" (p. 101).

Though Mr. Woodhouse's report on the active life and sad health of Mr. Perry is no doubt extreme, Highbury, which is "reckoned a particularly healthy spot" (p. 22), is indeed touched both directly and indirectly by illness. Mrs. Churchill's illness and death cause repercussions in the community. Harriet misses dinner with the Westons because she has a severe cold. And Jane Fairfax, who has not been quite well since Miss Campbell's marriage, returns to Highbury with the approval of the Campbells, who "depended more on a few months spent in her native air, for the recovery of her health, than on anything else" (p. 166). Her progress is slow.

In this community—with its illnesses and its talk of illnesses, imagined or real—we find Mr. Knightley, who has "a great deal of health" (p. 213). We also find Emma, "the complete picture of grown-up health." Mrs. Weston insists on this view of her friend:

> Such an eye!—the true hazle eye—and so brilliant! regular features, open countenance, with a complexion! oh! what a bloom of full health, and such a pretty height and size; such a firm and upright figure. There is health, not merely in her bloom, but in her air, her head, her glance. One hears sometimes of a child being "the picture of health"; now Emma always gives me the idea of being the complete picture of grown-up health. (p. 39)

Indeed, Emma "had an unhappy state of health in general" for the daughter of Mr. Woodhouse, "for she hardly knew what indisposition was . . ." (p. 336).

These three sets of comparisons and contrasts, detailed and quietly emphatic, are precise instruments in Jane Austen's hands.

II

Jane Austen's critics frequently comment on her use of comparisons and contrasts. Gilbert Ryle, for example, describes what he calls her "special wine-taster's technique of comparative character-delineation. . . . She pin-points the exact quality of character in which she is interested, and the exact degree of that quality, by matching it against the same quality in different degrees, against simulations of that quality, against deficiencies of it, and against qualities which though different, are brothers or cousins of that selected quality."[4] The theme of *Emma*, he suggests, is *"Influence and Interference"* or "more generically, *'Solicitude,'* "[5] and the characters "are systematically described in terms of their different kinds or degrees of concernment or unconcernment with the lives of others." Thus Mr. Woodhouse "tries in vain to influence his friends' needs and his grandchildrens' holiday resorts. He is ever solicitous and solicitous about trivialities, but he does not meddle, save, nearly, once. . . ."[6]

The comparisons involving teachers, rulers, and health provide an extension of such statements. They serve as instruments which Jane

Austen can use in the process of pin-pointing "the exact quality of character" which interests her; they allow her to compare ruler with ruler or one sick person with another and thus define a particular variety and degree of selfishness. But Jane Austen is interested in a social ideal as well as in character, and appropriately the comparisons enable her to focus sharply on individuals as they relate to each other and to the community.

In *Emma* social position is a fact of life. The emphasis on teachers and rulers expands the idea of subordination and firmly suggests that the world of the novel is characterized by the number and variety of authorities that it contains. Many authorities—all willing (and some eager) to exercise their power—attempt to guide, or dominate, or shape the character of individuals around them. Some are well qualified; others are not. Collectively they create a tension, a force, which makes this world seem difficult, even dangerous.

In this world Emma holds two positions of authority: she is both a teacher and a ruler. Comparisons and contrasts define Emma in both roles and in doing so illuminate the novel as a study of character and community.

Mrs. Goddard's school, we are told, was not "a seminary, or an establishment, or any thing which professed in long sentences of re-fined nonsense, to combine liberal acquirements with elegant morality upon new principles and new systems—and where young ladies for enormous pay might be screwed out of health and into vanity . . ." (p. 21). Nor do Mr. Knightley and the Campbells, whose educational programs Jane Austen supports, honor any system which leads to vanity. Mrs. Goddard's is a school "where a reasonable quantity of accomplishments were sold at a reasonable price, and where girls might be sent to be out of the way and scramble themselves into a little edu-cation without any danger of coming back prodigies" (pp. 21–22). Mr. Knightley and the Campbells have something better (and cer-tainly less casual) in mind for Emma and Jane Fairfax.

As teachers Mr. Knightley and the Campbells are motivated by a sense of duty based on friendship and love and are aware of the dangers involved in trying to form another person's character. To a surprising degree they are interested in enforcing the same lessons. They want their pupils to see themselves with clarity, for example, and to act in accordance with their situations. And they want even more. "Living constantly with right-minded and well-informed people, [Jane

Fairfax's] heart and understanding had received every advantage of discipline and culture; and Col. Campbell's residence being in London, every lighter talent had been done full justice to, by the attendance of first-rate masters" (p. 164). Mr. Knightley, as "right-minded" as Colonel and Mrs. Campbell, is obviously interested in a similar program. He, too, can appreciate lighter talents, and he places great value on the understanding and the principles of his rebellious student. With regret, for example, he tells Mrs. Weston that Emma "will never submit to any thing requiring industry and patience, and a subjection of the fancy to the understanding" (p. 37). And at Box Hill he says to Emma, after her heartless treatment of Miss Bates, "I cannot see you acting wrong, without remonstrance" (p. 374). *Wrong*, for him, is a very forceful word.

The value of principle, the regulation and improvement of the heart and understanding, the importance of self-knowledge, and awareness of situation—these are the lessons which Mr. Knightley and the Campbells, committed to their students, teach with love and a sense of responsibility. As a teacher Emma falls woefully short of this standard.

Her motive for setting herself up as Harriet's teacher is clear. "She would notice her; she would improve her; she would detach her from her bad acquaintance, and introduce her into good society; she would form her opinions and her manners. It would be an interesting, and certainly a very kind undertaking; highly becoming her own situation in life, her leisure and powers" (pp. 23-24). Every word betrays the self-love behind her decision to "improve" Harriet.

The lessons that Emma teaches are unlike those endorsed by Mr. Knightley and the Campbells. She gives Harriet notions of self-consequence, thus confirming Mr. Knightley's uneasiness. "I am much mistaken if Emma's doctrines give any strength of mind," he says, "or tend at all to make a girl adapt herself rationally to the varieties of her situation in life" (p. 39). Significantly, the Campbells also elevate their charge. Because they love Jane, they keep her with them, postponing the day when she will have to become a governess. Ultimately, however, she decides to seek her first position.

> The good sense of Colonel and Mrs. Campbell could not oppose such a resolution, though their feelings did. As long as they lived, no exertions would be necessary, their home might be her's for ever; and for their own comfort they would have retained her

wholly; but this would be selfishness:—what must be at last, had better be soon. Perhaps they began to feel it might have been kinder and wiser to have resisted the temptation of any delay, and spared her from a taste of such enjoyments of ease and leisure as must now be relinquished. (p. 165)

Their good sense, unselfishness, and love, their concern for Jane as a person, their keen awareness that she is to be a governess no matter how much they love her contrast emphatically with Emma's distortion of Harriet's situation and her view of her friend as "exactly the something which her home required" (p. 26).

Certainly Emma does little to give Harriet's heart and understanding the advantages of "discipline and culture" which Jane receives from the Campbells. In irresponsible fashion she steps between Harriet and Robert Martin and teaches her to have false hopes about Mr. Elton and (to Emma's astonishment) Mr. Knightley. She does intend to improve her friend's mind, but finds it "much pleasanter to let her imagination range and work at Harriet's fortune, than to be labouring to enlarge her comprehension or exercise it on sober facts . . ." (p. 69). In addition, though Emma, like the Campbells, has good principles, she encourages Harriet to appear ungrateful and rude to the Martins and sets a bad example for her by making uncharitable remarks about Miss Bates.

As Emma goes about the serious business of improving Harriet, it becomes clear that she is poorly qualified for her role: she lacks the proper motive, an understanding of the relationship of teacher and student, and any real sense of the social and moral implications of education. As a teacher, in fact, she represents a threat to Harriet's happiness and security, and, indeed, she succeeds in harming her. Her failure as a teacher neatly underscores her self-love, her irresponsibility, and her colossal blindness.

With the comparisons of rulers Jane Austen continues her exploration of self-love, the nature of commitment, and the uses of power. In the scene at Box Hill, for example, she allows Frank Churchill to create a mock court and place Emma at the center as ruler. "Ladies and gentlemen," he says, "I am ordered by Miss Woodhouse (who, wherever she is, presides,) to say, that she desires to know what you are all thinking of" (p. 369). When the response from the other members of the group is not encouraging, he continues:

Ladies and gentlemen—I am ordered by Miss Woodhouse to say, that she waves her right of knowing exactly what you may all be thinking of, and only requires something very entertaining from each of you, in a general way. Here are seven of you, besides myself, (who, she is pleased to say, am very entertaining already,) and she only demands from each of you either one thing very clever . . .—or two things moderately clever—or three things very dull indeed, and she engages to laugh heartily at them all. (p. 370)

Emma cooperates, and plays Frank's game so well that the "mock ceremony of her manner" (p. 371) momentarily deceives Miss Bates when she insults that good lady.

The scene is a striking one, rich with ironies growing out of the implied comparison between Emma, the ruler of Highbury, and Emma, the mock ruler elevated to artificial heights by Frank's manner. Frank says that Emma "presides wherever she is." But she fails to preside effectively over her mock court: the Eltons are indignant, Mr. Knightley is ironic, Miss Bates is hurt—and the court soon collapses. Ironically, the commands which Frank attributes to Emma point to her self-love and her desire to dominate, the very flaws which qualify her value as a ruler "wherever she is": she "demands" and "orders" and has the "right" to know what others are thinking, and "requires" something entertaining from everyone. Frank, however, successfully controls Emma, the mock ruler, just as he "controls" Emma, the ruler of Highbury. He creates the court; he elevates her; and he invents the commands which he says are hers. In addition, he knows her thoughts well, and Emma, who has the "right" to know, does not understand herself or the tensions which are rapidly developing around her.

The scene is a shrewd example of the comedy of self-deception. More important, it shows Emma's failure, as mock ruler, to recognize her obligations to her small community. Her duty, as Frank describes it for her, is to command and to be amused; her subjects in the court exist to flatter and entertain her. In effect, they do everything for her; she does nothing for them. Her misuse of power, her failure to make a responsible commitment to her subjects, cannot hold the group together, and gradually the members of the party drift away. Like the queen of the mock court, Emma, the ruler of Highbury, is flawed by self-love and the love of power; and she is a disruptive force as she mismanages the affairs of others. Just as Emma, the teacher, represents a threat to Harriet Smith, so Emma, the ruler, is a threat to the community.

But the question of rule is a complex one, and the scene at Box Hill does not exhaust its possibilities. Mrs. Churchill, for example, "governed her husband entirely" (p. 17), and Jane Austen uses this detail from the domestic life of this shadowy figure to establish an important comparison and contrast involving the Eltons and the Westons. Mrs. Elton refers to her husband as her "lord and master" and to herself as an obedient, "dutiful creature" (p. 457). This is no doubt a less than accurate description of the relationship of her affectation and self-deceit to his egotism. Mr. Knightley suggests his view of the problem when he discusses the Westons' marriage with Mrs. Weston. He points out to her that she understands "the very material matrimonial point" of submitting her own will and doing as she is bid (p. 38). And though his statement is couched in irony, his ideal—a marriage in which the will of the husband rules—shines through.

The Churchills and the Eltons obviously do not meet Mr. Knightley's standard; Emma must learn to meet it. Mr. Knightley reminds her that she opposed her will to his when she was a girl: "How often, when you were a girl, have you said to me, with one of your saucy looks—'Mr. Knightley, I am going to do so and so; papa says I may, or I have Miss Taylor's leave'—something which, you knew, I did not approve" (p. 462). She continues to exercise her willfulness throughout the novel, though "she had a sort of habitual respect for his judgment in general, which made her dislike having it so loudly against her . . ." (p. 65). She must learn to submit her will to his, first in friendship, then in marriage; she must learn the significance of his "commanding sort of manner" (p. 34).

There can be little doubt that she learns her lesson well. Her contrition and penitence after Mr. Knightley reprimands her for being thoughtlessly cruel to Miss Bates are encouraging signs. Equally encouraging is her desire "to grow more worthy of him, whose intentions and judgment have been ever so superior to her own" (p. 475). Even more hopeful are Emma's reflections on her willfulness. Aware of her love for Mr. Knightley and afraid that she will lose him, she thinks: "She had herself been first with him for many years past. She had not deserved it; she had often been negligent or perverse, slighting his advice, or even wilfully opposing him insensible of half his merits . . ." (p. 415). The intensity of her feeling is significant. Later,

with shame and regret, she reflects upon her relationship with Jane
Fairfax. "Had she followed Mr. Knightley's known wishes, in paying
that attention to Miss Fairfax, which was every way her due . . . she
must, in all probability, have been spared from every pain which
pressed on her now" (p. 421). Her preoccupation with her willfulness
at a time when her suffering enforces what she sees, her emotional
as well as intellectual assessment of the damage that she has done by
opposing her will to Mr. Knightley's,[7] points to a marriage in which
he will rule.

But before Emma can marry Mr. Knightley, Jane Austen introduces two more rulers—loneliness and melancholy—and allows her
heroine a hard look at a very bleak contrasting possibility.

From the beginning Emma is uneasy about the possibility of
solitude, as her response to Miss Taylor's marriage indicates:

> How was she to bear the change?—It was true that her friend was
> going only half a mile from them; but Emma was aware that great
> must be the difference between a Mrs. Weston only half a mile from
> them, and a Miss Taylor in the house; and with all her advantages,
> natural and domestic, she was now in great danger of suffering
> from intellectual solitude. She dearly loved her father, but he was
> no companion for her. He could not meet her in conversation, ra-
> tional or playful. (pp. 6–7)

On occasion she collects Mrs. Bates, Miss Bates, and Mrs. Goddard
for her father's amusement, but they are "no remedy for the absence
of Mrs. Weston" and "the quiet prosings of three such women made
her feel that every evening so spent, was indeed one of the long evenings
she had fearfully anticipated" (p. 22). At this point Emma feels a
need for companionship which she does not understand. She insists
on defining "solitude" in superficial terms; what she fears is boredom
or, more specifically, having no one to talk with her on her own intellectual level. She thinks of solitude again when she fails to receive
an invitation to the Coles's dinner party and sees herself "being left in
solitary grandeur." Her original response to the idea of being invited is thoroughly snobbish. When she is apparently excluded, however, the thought that the party would consist "precisely of those whose
society was dearest to her" occurs to her repeatedly (p. 208). Again
she feels a need and fails to comprehend it, as her recollections the
next day indicate: what she lost "on the side of dignified seclusion"

by going to the party, she thinks, was "amply repaid in the splendour of popularity" (p. 231).

Ultimately she does learn to understand the nature of solitude. Aware at last that she has acted toward everyone with "insufferable vanity" (p. 412) and "unpardonable arrogance" (p. 413) rather than with responsibility, aware too of her own heart, of her affection for Mr. Knightley, and afraid that she has no hope of his returning her love, Emma spends a long and thoroughly unhappy evening at Hartfield. The weather—the cold, stormy rain—simply adds to her gloom. Wretched, she looks into the future and sees a disheartening prospect: "If all took place that might take place among the circle of her friends, Hartfield must be comparatively deserted; and she left to cheer her father with the spirits only of ruined happiness" (p. 422). Her thoughts then focus on Mr. Knightley: "All that were good would be withdrawn; and if to these losses, the loss of Donwell were to be added, what would remain of cheerful or of rational society within their reach?" (p. 422). The next morning nothing has changed. "The weather continued much the same . . .; and the same loneliness, and the same melancholy, seemed to reign at Hartfield—but in the afternoon it cleared; the wind changed into a softer quarter; the clouds were carried off; the sun appeared; it was summer again" (p. 424).

The weather does indeed change. The sun appears, and with it Mr. Knightley and his love. Before this happens, however, Emma's idea of solitude takes on a dimension which it does not have at the beginning of the novel. Faced with the possibility of a comparatively deserted Hartfield and the loss of all cheerful or rational society, she focuses the emotions which have been building up in her ever since she discovered her love and her folly. And Emma, who has opposed her will to Mr. Knightley's and attempted to dominate society, experiences the alternative to the rule of a husband and proper commitment to the community; she *feels* the power of loneliness and melancholy, the rulers who seem "to reign" at Hartfield. Her insight seems clear. Solitude, she now sees, is neither boredom nor unpopularity. It is, rather, a frustrating and tormenting loneliness characterized by a profound sense of loss: it is loving without hope of having the love returned; it is recognizing the value of commitment to the group when there is no group. In a word, it is incompleteness.

Emma's intensely personal experience with the rule of loneliness and melancholy marks the climax of the learning sequence which begins when she recognizes that she loves Mr. Knightley. An important though less dramatic discovery that she makes about herself earlier in this same sequence is related to the question of health.

Here, by virtue of her illness and death, Mrs. Churchill serves as a key figure.

> Goldsmith tells us, that when lovely woman stoops to folly, she has nothing to do but to die; and when she stoops to be disagreeable; it is equally to be recommended as a clearer of ill-fame. Mrs. Churchill, after being disliked at least twenty-five years, was now spoken of with compassionate allowance. In one point she was fully justified. She had never been admitted before to be seriously ill. The event acquitted her of all the fancifulness, and all the selfishness of imaginary complaints. (p. 387)

But the event does not acquit her of the selfishness of real complaints; nor does it remove the possibility of earlier imaginary illnesses. Mr. Weston suggests that she has "no more heart than a stone to people in general" (p. 121), and indeed her selfishness is easily apparent in her heartless domination of those around her. Mr. Woodhouse is a clear illustration of "the selfishness of imaginary complaints." A hypochondriac, he views everything as a threat to himself. He distrusts food, weather, walking, and driving. He is fond of people that he is accustomed to, but, no doubt to protect his equanimity, he assumes that they feel as he does. In addition, fearful of change of any kind, he hates to part with anyone. His nervousness, anxieties, and fears are all characteristics of his "gentle selfishness" (p. 8).

Jane Fairfax provides a variation on the theme of selfishness. Her difficulties with her health begin at Weymouth when she agrees to a secret engagement with Frank Churchill. She makes her commitment to him out of love. In doing so, however, she exhibits a selfish disregard for her obligations to others. "Do not let any reflection fall on the principles or the care of the friends who brought me up," she says. "The error has been all my own; and I do assure you that, with all the excuse that present circumstances may appear to give, I shall yet dread making the story known to Colonel Campbell" (p. 419).

The consequences of Jane's selfish act of love are far reaching. Unattached, she can look forward only to an unhappy career as a governess. "If a woman can ever be excused for thinking only of herself," Emma says, "it is in a situation like Jane Fairfax's.—Of such, one may almost say, that 'the world is not their's, nor the world's law' " (p. 400). Though Emma speaks with feeling, she carefully implies that there is, after all, only one law—the world's. And when Jane chooses to follow her own, she deliberately separates herself, in a way, from the world—a division emphasized by the life of conscious deception that she leads after her engagement. Mr. Woodhouse, with his imaginary complaints, is also apart from the world. His hypochondria, in fact, suggests such a fear of reality[8] that we are inclined to accept his words literally when he says, "But I live out of the world, and am often astonished at what I hear" (p. 252). Similarly, Mrs. Churchill's withdrawal from society is linked with her "complaint." Frank Churchill reports, for example, that at Enscombe "their visitings were among a range of great families, none very near; and that even when days were fixed, and invitations accepted, it was an even chance that Mrs. Churchill were not in health or spirits for going . . ." (p. 221).

Mrs. Churchill, Mr. Woodhouse, Jane Fairfax—an unlikely grouping. And yet all three suffer from real or imaginary complaints which have a common base—selfishness. Mrs. Churchill and Mr. Woodhouse fail to see their responsibilities to individuals and society; Jane sees her obligations but deliberately chooses not to honor them. And each character, accordingly, is separated from the world.

According to Mrs. Weston, Emma is "the complete picture of grown-up health" (p. 39). And indeed her vitality and energy create the impression of physical well-being. In the painful process of getting to know herself better, however, Emma learns something about her health which links her with Mrs. Churchill, Mr. Woodhouse, and Jane Fairfax and places her in sharp contrast with Mr. Knightley, who has "a great deal of health" (p. 213) and is indeed much closer to being a complete picture of grown-up health than she is.

Just before the long stormy evening which she spends so wretchedly, Emma receives a visit from Mrs. Weston, who wishes to give an account of her interview with Jane Fairfax. In the course of the conversation, Emma falters and seems confused, and Mrs. Weston asks, "Are you well, my Emma?" She replies, "Oh! Perfectly, I am always well, you know" (p. 420). Her conscious irony suggests that she now sees herself as significantly unwell.

Mrs. Weston's remarks increase Emma's compassion and esteem for Jane and also stir her feelings of guilt. But Emma finds it difficult to concentrate on what her friend is saying, for her mind is elsewhere.

The one subject which had dominated her thoughts for twenty-four hours is Mr. Knightley. Inextricably linked with her thoughts of him is her recent realization that she has been guilty of vanity and arrogance and deficient in her knowledge of herself and others. When Emma stumbles in her conversation with Mrs. Weston, her faults and the consequences of her faults are uppermost in her mind. When she recovers by saying, "I am always well, you know," she is passing harsh judgment on herself—on her selfishness, her failure to see her responsibilities, her separation from everyone. From this position, filled with self-disgust, Emma moves into her long night and discovers the implications of the solitude which she fears is her destiny.

But the novel is, after all, a comedy, and Emma's punishment and suffering last only long enough to secure her emotional as well as intellectual acknowledgment of her errors and their consequences. Once this has happened, she can marry Mr. Knightley and "the small band of true friends" can rejoice in "the perfect happiness of the union" (p. 484). This comedy, however, has grave implications about character and community. As one means of defining them, Jane Austen asks three questions: What is a teacher? what is a ruler? what is good health? Her answers contribute to the complex possibilities of the novel as a study of self-love, the uses of power, and the nature of commitment.

Notes

1. Edgar F. Shannon, *"Emma:* Character and Construction," *PMLA,* LXXI (1956), 650.

2. Malcolm Bradbury, "Jane Austen's *Emma," Critical Quarterly,* IV (1962), 345.

3. *Emma,* in *The Novels of Jane Austen,* ed. R. W. Chapman, 3rd ed. (London, 1952), p. 39. Subsequent references are to this edition and appear parenthetically in the text.

4. Gilbert Ryle, "Jane Austen and the Moralists," in *Critical Essays on Jane Austen,* ed. B. C. Southam (London, 1968), p. 108.

5. Ibid., p. 110.

6. Ibid., p. 111.

7. Emma's tears at Box Hill "signify an emotional as well as a mental commitment to a new mode of conduct and to the necessity of Mr. Knightley's approval" (Shannon, p. 641).

8. "Mrs. Percival (in *Catharine or The Bower)* is the first hypochondriac in Jane Austen's fiction, and here—as in future works—the hypochondria is used as an emblem for fear of reality" (A. Walton Litz, *Jane Austen: A Study of Her Artistic Development,* London, 1965, p. 37).

Nigel and the Historical Imagination

C. HUGH HOLMAN

The publication in 1814 of *Waverley,* Walter Scott's first novel, stands like a continental divide in the history of fiction. Before Scott there was novelistic accomplishment of tremendous magnitude, contemporary with him was the almost perfect artistry of Jane Austen, and yet the novel, in whatever language, was not to be the same again after *Waverley* had made its way into the reading world. It was not merely that no one for the rest of the century was to be free of his influence, that Dickens, Thackeray, and George Eliot in England, Cooper and Hawthorne in America, Manzoni in Italy, Hugo, Balzac, and Dumas in France, Tolstoi and Pushkin in Russia, and historians like Leopold von Ranke and Macaulay were to adapt his method and something of his subject matter. If the novel is a study of man, then the Waverley Novels represent in that study a "turn" in the Aristotelian sense, a reversal the consequences of which were permanent. For the image of man, either alone or in society, gained in Scott's work a new dimension and a new direction. From Scott's work stems the sense of man in history.

These seem extravagant claims for a writer today often neglected even in courses in the history of the novel, one whose grievous faults are the easy possession of supercilious schoolboys, and one who invented a form currently held in critical disrepute. It is easy to see his faults; they are large and unmistakable, but an awareness of them is no modern discovery. Reviewers were pointing them out in the

[65]

quarterlies while the Waverley Novels were still being written. Scott himself pointed out many of them and passed on his own work some of the harshest of judgments. In an anonymous review of *The Antiquary,* he wrote, "Waverley, Brown, or Bertram in Guy Mannering, and Lovel in the Antiquary, are all brethren of a family; very amiable and very insipid sort of young men." [1] He repeatedly declared himself the willing victim of the taste and wishes of his public. He praised Jane Austen for "describing the involvements and feelings and characters of ordinary life," while he acknowledged his to be "The Big Bow-wow strain." [2] What gave the Waverley novels an influence unequalled in the history of the genre was not connected with these faults but with special virtues that transcend them. It resulted from the presence in them of a new kind of imagination, the historical imagination. Scott showed man in time and place, showed him as both maker and product of historical forces, showed him imprisoned and defined by actions and manners, and, above all, depicted him as a part of society in process.

Walter Scott was in his forty-third year when he took up the incomplete manuscript of *Waverley,* brought it to a conclusion, and published it anonymously. Behind him was a distinguished career as student, scholar, critic, collector of ballads, amateur but committed historian, and author of some of the most popular long narrative poems ever written, including *The Lay of the Last Minstrel, Marmion,* and *The Lady of the Lake.* He was partially crippled by infantile paralysis when a baby and consequently became an omnivorous reader. Although trained to the law, he was an indifferent lawyer. He had a deep love for Scotland and its craggy past. And he was a man to whom writing was as natural as breathing and seemingly as easy. Although he was late in finding his vocation, Scott was a born novelist. He fused a perennially boyish delight in action and adventure, a memory as phenomenal as any to be encountered in literary biography (he could repeat long poems verbatim after hearing them once), a love for place, a very real devotion to the common and the earthy and to the ballads and bare facts of the lives of simple people, with a pervasive and exact knowledge of history and an interest in social forces in the past.

In 1808 Scott completed an unfinished historical novel, *Queenhoo Hall,* which his late antiquarian friend Joseph Strutt had begun. It was laid during the reign of Henry VI and designed to "illustrate the manners, customs, and language of the people of England during that period."[3] Despite Strutt's adequate knowledge of the period and Scott's literary skill the work was not successful, and Scott felt that its failure resulted from Strutt's not having rendered his "antiquarian knowledge" in language "easily comprehended." It was probably as a result of this experience that Scott wrote the first seven chapters of *Waverley* at that time. For in attempting *Waverley,* he was wrestling with the problem of illustrating "the manners, customs, and language" of a bygone period in a form readily available to the general reader. He succeeded magnificently. *Waverley* was tightly bound to the Scotland of sixty years before, but, despite its extensive use of dialect, it was "easily comprehended." He informed the reader of *Waverley* that the book he held in his hand was, at least in the intention of its author, something new. He had chosen "an uncontaminated name," without romantic associations, and had avoided "the castle of Udolpho" and "Rosycrucians and Illuminati," sentimental heroines, and "dashing sketch[es] of the fashionable world." He said, "I would have my readers understand, that they will meet in the following pages neither a romance of chivalry nor a tale of modern manners."[4] The almost incredible success of *Waverley* showed that the public recognized and valued this newness. It led to that long chain of thirty-one other novels and tales "by the author of Waverley," which are still known as "The Waverley Novels."

As if these works were not enough, after 1814 Scott also wrote two long narrative poems, edited Swift's works, wrote a series of critical biographies of English novelists, wrote a life of Napoleon, and, as a partner in the publishing firm of the Ballantynes, underwent financial ruin from which he extricated himself by devoting the remainder of his life to working to repay his creditors. On September 21, 1832, he died at his beloved Abbotsford, which he had made into a veritable historical museum.

All the evidence shows that Scott was a truly virtuous, scrupulously honest, and courageous man. Extreme good-will and good-nature have been called his greatest flaws. But he was also a naive, ingenuous, and in certain ways immature man, who played at life with boyish enthusiasm, hiding his identity behind ridiculous masks, bankrupting himself to create a feudal estate, and often harnessing a magnificent novelistic talent to the whims of a casual public. In the closing years of his life, when the fruits of his immaturity and his universal benevolence came home to him in financial ruin, he shouldered his burdens with a display of moral courage greater than he assigned most of his heroes. But the significant and enduring accomplishment of this admirable life was not narrative poetry or Abbotsford but the Waverley Novels.

In *Guy Mannering* (1815), *The Antiquary* (1816), and *The Black Dwarf* (1816) he continued to write of eighteenth-century Scotland, as he had in *Waverley*. In *Old Mortality* (1816) he moved to Scotland at the time of the Covenanters' insurrection in the seventeenth century. In *Rob Roy* (1817) and *The Heart of Midlothian* (1818) and *The Bride of Lammermoor* (1819) he wrote of Scotland in the early eighteenth century. *A Legend of Montrose* (1819) moved back to the seventeenth century and the Civil War. Scott turned from Scotland to England and from the modern ages to the medieval period for the first time in *Ivanhoe* (1820) because he feared that his readers would grow tired of the same fare. Its success was phenomenal. *The Monastery* (1820) and *The Abbot* (1820) dealt with the days of Mary, Queen of Scots, and *Kenilworth* (1821) with the reign of Elizabeth. *The Pirate* (1821) was laid in the Shetland and Orkney Islands in the early eighteenth century. *The Fortunes of Nigel* (1822) was laid in England in the reign of James I. *Peveril of the Peak* (1822) was concerned with the Popish plot in 1678. *Quentin Durward* (1823) occurred in the France of Louis XI. *St. Ronan's Well* (1824) was a contemporary story. *Redgauntlet* (1824) was laid in eighteenth-century Scotland. *The Betrothed* (1825) and *The Talisman* (1825) are tales of the Crusades. *Woodstock* (1826) dealt with the Civil War and the Commonwealth. *The Fair Maid of Perth* (1828) was laid in Scotland during the reign of Robert III. *Anne of Geierstein* (1829) concerned fifteenth-century Switzerland. *Count Robert of Paris* (1831) dealt with the Crusaders at Byzantium, and *Castle Dangerous* (1831) was laid in Scotland in the days of the "Black Douglas."

Even so brief a listing of period and setting for the Waverley Novels as this shows that Scott was most often the recorder of the recent and fairly recent history of his beloved Scotland. The bulk of his best fiction is laid in his native land during the seventeenth and eighteenth centuries. Yet much of his fame rested and rests on stories like *Ivanhoe, Kenilworth, Quentin Durward,* and *The Talisman,* laid in England, the continent, and the Holy Land in medieval and Renaissance times. Certainly, although many of his finest creations speak with a Scottish burr, the range of his people is remarkably broad, and the variety of his situations is truly astounding. Careless though he often was in constructing his central plots, he was wonderfully fertile in concocting convincing and dramatic episodes.

Critics have selected various of these novels for their special praise, most often choosing the comparatively early Scottish stories, such as *The Heart of Midlothian* and *Old Mortality*. Some have praised *Quentin Durward, Redgauntlet,* and *St. Ronan's Well.* Scott himself preferred *Rob Roy.* In recent years *Waverley* has had several strong admirers. In selecting a representative Waverley Novel, one uses these favorites, as well as such well-known tales as *Ivanhoe* and *The Talisman,* only with partial success; for, despite their excellence—perhaps, even, because of it—they do not show Scott's range or his historical breadth.

The Fortunes of Nigel has had relatively few who claim for it superlative qualities. Hesketh Pearson called it "Scott's most varied and richly coloured romance,"[5] and Edward Wagenknecht said that it is "one of the best adventure stories ever written."[6] It has many claims to being, if not superior, clearly representative. It was written when Scott was at the peak of his fame and power. It is laid in England in the days when it had a Scottish king and is crowded with Scottish people seen in sharp contrast to the English. It is modeled in part on the rich portrayal of criminal life in Alsatia in English drama, particularly in the plays of Shadwell. It hinges upon complex and intricately convoluted problems of Scottish law. Despite an incredibly circumstantial central plot, its adventure story is as exciting as Scott ever wrote, and it is crowded with scenes that are vivid and convincing. And it contains in the portrait of James I Scott's greatest portrayal of a historical figure. Through its examination the essential nature of the Waverley Novels and the primary characteristics of his method as a writer can be illustrated.

First we need to examine the nature of Scott's special use of history in fiction. Shakespeare's Caesar, Lear, Macbeth, Hamlet, Henry IV exist as persons in an absolute world of motives, emotions, actions, and deeds free of the trammels of historical time or special place—or, perhaps, like Tennyson's Arthur, bound by the trammels of their author's time and place. On the other hand, Scott's Richard the Lion-Hearted, Louis XI, James I, Elizabeth, and even the simplest of his Scottish peasants exist in the confines of a very particular time and place. On the simplest level, this is merely freedom from anachronism. Shakespeare writing today might send Washington across the Delaware in a motor-driven landing craft; but Scott would know the exact structure of the boat Washington used and would have at least a generalized knowledge of how the oarsmen talked to each other. Yet freedom from anachronism is a negative virtue, and greatness is always positive. Shakespeare might say profound things about man and patriotism through his anachronistic Washington, and a literal and accurate description might be trivial.

What Scott said through his use of history struck his century as profoundly meaningful. This is not to say that Scott aspired to or had a philosophical mind or that truths of an abstract sort are to be found very often in his works. Although Thomas Carlyle felt that they "taught all men this truth . . . that the bygone ages of the world were actually filled by living men, not by protocols, state-papers, controversies, and abstractions of men," he could find in the novels none of that philosophical depth to which his own soul aspired, "no opinions, emotions, principles, doubts, beliefs, beyond what the intelligent country gentleman can carry along with him."[7] Yet Coleridge saw in the pattern of these novels a conflict that was deeply significant. He defined it as "the contest between the two great moving principles of social humanity: religious adherence to the past and the ancient, the desire and the admiration of permanence, on the one hand; and the passion for increase of knowledge, for truth, as the offspring of reason—in short, the mighty instincts of *progression* and *free agency,* on the other."[8] It was in imposing upon man's awareness of himself a sense of a continuum of time and institution and of the shaping power of the events of history that Scott gave the novel a new grasp upon the reality of man's accelerating contest with his society, a contest which marked the nineteenth century.

In achieving this sense of history as process, the selection of an appropriate historical period was of cardinal importance. As Walter Raleigh said, "The historical novelists who preceded Scott chose a century as they might have chosen a partner for a dance, gaily and confidently, without qualification or equipment beyond a few outworn verbal archaisms."[9] But Scott chose a period for qualities directly associated with his concept of history and of the novel which he planned to write to illustrate it. For him an age of great contrast afforded the most satisfactory basis for a social study. As he said of *Ivanhoe,* "The period . . . afford[ed] a striking contrast betwixt the Saxons, by whom the soil was cultivated, and the Normans, who still reigned in it as conquerors, reluctant to mix with the vanquished, or acknowledge themselves of the same stock." [10] In the Introduction to *The Fortunes of Nigel* he explained his choice of the period of James I:

> . . . the most picturesque period of history is that when the ancient rough and wild manners of a barbarous age are just becoming innovated upon and contrasted by the illumination of renewed or reformed religion. The strong contrast produced by the opposition of ancient manners to those which are gradually subduing them affords the lights and shadows necessary to give effect to a fictitious narrative. . . . The state of society in the reign of James I was also strangely disturbed, and the license of a part of the community was perpetually giving rise to acts of blood and violence. [11]

This contrast inherent in the time setting of the novel was further heightened by introducing into a sophisticated but morally decadent London a band of grim and warlike Scots, who make the implicit conflict between Puritan religious fervor and moral rectitude and the growing license of the established Church a physically embodied and individually comprehended difference.

The period of James I also gave him almost unlimited variations on the contrasts of old and new ways. As he said, "Some beams of chivalry, although its planet had been for some time set, continued to animate and gild the horizon." [12] At the same time the new class born of the triumphs of Elizabeth's navy was starting the trend which was to make England a nation of little shopkeepers and bankers. Scott saw the beginnings of capitalism in the seventeenth century and depicted them. For this burgeoning world of trade and handicraft, of industry and banking is very much a part of Nigel's London. The novel opens with a sharply dramatic scene in which David Ramsey, horologue to the king, and his apprentices, Jenkin Vincent and Frank Tunstall, are conducting business in the rowdy and bustling world of a London tradesman within Temple Bar, where 'prentices are likely to brawl with Templars and aristocrats; and it quickly moves to the home of George Heriot, middle-class Scotsman and banker to the king.

Such contests between old and new, between chivalry and capitalism are realized in dozens of separate ways, some of them dramatic microcosms of the sweep of English history in the seventeenth century. For example, John Christie, a stern Puritan, is deeply wronged by the "new ways" of the Cavaliers when his wife Dame Nellie is seduced, and he is pathetic in his grief, although Scott had a lot of comic delight in suggesting Dame Nellie's readiness for seduction. Then Christie changes from pathetic to awesome as he takes revenge for the wrong and then extends forgiveness to his wife. The contest between Puritan and Cavalier is here realized in simple, individual lives and made movingly personal in an incident almost casual to the main plot.

But the contrasts go, if not deeper, at least much further. Nigel Olifaunt, Lord of Glenvarloch, inhabits a world of Scots set down in the shadow of the court of an English monarch who is himself a Scot. The rough manners and rudely honest ways of the Scotsman are sharply contrasted with the smoother manners and more ingenious ways of the English. Lord Huntinglen, a Scot, defines the difference well when he says, ". . . my grey beard falls on a cambric ruff and a silken doublet, my father's descended upon a buff coat and a breastplate."[13] George Heriot, looking at Huntinglen and his son, Dalgarno, declares, "There live . . . the old fashion and the new. The father is like a noble old broadsword, but harmed with rust, from neglect and inactivity; the son is your modern rapier, well-mounted, fairly gilt, and fashioned to the taste of the time."[14] Dalgarno is, ironically, the villain, and his temporary triumph over the Scotsmen would finally fall before the historical clash of Puritan and Cavalier even if Scott had not chosen to destroy him in the melodramatic plot. His fall, however poorly handled as melodrama, is inevitable as history. Yet an important part of the new way, represented by the Ramseys and the Heriots, is to survive and finally to triumph. Scott's solutions are seldom simplistic.

This contrast goes still further in the person of James I, whose portrait is usually praised as Scott's greatest characterization of a historical figure. (Coleridge, however, disagreed, thinking it more "burlesque" than portrait.[15]) James is a Scotsman from his dialect to his daily actions, a chieftain from an earlier time who is, for all his Latinate learning and curious lore, out of place away from Scotland's crags and brusk warriors. He is trapped in the financial maze of the new way, just as he and his land are also trapped in the religious conflict. James I stands at a halfway house between the old and the new in chivalry, in monarchy, in business affairs, in national loyalties, and in religion. In his comic way he is as lonely a figure as "The Disinherited Knight" riding to do battle for Saxon honor in Norman armor in *Ivanhoe*. Scott lavished upon his portrait both love and skill.

In 1819 Abel Moysey had published a novel, *Forman*, laid in the reign of James I, and Scott had taken exception to its picture of the monarch. He wrote Moysey, "The 'wisest fool in Christendom' ought to have had a more marked character. I have sometimes thought his wit, his shrewdness, his pedantry, his self-importance & vanity, his greed & his prodigality, his love of minions & his pretensions to wisdom made him one of the richest characters for comedy who ever existed in real history."[16] In the comic person of this ruler, Scott found a most effective personal portrait of the conflicts of the age and one that he could treat with both sympathy and amusement, for *The Fortunes of Nigel* is an adventure story which hinges on sharp points of law and shrewd business practices; it belongs to a world to be won at the Exchange and not at a passage of arms. And James I, greedy for glory and stripped for cash, kiting his royal warrants like a modern business man desperately kiting checks, sums up in his person the essence of his age, as he carries out day by day the policies that bring ever closer the catastrophe of the Civil War.

The Fortunes of Nigel is comic in mood like most of Scott's fiction, except a few pieces such as *The Bride of Lammermoor, The Fair Maid of Perth,* and "The Two Drovers." It is comic not only because within its limits all ends well and rewards and punishments are distributed with all the unembarrassed profusion of the writer of comedy; it is comic because the center of the novel is James I, the magnificence of whose portrait is that he is both the wisest fool in Christendom and a believable ruler with strength and royal honor. Yet behind this hurried and comic story of a transitional age, the reader with even the faintest awareness of history senses the portentous quality of the events. "Baby Charles" and "Steenie" and the depleted royal coffers keep before us the sense of that next installment, in which Cromwell and Civil War are to be the fruits of these days and deeds. Hence a kind of tragic irony underlies this pleasant exterior. The inexorable and deadly rush of time can be faintly heard off stage. But it, too, is embraced in the author's genial good will.

If, as Georg Lukács says in one of the finest studies of Scott,[17] the "Glorious Revolution" of 1688 was the perfect embodiment of the English social ideal, Scott's choice of the reign of the first of the Stuarts and his emphasis on that monarch's part in the rise of capitalism is a significant beginning for the progress of modern British history, and one which ultimately justifies the pleasant tone of comedy about an age in which much that is good and admirable is overshadowed by the bloody threat of war in the near future. Thus the choice of period in *The Fortunes of Nigel* not only serves dramatic and fictional purposes; it is consonant with an idea of historical progression, however unarticulated, and appropriate to a mood that can see James as "one of the richest characters for comedy who ever existed in real history." Scott chose well in selecting his period.

Yet having chosen it, he used very few historical events and, in fact, gave it a very indefinite location in time. Although critics of the novel have assigned it dates from 1603 to 1624, locating its exact time-setting is impossible. Charles ı was born in 1600 and he is a young man in this novel. The King James Version of the Bible, translated in 1611, is referred to as an accomplished fact. George Villiers, although eight years older than Charles, did not arrive at the English court until 1614, and Charles' brother died in 1612. Villiers was married in 1620, although he is single in the novel. He was not made Duke of Buckingham until 1623, yet he is given this title consistently in the novel. His famous trip to Spain took place in 1623, so the one which figures faintly in *The Fortunes of Nigel* must have been earlier but just when is uncertain. Sir Thomas Overbury died in 1613, and Mistress Turner, of the yellow starch, was executed in 1615, and both are dead at the time of action of the novel. Measured by these events the novel appears to be laid sometime between 1616 and 1620, a dating in no way aided or injured by the facts about the one major historical figure other than those already named, George Heriot. Yet a date this late casts an air of uncertainty on Nigel Olifaunt, whose father's claim against James has lain dormant since 1603, when James mounted the English throne. Scott is not being cavalier with time or history (although he was perfectly willing to do so, as he showed when he had a Shakespeare play performed on a Queen's progress in the 1570s in *Kenilworth*). It is simply that he has fused a number of aspects of the Age of James in this study of the manners, lives, and hopes of his English and Scottish citizens.

Scott seems to have been influenced to write the novel by two different immediate motives. He amused himself in 1821 by writing a series of "Private Letters," supposedly recently discovered, that gave a picture of manners in the reign of James ı, and finally decided to put this matter to novelistic use in a tale about "Gentle King Jemmy our Scottish Solomon."[18] But there is no reason to question—and there is, indeed, every reason to accept—Scott's statement in the Introduction to *The Fortunes of Nigel* that he wanted to write a novel with a simple and good hero, not of noble birth but of great worth of character, and that George Heriot, Scottish goldsmith and banker to James I, who followed his monarch to London and there came to be known as "Jingling Geordie," was the figure around whom he decided to weave the story. Heriot died in 1624 a rich but childless man, and left a huge bequest to educate the freemen's sons of Edinburgh at a "hospital," now called a "Boys' School." Scott's plan was to show Heriot's "efforts directed to the benefit of a young nobleman, misguided by the aristocratic haughtiness of his own time."[19] Heriot was a financier, a philanthropist, and very plainly an early but major capitalist. In the novel he is counterpoised against King James, and he serves as a true representative of the "world-historical individual" whom Hegel calls "the hidden Spirit knocking at the door of the present, still subterranean, still without a contemporary existence and wishing to break out, for whom the contemporary world is but a husk containing a different kernel from the old."[20]

That one may say this much about the nature and meaning of *The Fortunes of Nigel* without referring in any detail to its ostensible protagonist, its central plot, or the desperate adventures into which its titular hero is tossed is a significant commentary on the basic nature of the Scott novel and the role of imaginary and real personages in it, and on his special use of history and historical events.

The two principal figures of the novel are James and Jingling Geordie; they absorb our imagination and embody much of what Scott has to say of history. But the novel is not about either of them; it is about a group of imaginary personages upon whom they act. James and Heriot, Charles and Buckingham make their times; the central figures of the fictional narrative are made by those times. Although Margaret Ramsey, a vivaciously charming commoner, is a livelier heroine than Scott usually casts in the central feminine role, both she and Nigel really belong to the group of Scott's insipid young lovers, and they seem but instruments of the plot. Nigel, when a fugitive in Alsatia and at the lowest point of his life, broods over his situation in terms that describe very effectively and directly his role in the novel. He says:

"I am ashamed to have suffered the same habit of throwing my own burden upon others, to render me, since I came to this city, a mere victim of those events which I have never even attempted to influence—a thing never acting, but perpetually acted upon—protected by one friend [Heriot], deceived by another [Dalgarno]; but in the advantage which I received from the one, and the evil I have sustained from the other, as passive and helpless as a boat that drifts without oar or rudder at the mercy of the winds and waves. I became a courtier, because Heriot so advised it; a gamester, because Dalgarno so contrived it; an Alsatian, because Lowestoffe so willed it. Whatever of good or bad has befallen me hath arisen out of the agency of others, not from my own."[21]

Nigel is not only accurate in this estimate of himself, he describes the standard function of the protagonist in Scott's novels.

However weak such a protagonist may be, passivity is a direct function of Scott's view of history and of life.[22] Historical man is the product of social forces; he stands in his time and place unique to his nationality and his manners, a product more than a producer. It is Scott's interest in these shaping forces which constitutes his special contribution to the novel, but it is an interest not in the forces themselves so much as in their impact on common men living under them. The question that he seems always to be asking is not who won what famous victory or how, not the origin or progress of some great affair of state, not huge military strategies or even diplomatic coups. His question is simpler, more fundamental, and vastly harder to answer. It is, What was it like to have lived then, under such conditions, driven by such forces? James's parsimonious yet spendthrift ways, his methods of finance, his love of minions, his blindness to the flaws in favorites had enormous ramifications for the English people and wrote with a bloody scrawl across the pages of their history in the seventeenth century. These large consequences Scott takes it for granted that we know. But in Nigel and Moniplies, in Heriot and Huntinglen, in Margaret and Hermione, in Sir Mungo Malagrowther, in Duke Hildebran and Martha Trapbois he shows what it was like to live as a common, historically faceless citizen in those days. To the extent that a way of life is the determinant here, Scott is a novelist of the manners of past ages. In fact, Ernest A. Baker has argued that the Scott novel is essentially a novel of manners laid in the past, with the three constituents of a thorough knowledge of the period, a sufficiency of human figures, and a plan of action "as the machinery to set things going."[23] But it is more accurate to say, as Karl Kroeber does, that a

Scott novel is a "story of changing styles of life in which the individuals are significant as representatives of supra-personal forces."[24]

The result is that, as Louis Reynaud says, "Ses personnages ne sont pas libres. Ils sont presque exclusivement des produits de leur hérédité, de leur milieu, de leur profession, qui les dominent."[25] If Scott had stopped there, with the fictional personages who always carry his plots drawn simply as the products of forces outside themselves, he would have come very close to late nineteenth-century naturalism. And, indeed, his protagonists certainly anticipate a character like Dreiser's Carrie Meeber in their passivity, if in nothing else. But for Scott there was another dimension. It was consistency of human character and personality. He not only saw man as shaped by social and political forces, he also believed in the unchanging quality of human nature and in a persistent moral order. Man he saw as a great constant in a perpetually changing equation of politics, customs, and manners. In *Waverley* he said:

> The object of my tale is more a description of men than manners
> . . . throwing the force of my narrative upon the character and
> passions of the actors—those passions common to men in all stages
> of society. . . . Upon these passions it is no doubt true that the state
> of manners and laws casts a necessary colouring; but the bearings,
> to use the language of heraldry, remain the same, though the tinc-
> ture may be not only different, but opposed in strong contradistinc-
> tion. . . . The deep-ruling impulse is the same . . . and the proud
> peer who can now only ruin his neighbor according to law, by pro-
> tracted suits, is the genuine descendant of the baron who wrapped
> the castle of his competitor in flames, and knocked him on the head
> as he endeavored to escape from the conflagration.[26]

In the Dedicatory Epistle to *Ivanhoe,* he declared, "The passions . . . are generally the same in all ranks and conditions, all countries and ages; and it follows, as a matter of course, that the opinions, habits of thinking, and actions, however influenced by the peculiar state of society, must still, upon the whole, bear a strong resemblance to each other."[27] Although in the coy Introductory Epistle to *The Fortunes of Nigel* Scott said, "I am no great believer in the moral utility to be derived from fictitious composition,"[28] and Walter Bagehot is correct in his conclusion that "Sir Walter had no thesis to maintain,"[29] Scott believed that there was a moral order in the universe and the shadowy but strong outlines of that order are everywhere evident in his work. As Bagehot also observed, "You can scarcely lay down any novel of his without a strong feeling that the world in which the fiction has been laid . . . is one subject to *laws* of retribution which, though not apparent on a superficial glance, are yet in steady and consistent operation."[30]

It is this aspect of Scott's view of man that is omitted from the highly appreciative Marxist interpretations of Scott, and most notably those of Georg Lukács, who thinks that "Scott's greatness lies in his capacity to give living human embodiment to historical-social types,"[31] and argues that "Scott then becomes a great poet of history because he has a deeper, more genuine and differentiated sense of historical necessity than any writer before him."[32] Certainly this is true, but equally certainly it is a limited truth that sees but half of Scott's world. Karl Kroeber asserts that Scott had a method of characterization that "depends upon the double perception of individual personality and social role,"[33] and he is much closer to Scott's essence.

Here the richness of Scott's characterization finds its source in the recognizable common characteristics of men and the endless variety of their special ways of life, crafts, settings, and heritages. Virginia Woolf praises Scott's characters for their dialect, their metaphors, their "immense vivacity," and asserts that we know them as though they were real people and that they vary from reading to reading as real people do from meeting to meeting. They form for her "a host of observations, subtle and profound enough, should we trouble to spread them out; and next this transparent stream through which we see stones, weeds, and minnows at the bottom, becomes without warning the sea, the deep, the inscrutable, the universal ocean on which we put out with the greatest only."[34]

Certainly when we praise Scott's characters we are talking primarily about the vast horde of figures in the background and immediate foreground of his works. Dame Nellie Christie, Ursula Suddlechop, Martha Trapbois, the bewildered Templar Reginald Lowestoffe, the scrivener Andrew Skurliewhitter, Jenkin Vincent, Frank Tunstall, Lutin the page, Richie Moniplies, Mr. Linklater, the King's cook—these are struck off by a novelist with the richest sense of character and person. We have no difficulty believing Scott when he says, ". . . we never found ourselves in company with the stupidest of all possible companions in a post-chaise, or with the most arrant cumber-corner that ever occupied a place in the mail-coach, without finding that, in the course of our conversation with him, we had some ideas suggested to us, either grave or gay, or some information communicated in the course of our journey, which we should have regretted not to have learned."[35]

The principal glory of *The Fortunes of Nigel* is James I—as Hugh Walpole says, ". . . a king in spite of his clumsy clothes and his cowardice, but . . . also a weak, humorous, vain old man such as Scott may have seen at any moment stumbling down Princes Street."[36] But among the special glories of the novel is the wealth of characters and social classes—an almost endless variety of persons stretching from the court to Alsatia, from threadbare serving men to rumpled kings and sparkling courtiers, so that we have a sense of the whole crowded life of the London of James I. Of *The Fortunes of Nigel* Edwin Muir writes, "If Balzac had concentrated his powers to fill such a canvas, he would have done it in sections, devoting a separate book to each. Scott gathers the endless variety into one colossal whole. He does this without falling into confusion. The characters are thrown together pell-mell in the action; the classes intermingle in all sorts of ways; yet each figure remains . . . firmly in his station."[37]

Actually, these are, with the exception of King James, minor or secondary characters. When we turn to the central story the passivity of Nigel is reflected again and again, and the characters function more in terms of the plot than of the demands of human nature or historical force, illustrating one of Scott's great weaknesses as a novelist. In the Introductory Epistle to *The Fortunes of Nigel,* he quotes Bayes from *The Rehearsal,* " 'What the devil does the plot signify, except to bring in fine things?' "[38] It is an appropriate remark, for the plot is strange to the point of being preposterous.[39] Snarled and tangled in Scottish law, the story is strung around a colorless, ineffectual, and somewhat snobbish protagonist. The plot moves through the villainous machinations of Lord Dalgarno, who would be more at home in a melodrama than a serious novel. For, with all his charm and glitter, he is a cynical man of unmitigated evil, and he plays his role with stylized but mounting depravity. Few readers will lend him credence for long, and if the central plot really mattered, his portrayal would irremediably rend its fabric. This plot is unravelled by as unbelievable a deus ex machina as we are likely to find—the totally unconvincing, mysterious lady in white, Hermione, who finally is the means of dooming Dalgarno, salvaging Nigel's fortunes, and setting all to rights, except her own unhappy life. The comedy-like ending—with rewards and punishments distributed in a pattern of poetic justice—is at variance with the ominous historical overtones that threaten civil war and sudden death. Not only is the central plot comic in thrust and sentimental in structure; it is intricately interwoven with coincidences, newly discovered former acquaintances, and undisclosed relationships that, if put to the test of simple credibility, are preposterous.

But Scott takes this plot little more seriously than we do. It is a complex structure designed to "bring in fine things." And these fine things are not the Lady Hermione or her mysterious Spanish adventures, not even the charming Margaret Ramsey and her plots to save Nigel. In each case a servant breathes with a more intense life. Who would not choose Monna Paula over Hermione or Jenkin Vincent over Margaret as figures in a novel?

We read this novel for the richness and variety of the life which it portrays and for the dramatic intensity and success of its separate scenes. Particularly in its scenes in Alsatia, in the apprentices' stalls, in the Tower, and in the Christies' home an inventive novelistic power is at work. Scott has vigor and force, the ability to fashion a character with a few words, a speech or two, and a few indelible gestures that is equalled in the English novel only by Dickens.

Another of Scott's glories is his dialogue. When he is writing of non-Scottish aristocrats, his people often speak a stiff and unbelievable Wardour Street English. But when his characters are Scots, speaking the dialect which their author himself knew, their words come vigorously to life. Balzac, commenting on Scott's innovations, said they were the delineation of manners, the dramatic character of action, and the new and important role of dialogue in the novel.[40] In this quality *The Fortunes of Nigel* is particularly rich, for from King to lowly commoner, its cast of characters has a high percentage of Scotsmen, and Scott delights in their talk, particularly in that of King James.

This use of dialect is consistent with Scott's method of the dramatic portrayal of character. For we see these characters from the outside; we watch their actions; we hear their words; but we do not penetrate very often their secret innerselves. This is a part of Scott's success with James: we see him in action but never in private. Scott shows us a living James but avoids what Lukács calls "the detailed analysis of small, human peculiarities which have nothing to do with the historical mission of the person concerned."[41]

Scott's use of the soliloquy, while acknowledging that it is a dramatic convention that is unreal, betrays his unwillingness to write introspectively of his characters. At one place in *The Fortunes of Nigel* he wrote:

> I choose to present to my dearest reader the picture of my hero's mind, his reflections and resolutions, in the form of a speech rather than that of a narrative. . . . There are no such soliloquys in nature, it is true. . . . In narrative, no doubt, the writer has the alternative of telling that his personages thought so and so, inferred thus and thus, and arrived at such and such a conclusion; but the soliloquy is a more concise and spirited mode. . . .[42]

Thus *The Fortunes of Nigel* is a picture of actions and words and through these actions and words, of the forces at work on a world in a state of change. It attempts to portray the history of the reign of James I in terms not of parliamentary debates or diplomatic missions, but of the life of London—and particularly of Scotsmen in London—at that time. It shows the tensions, the moral decay, the rapidly collapsing class structure of the time, not through a record of great events or historical occurrences but through a fable which is wild enough and tortuous enough to take its passive protagonist from the secret chambers of the king to the lowest depths of Alsatia, from the quiet chapel of Heriot to the gambling house of St. Priest de Beaujeu, from the godly home of John Christie to the Tower of London.

We emerge from reading *The Fortunes of Nigel* with a world in our imaginations. It is a real world peculiar to its time and place, and we know its social conditions with a very direct and personal knowledge. Scott has centered on what he believed to be permanent in human nature and conduct and was, therefore, common to King James's world, to Scott's, and to ours. Then he took that common body of "passions" and actions, clothed them with the flesh and blood of imagined but believable persons, and set them down to experience the life of their age. His plot is a convenience; his hero is powerless in a world he never made; but it does not matter. The important part of the narrative is centered in the small and frequently trivial details upon which life marches. The tone is essentially comic, not only because Scott's ebullient good nature usually denied him the luxury of tragedy, but because comedy is the mode of limitations and frailty, and the characters of Scott's world are creatures of limits.

His James is his greatest historical creation, but his James came to him from history ready made and we never see him perform an act that would be recorded in a history. The conclusion of the novel is a magnificent summary of its historical thrust. Nigel marries a commoner; his serving man Richie Moniplies marries the daughter of Trapbois. The King decides to knight Richie and clumsily almost runs him through with the knighting sword, but he declares, "Rise up, Sir Richard Moniplies, of Castle-Collop!—And, my lords and lieges, let us all to our dinner, for the cock-a-leekie is cooling."[43] It is a magnificent scene, both in its comedy and in its historical meaning. It does not need, although it is illuminated by, Mistress Moniplies declaring. " 'There are fools, sire . . . who have wit, and fools who have courage —aye, and fools who have learning and are great fools notwithstanding. I chose this man because he was my protector when I was desolate, and neither for his wit nor his wisdom. He is truly honest."[44] Brave words to be spoken before the "wisest fool in Christendom," but Scott's lowly people often speak with the pungent courage of history itself. Only a generous man could have written this scene; only a man as gay at heart as Chaucer would have revealed the tragedy of change and pain through so genial an action.

But Scott did this as a portrayer and depicter not as a rhetorician or an allegorist. Two things are at the center of Scott's novels: men and actions, never Man and abstraction. We must be willing to find his meaning in what happens and how men react to it, not in what they say of its meaning or in what cosmic truths it states. If Scott's subject is history, it is history in motion; if his uniquely fresh contribution is an idea of history, it is still not a philosophy of history. Those—and they are many—who label Scott a "realist" or a "proto-realist" will find here the strongest argument for their label: that Scott has no interest in abstractions or in much of anything that is not concrete, personal, and immediate. The rich humanity of his teeming world, the variety and throbbing life of his people on all levels have led some critics to see him as much like Shakespeare. But he lacks Shakespeare's philosophical penetration, and he has few of Shakespeare's darker shadows. If we must look backward for the English writer whom he is most like, it is Chaucer—in his warm humanity, in his great social breadth, in his awareness that a man's trade and station tell us a great deal about him, and—above all—in the warm, clear, open, and optimistic daylight that covers his world, illuminating and gracing alike priest, peasant, warrior, and rogue. His essential mode is comic, and if in his comic vision of experience, he knows that "This too shall pass away," he can lament its going without yielding up his supremely hopeful confidence in the process by which it is made to depart.

Notes

1. *Quarterly Review*, XVI (1817), 431.

2. *The Journal of Sir Walter Scott* (New York, 1890), I, 155.

3. Walter Scott, "General Preface to the Waverley Novels," *Waverley*, in *Scott's Complete Works*, Riverside edition, 25 vols. (Boston, 1923), I, xxiii. All citations to Scott's works will be by title and page in this edition, which has unnumbered double volumes.

4. *Waverley*, I, 1–4.

5. *Walter Scott: His Life and Personality* (London, 1954), p. 185.

6. *Cavalcade of the English Novel* (New York, 1943), p. 158.

7. "Sir Walter Scott," *Critical and Miscellaneous Essays* (New York, 1901), V, 54–77.

8. *Coleridge's Miscellaneous Criticism*, ed. T. M. Raysor (London, 1936), pp. 341–342.

9. *The English Novel* (New York, 1894), p. 279.

10. *Ivanhoe*, I, xii.

11. *The Fortunes of Nigel*, I, xi–xii. Hereafter referred to as *Nigel*.

12. Ibid., I, xii.

13. Ibid., I, 172.

14. Ibid., I, 187.

15. *Coleridge's Miscellaneous Criticism*, p. 333.

16. *The Letters of Sir Walter Scott*, ed. H. J. C. Grierson (London, 1933), V, 398.

17. *The Historical Novel*, trans. Hannah and Stanley Mitchell (Boston, 1963), p. 32.

18. John G. Lockhart, *Memoirs of the Life of Sir Walter Scott, Bart.* (Edinburgh, 1837), V, 138; *Letters*, VIII, 16.

19. *Nigel*, I, ix–x.

20. Quoted in Lukács, pp. 39–40.

21. *Nigel*, II, 79.

22. Alexander Welsh, in *The Hero of the Waverley Novels* (New Haven, 1963), makes a detailed study of Scott's "weak" and "strong" protagonists and his "light" and "dark" heroines. Nigel is to Welsh an archetypal weak hero, but the roles of light and dark heroines are reversed in the novel. Welsh's study is essential for anyone interested in the role and meaning of the passive hero in Scott.

23. *The History of the English Novel* (London, 1935), VI, 135–138.

24. *Romantic Narrative Art* (Madison, Wis., 1960), p. 184.

25. *Le Romantisme: ses origines anglo-germanique* (Paris, 1926), p. 184.

26. *Waverley,* I, 4–5.

27. *Ivanhoe,* I, xxxii–xxxiii.

28. *Nigel,* I, x.

29. "The Waverley Novels," *Literary Studies* (Everyman Library; London, 1911), II, 133.

30. Ibid., p. 147.

31. Lukács, p. 35.

32. Ibid., p. 58.

33. Kroeber, p. 173.

34. *New Republic,* XLI (Dec. 3, 1924), 42.

35. *Nigel,* II, 152–153.

36. "After a Hundred Years," in *The Waverley Pageant,* ed. Hugh Walpole (London, 1932), p. xxxix. But Coleridge *(Miscellaneous Criticism,* p. 33) thinks he was modeled poorly on Shakespeare's Holofernes.

37. "Walter Scott: The Writer," in *Sir Walter Scott Lectures 1940–1948* (Edinburgh, 1950), pp. 71–72.

38. *Nigel,* I, xxvi. This Introductory Epistle, in which Scott seems to glory in all his weaknesses, has been used against him repeatedly, despite its tongue-in-cheek quality, and despite the fact that Scott essentially disavows its seriousness in the later Introduction to the novel (ibid., I, xvii–xviii).

39. Francis R. Hart, in *Scott's Novels: The Plotting of Historical Survival* (Charlottesville, 1966), examines Scott's plots in terms of "cultural continuity in historical change," but he says little about *The Fortunes of Nigel* because he thinks its "historicity" is "inorganic" and that the role of Nigel is peculiarly weak. (See pp. 198–203.)

40. Lukács, p. 31.

41. Ibid., p. 47.

42. *Nigel,* II, 78.

43. Ibid., II, 344.

44. Ibid., II, 343.

Dickens and Copperfield:
The Hero as Man of Letters

SAMUEL G. BARNES

Lord David Cecil, in his *Victorian Novelists,* calls attention to the obvious: "It is not to be avoided—a book on the Victorian novelists must begin with Dickens."[1] But then Cecil avoids the next and most pressing responsibility—where in Dickens? Limited to pinpointing one work in the panorama that runs from the joyous *Pickwick Papers* to the brooding and unfinished *Edwin Drood,* any critic would blanch. Thus George Ford, towards the end of his exhaustive effort to synthesize divergent estimates of the novelist and relate this picture of Dickens and his readers to the general sweep of critical theories of prose fiction, plaintively wonders "if the complete Dickens does exist anywhere in criticism."[2] As a policy of cowardice, then, the proper resort is to turn to the master's own words: "Like many fond parents, I have in my heart of hearts a favorite child—and his name is *David Copperfield.*"[3]

Once chosen, this mid-career novel swiftly begins to acquire validity as a representative and important work. First, of course, is the autobiographical quality of the novel. In 1845, still a young man, though flushed with his literary success, Dickens started to write an autobiography. The effort was soon abandoned, to be superseded by *David Copperfield.* Secondly, the 1840s was a decade when England was forced to examine her past and seek reforms to avert imminent revolution. Third, the timing of *David Cooperfield* falls midway between *The Chimes* (1844) and *Hard Times* (1854), that period which Lionel Stevenson calls Dickens' "dark decade," from which the mature novelist emerged.[4] Fourth, this period is the decade which Kathleen Tillotson chooses to find pivotal in the development of the nineteenth-century novel.[5] And finally, the decade closed with Dickens' ultimate tribute to his philosophical father—Thomas Carlyle.

Hence the premise of this study: *David Copperfield* marks the emergence of Dickens as—in Carlyle's terms—the Heroic Man of Letters.[6] Such an estimate would shed light on other developments of the century: the rise to cultural dominance of the middle class, the rise of the novel to dominance as a literary form, and the subsequent reinterpretations of the role of the novelist. If the 1840s were pivotal in English history, pivotal in the development of the Victorian novel, and pivotal in the career of Charles Dickens, then an examination of *David Copperfield* should be illuminating.[7]

Central to this examination, of course, is the added point that *David Copperfield* was pivotal in Dickens' assimilation of Carlylean philosophy. Since the "dark decade" began with Dickens' comic effort to impress Carlyle with *The Chimes* and ended with his confident dedication of *Hard Times,* some resolution must have occurred within Dickens' own mind. That resolution should be sought in *David Copperfield,* Dickens' own story of "how I became a novelist."

First, then, to a consideration of Dickens' discipleship.

The lifelong admiration of Charles Dickens for Thomas Carlyle and the enduring affection of Carlyle for "little Dickens" are too well known and too frequently remarked to be questioned. But the temperamental incongruity of the two men, the fact that they worked in different literary forms, and the outdistancing of Carlyle's career by the success of Dickens have precluded, for the most part, any serious analysis of the relationship beyond the period of Dickens' formative years. That Carlyle's *Chartism, Past and Present,* and *The French Revolution* influenced specific novels has been admitted—necessarily because Dickens said so. Furthermore, as popularizer of the social purpose novel, Dickens joined his master in concern over "the condition of England question." Both men despaired of the English aristocracy. Both doubted the efficacy of Parliament's reform. Beyond such parallels, however, the usual critical agreement is that Dickens, because of his sentimental sympathy for pathetic victims in the lower class, rejected Carlyle's doctrine of heroes and hero-worship.

Yet Dickens himself believed that he was steeped in Carlylean thought. In 1854, when seeking permission to dedicate *Hard Times* to his teacher, Dickens asserted: "I know it contains nothing in which you do not think with me, for no man knows your books better than I." How could he speak so confidently? Perhaps because of the conviction that arose within him at the end of *David Copperfield.*

The acquaintance with Carlyle, begun in 1840 after years of admiration on the part of Dickens, had flourished with the latter's success. As early as *Chartism* (1839), Jack Lindsay notes that Carlyle was furnishing Dickens with "philosophic support for his feeling that something was radically wrong, the feeling that he had put into the symbolism of *The Old Curiosity Shop.* . . ."[8] In the summer of 1844, as Dickens posted home from Italy the installments for *The Chimes,* his writing, according to John Forster, had taken on a new gravity, startlingly "impressed on him in Carlyle's writing."[9] Late in October 1844, in correspondence with Forster, Dickens first hinted at a wish to see his friends during a complete reading of his new Christmas book. In his next letter Dickens revealed more complete plans, as well as a concern for the impact of the tale:

> Shall I confess to you, I particularly want Carlyle above all to see it before the rest of the world, when it is done; and I' should like to inflict the little story . . . with my own lips. . . . Now if you was a real gent, you'd get up a little circle for me, one wet evening, when I come to town. . . . I shall be under sailing orders the moment I have finished. And I shall produce myself (please God) in London on the very day you name.[10]

In a letter dated November 4, Dickens furnished further specifications for the reading: "Don't have anyone, this particular night, to dinner, but let it be a summons for the special purpose at half-past 6. Carlyle, indispensable, and I should like his wife, of all things, *her* judgement would be invaluable."[11]

And Carlyle was there, but without his wife, because Forster decided to have no women present. Forster and Dickens felt the reading was a success—so much so that it was repeated for another group within the week, before the novelist returned to Italy. But of the first reading Forster remembers only the "grave attention" of Carlyle; obviously the Scotch philosopher was disappointed in the work he had purportedly influenced.

Lindsay shrewdly identifies the humanitarian message of this second Christmas book as the point of divergence of the two men. He explains Carlyle's "grave attention" by a remark made on a later occasion: "But Carlyle was probably feeling something like the disgust which he later let out when he said, 'His theory of life was all wrong. He thought men ought to be buttered up, and the world made soft and accomodating for them, and all sorts of fellows have turkey for dinner.' "[12]

Apparently Dickens felt that Carlyle's grave attention was sufficient. Not until ten years later—in the strident insistence of the letter about *Hard Times*—do we sense that he may have felt a lack of enthusiasm on the part of Carlyle. And even then the suggestion is not of a divergence of thought but rather a difference in emphasis. Why did Dickens so confidently dedicate *Hard Times* to Carlyle ten years after the lukewarm approval of *The Chimes?* Because in the dark decade a period of self-searching had borne fruit in *David Copperfield*, the self-appraisal which convinced the novelist that he thought with Carlyle.

The confidence of 1854 was no longer based upon enthusiastic hero-worship of his elder, but upon an understanding of himself, an understanding which had come with the catharsis of an autobiographical novel. For in attempting his abortive autobiography, then fictionalizing the events in *David Copperfield*, Dickens had followed the advice Carlyle offered in *Sartor Resartus*: "To each is given a certain inward talent; a certain outward Environment of Fortune; to each, by wisest combination of these two, a certain maximum of Capability. But the hardest problem were ever this first: To find, by a study of yourself, and of the ground you stand on, what your combined inward and outward Capability specially is."[13]

Charles Dickens at mid-career, examining his "inward talent" and his "Environment of Fortune" to determine "the maximum of Capability," puts his protagonist through an illuminating experience. Late in *David Copperfield*—with Dora dead, his friends rehabilitated, and no hope for the hand of Agnes Wickfield—David goes to Switzerland. There, symbolically surveying the prospect of a great valley, he writes his second novel, the work which is to crystallize his career as a writer. Significantly—for Dickens, for the Victorian novel, and as a credo for imitators and rivals—David defines the role of the novelist: "I wrote a story, with a purpose growing, not remotely, out of my experience . . ." (p. 861).

When, in 1848, Charles Dickens chose to make an examination of his "inward talent" and how it evolved, the "outward Environment" of England was close to revolution. The Chartist Movement, then at its peak of potential violence, had brought Carlyle and Dickens back on a pendulum swing from complete scorn for the aristocracy to a deep concern that democracy might produce anarchy. Carlyle, contemptuous of Democracy as another "Morrison's Pill," was embracing ever more strongly his doctrine of pragmatic, working heroes; his *Past and Present* was an authentic but idealized portrait of such a hero. Dickens had seen—with distaste—the working out of democracy in America; his *American Notes* and *Martin Chuzzlewit* reflect his rejection of political democracy.

Beginning with *The Chimes* Dickens' work reflected this new and Carlylean gravity. The novelist rejected the cold mechanism of a system, to emphasize the solidarity possible within the working class through a humanitarian attitude. Later, in *Dombey and Son,* he pointed out the empty promise of any hope for reform from the aristocracy, despite his recognition of their heroic potential. A compromise between these two views and a possible solution to "the condition of England question" that would extend through all classes is reached in *David Copperfield.* The novel is a story of work and success, of working people standing together, of charity to one's fellow men, of success at "clearing a forest of difficulties" with one's own axe. But it is also a story of idleness, parasitical exploitation, and failure; of the aristocracy and their retinue standing together to exploit the lower classes; of hero-worship of aristocracy at the expense of one's fellow men; and of failure through waiting in expectation that "something will turn up." Other literary works of this dark decade—*Bleak House,* in particular—continued this analysis until Dickens arrived at his "maximum Capability," but the most thorough presentation came in *David Copperfield.*[14]

That Dickens, while struggling to find "the ground you stand on," was aware of Carlyle's parallel effort seems suggested by the work he drew upon for inspiration. He did not go to *Sartor Resartus,* though he was writing a novel of apprenticeship; nor to *Signs of The Times, Characteristics,* or *Past and Present,* though he was seeking a formula for reform. Instead, while writing his novel at Devonshire Terrace he was reading "that wonderful book," Carlyle's *The French Revolution,* "again for the 500th time." Now *The French Revolution* was, at once, Carlyle's most difficult writing effort and his most ingenious philosophical resolution, for he necessarily had to reconcile popular revolution with an innate disdain for democracy, his theory of heroes with his scorn for the aristocracy. In the England of 1848 Carlyle and Dickens faced a similar concern—reform without revolution. Carlyle sought heroes and hero-worship; Dickens sought humanitarianism.

In the novels which preceded *David Copperfield* Dickens wrote in sentimental protest, often choosing a single evil for his target; subsequently he urged personal reform on broad and general terms. The change in emphasis is slight but significant; carried further it might have produced another social commentator, another Thackeray. Fortunately, rather than be a social commentator, Dickens felt the need to preach what Carlyle had urged in the conclusion of *Signs of The Times:* "To reform a world, to reform a nation, no wise man will undertake; and all but foolish men know that the only solid, though a far slower reformation, is what each begins and perfects on himself."

As Charles Dickens saw it, the solution of the "condition of England question" lay in personal reform diffused through all classes of society, and two aspects of his particular version of personal reform, work and humanitarianism, were fictionalized in novels after *David Copperfield.* "He who labors, prays," Carlyle had said, and Dickens, examining the events of his life to the age of thirty-six, carefully divided his acquaintances into workers and non-workers. The Carlylean doctrine of labor becomes the criterion for characterization in *David Copperfield.* Thus David, Traddles, Peggoty, Ham, and Dr. Strong are good because they work productively. On the other hand, Emily, Malden, Mr. Wickfield and others are lost through idleness. Salvation comes to Mrs. Gummidge, Micawber, and Mr. Dick when they turn to productive work. Furthermore, the villains Murdstone, Heep, Littimore, and—in a lesser sense—Spenlow are painted blacker by their roles as parasites rather than producers. The secret of David's success, he finds in retrospect, is work; the hope of the lower classes, in sorrow, in bankruptcy, or in illness, is work—even if by emigration.

But there is a difference between working and merely being busy, as Dickens was to point out frequently—in the Doctor's Commons, of *David Copperfield;* or the Chancery Court, of *Bleak House;* or the Circumlocution Office, of *Little Dorritt.*

Carlyle had identified as labor that "which lies nearest at hand" —needed, productive work. By 1848 Dickens had become appalled at the new class of entrepreneurs, those members of the middle class who exploited others and who held a vested interest in systems and bureaucratic operations. Thus in *David Copperfield* he attacks, by characterization, three classes of people who are busy but are not workers: those who lived on and thus supported the idle aristocracy—Littimore, Rosa Dartle, and the early Miss Mowcher; those who busied themselves making work (Spenlow and the associates of Doctors' Commons) rather than doing work (Traddles); and those who were busy exploiting the other members of their class—Micawber (in theory), and Tungay, Murdstone, Creakle, and Heep (in practice).

Early in the novel Mr. Wickfield raises the point of "busyness" versus work, in a discussion with Dr. Strong about Jack Maldon's career. As the scene opens, Dr. Strong has just pointed out that Maldon is "needy and idle, and of those two bad things worse things sometimes come." He then quotes Doctor Watts on Satan and idle hands, to which Mr. Wickfield replies: " 'Egad, Doctor . . . if Doctor Watts knew mankind he might have written with as much truth, Satan finds some mischief still for busy hands to do. The busy people achieve their full measure of mischief in the world, you may rely upon it. What have people been about who have been the busiest in getting money and in getting power, this century or two? No mischief?' " (p. 238f.). Here, with "this century or two," we can suspect Dickens of more than an intent to "think with" Carlyle. For in a rebuke of contemporary Mammonism in *Past and Present* are found almost the same words and the same indictment: in the chapter on "Reward" Carlyle laments the fact that for the past two centuries all work in England has been done only for money and power.[15]

Dickens carefully details the "busyness" of the people of mischief in *David Copperfield*. Thus Murdstone is not "actively concerned in any business" but had an annual charge upon the profits of a concern. Miss Murdstone does "all sorts of things" and gropes "into all sorts of places" to spare David's mother—and in doing so takes over the resources of the Copperfield home. Steerforth, clear-eyed about the evils of the day which he will not correct, scornfully refuses to bind himself "to any of the wheels on which the Ixions of these days are turning round and round." Steerforth also first alerts David to the empty "busyness" of Doctors' Commons: ". . . but it's always a very pleasant, profitable little affair of private theatricals. . . ." Mr. Spenlow's shocking explanation of how the Commons is "conveniently organized" to provide work and profit for all does not impress young David, but neither did David's theory for abolishing the Prerogative Office impress Mr. Spenlow: "I had not the hardihood to suggest to Dora's father that possibly we might improve the world a little, if we got up early in the morning, and took off our coats to the work; but I confessed that I thought we might improve the Commons. Mr. Spenlow replied that he would particularly advise me to dismiss that idea from my mind, as not being worthy of my gentlemanly character . . ." (p. 503).

The distinction that Dickens draws between workers and non-workers, between producers and exploiters, is further illustrated in the character of Miss Mowcher, another portrait which has bothered the critics. Forster's account of how Dickens altered his treatment of Miss Mowcher in response to readers' criticism of the earlier episodes is well known, but notice how Dickens enhances her character. In the clearing and ennobling of Miss Mowcher, from her first appearance in the story to the later sequences, can be seen Dickens' reliance upon work and the humanitarian motive as a force to cure or purify. He not only has her perform a noble act, but he gives her a lengthy monologue in which she explains her eccentricities by her difficulty in obtaining work—work to support similarly afflicted kinfolk: " 'I have worked for sister and brother these many years—hard, Mr. Copperfield, all day. I must live, I do no harm. If there are people so unreflecting or so cruel as to make a jest of me, what is left for me to do but to make a jest of myself, them, and everything? If I do so, for the time, whose fault is that? Mine?' " (p. 485).

That young David, too, could distinguish between "busyness" and work seems evident when he makes a jest about his own over-application. Aunt Betsy's financial crisis had brought out a new earnestness in David: "What I had to do was to take my woodsman's axe in my hand and clear my own way through a forest of difficulty. . . ." This resolution explains the extra job with Dr. Strong, the self-training in shorthand, and the new economy. But the new-found earnestness almost turned to unproductive asceticism: "I made it a rule to take as much out of myself as I possibly could, in my way of doing everything to which I applied my energies. I made a perfect victim of myself. I even entertained some idea of putting myself on a vegetable diet, vaguely conceiving that, in becoming a graminivorous animal, I should sacrifice to Dora" (p. 565).

In the Carlylean philosophy, work is more than a distinguishing mark of good character; it is also a curative. Thus in the stories of Mrs. Gummidge, Mr. Dick, and, particularly, Micawber, turning to work brought new strength to character and an end to troubles. Mrs. Gummidge is a "poor lorn creature" until the crisis of Emily; then, as David tells it,

> What a change in Mrs. Gummidge in a little time! She was another woman. She was so devoted, she had such a quick perception of what it would be well to say, and what it would be well to leave unsaid; she was so forgetful of herself, and so regardful of the sorrow about her, that I held her in a sort of veneration. The work she did that day! . . . As to deploring her misfortunes, she appeared to have entirely lost the recollection of ever having had any. She preserved an equable cheerfulness in the midst of her sympathy, which was not the least astonishing part of the change that had come over her. . . . In short, I left her, when I went away at night, the prop and staff of Mr. Peggoty's affliction; and I could not meditate enough upon the lesson that I read in Mrs. Gummidge, and the new experience she unfolded to me. (p. 482)

Furthermore, in return for the lesson and the new experience, as all too often, Dickens, the novelist, rewards Mrs. Gummidge with the supreme benediction for a nineteenth-century widow—a proposal of marriage.

Mr. Dick's rehabilitation, too, is due to a combination of work and a humanitarian impulse:

> He was like one under the propitious influence of a charm, from the moment of his being usefully employed; and if there were a happy man in the world, that Saturday night, it was the grateful creature who thought my aunt the most wonderful woman in existence, and me the most wonderful man.
>
> "No starving now, Trotwood," said Mr. Dick, shaking hands with me in a corner. "I'll provide for her, sir," and he flourished his ten fingers in the air, as if they were ten banks. (p. 556)

But it is in the delineation of Micawber's rehabilitation that Dickens is most insistent on the humanitarian impulse as concomitant with useful work. In his early efforts Micawber's plans for success are selfishly self-centered. Any reader aware of the Carlylean faith in the saving grace of unselfish labor should be able to predict the future of the three men from the characterizations given here: Traddles will succeed, Steerforth will fail, and Micawber must reform.

David first encounters Traddles, who has begun to demonstrate his personal heroism. Unprepared for life ("I had never been brought up to any profession, and at first I was at a loss what to do for myself"), Traddles has turned to what is at hand ("However, I began, with the assistance of the son of a professional man . . ."), and has prospered ("For I am a plodding kind of fellow, Copperfield, and had learned the way of doing such things pithily"). Career and marriage are "a pull" for Traddles, and he is to be exploited for many more years by the curate's family, "but our motto is, 'Wait and hope.' " Traddles' "Wait and hope" is not the passivity of Micawber, however; the young man continues to labor at that which is nearest at hand—copying, compiling, journalism, etc. (p. 425).

Micawber is brought onstage almost immediately, as a contrast. Characteristically, he is waiting for the world to put him to work: "You find me fallen back *for* a spring," he tells David, "and I have every reason to believe that a vigorous leap will shortly be the result." Dickens employs Mrs. Micawber to puncture her husband's hypocrisy: "Now I am convinced myself, and this I have pointed out to Mr. Micawber several times of late, that things cannot be expected to turn up of themselves. We must, in a measure, assist them to turn up. I may be wrong, but I have formed that opinion" (p. 440).

"Both Traddles and I applauded it highly," reports the author, but then Mrs. Micawber identifies herself with those who, though not disdaining labor, expect the impulse to come from environment: "And here is Mr. Micawber without any suitable position or employment. Where does that responsibility rest? Clearly on society. . . . What Mr. Micawber has to do, is to throw down the gauntlet to society . . . to advertise in all the papers . . . and to put it thus: 'Now employ me, on remunerative terms, and address, post-paid, to W. M., Post Office, Camden Town' " (p. 441).

Not until the great scene which ends the explosion of Heep does a humanitarian motive become joined to Micawber's deeds: "I must do Mr. Micawber the justice to say," Traddles began, "that although he would not appear to have worked to any good account for himself, he is a most untiring man when he works for other people." Here Dickens has turned, in his use of the Carlylean doctrine of labor, from characterization to plot. The reformation is carefully recorded: Micawber joins the emigration party ("His whole family, if I may so express it, were cleared for action"), and prepares for the labor that lies nearest at hand ("Both Mr. Micawber and his eldest son wore sleeves loosely turned back at the wrists, as being ready to lend a hand in any direction, to 'tumble up,' or sing out 'Yeo—Heave—Yeo!' on the shortest notice").

In a similar demonstration, humanitarian work is the reformation of Martha. Once her moral decision is made—humane because it is a desire to help Mr. Peggotty find Emily—she has no difficulty finding gainful employment. Early in the novel Dickens had already touched upon the necessary combination of a good heart and labor. Emily, already conscience stricken by her secret relation with Steerforth, has changed. Thus Mr. Omar reports, "It ain't that she don't work as well as ever, for she does. She was worth any six, and she *is* worth any six. But somehow she wants heart . . . what I mean in a general way by the expression, 'A long pull, and a strong pull, and a pull altogether, my hearties, hurrah!' I should say to you, that that was—in a general way—what I miss in Em'ly" (p. 461). Consistent to the end, late in the novel Dickens shows us "two interesting penitents" in a scathingly satirical scene on model prisons that is obviously borrowed from a Carlylean essay.[16] Here readers are made well aware that the two parasites have merely discovered a new technique for prospering without work—honest work motivated by a humane impulse.

In the summing-up of 1848, from personal experience—or perhaps wishful thinking—Dickens saw traits of sincerity, generosity, and helpfulness in the lower class. This humane concern for others, a corollary of personal reform that Dickens saw in his own life and which he employed consistently in the characterization and plotting of *David Copperfield,* appears to be the most subtle concept by which the novelist "thinks with" Carlyle. Dickens' positive program for personal reform—work from a humane impulse—is the transmutation of Carlyle's hero-worship into a code of conduct. But so subtle is the Dickens message that even Carlyle failed to see the resemblance. Hence the insistent claim of the dedication of *Hard Times,* after Carlyle's unenthusiastic response to *The Chimes:* Carlyle's hero-worship had become Dickens' humanitarianism.

The failure of the Scotch philosopher to identify himself with the English novelist seems absurd, if we grant to Dickens his claim that he knew the master's books well. The path from hero-worship to humanitarianism can be easily traced.

Hero-worship, because of Carlyle's later, frenetic search for true heroes, came to mean for many the mass following of a leader, some hero gifted with transcendental wisdom. But from the first, and in every subsequent restatement of his philosophy, Carlyle maintained a universal and classless appeal: all men were potential heroes, and hero-worship was the recognition of that truth:

> This body, those faculties, this life of ours, is it not all as a vesture for that Unnamed? "There is but one Temple in the Universe," says the devout Novalis, "and that is the Body of Man. Nothing is holier than that high form. Bending before men is a reverence done to this Revelation in the Flesh. We touch Heaven when we lay our hand on a human body!" This sounds much like a mere flourish of rhetoric; but it is not so. If well meditated, it will turn out to be a scientific fact; the expressing in such words as can be had of the actual truth of the thing. *We* are the miracle of miracles—the great inscrutable mystery of God. We cannot understand it, we know not how to speak of it; but we may feel and know, if we like, that it is verily so.[17]

Through the catharsis of *David Copperfield,* in particular, and the use of the fiction form, in general, Dickens learned "how to speak of it," for he found this "revelation in the flesh" in the characters he drew from the lower classes of England. And again he was "thinking with" Carlyle, who said: "Hero-worship exists for ever, and everywhere; not Loyalty alone; it extends from divine adoration down to the lowest practical regions of life. 'Bending before men,' if it is not to be a mere empty grimace, better dispensed with than practised, is Hero-worship—a recognition that there does dwell in that presence of our brother something divine; that every created man, as Novalis said, is a 'revelation in the Flesh.' "[18]

"Revelation in the flesh" becomes the motivation for Dickens' great humanitarianism; thus sincerity, generosity, and kindness are the transmutation of "hero-worship." Repeatedly, in his public addresses Dickens asserted his intent to carry hero-worship "down to the lowest practical regions of life":

> I was anxious to show that virtue may be found in the by-ways of the world; that it is not incompatible with poverty and even with rags. (Speech at Edinburgh, June 1841)

> I believe that Virtue shows just as well in rags and patches as she does in purple and fine linen. I believe she dwells rather oftener in alleys and byways, than she does in courts and palaces. (Speech in Boston, 1842)

What the working class have found me towards them in my books, I am throughout my life. Whenever I have tried to hold up to admiration their fortitude, patience, gentleness, and the reasonableness, so accessible to persuasion, and their extraordinary goodness toward one another, I have done so because I have first genuinely felt that admiration myself. (Speech in Birmingham, 1853)

It is through this "bending before men" that Dickens seems to depart from Carlyle and lay himself open to the charge of Christmas sentimentality. But Dickens is no Richardson or Mackenzie: his man of sentiment is heroic and a hero-worshipper. For Dickens there is latent heroism in all men—Sidney Carton, for example—and dynamic hero-worship of the divine in our fellow men by the members of the lower class. Such confidence in the natural impulse of humanitarianism appears equivalent to the views of Shaftesbury, but the philosophic conviction, from Dickens' own insistence, must stem from Carlyle's hero-worship.

"Bending before men" as a code of conduct is transmuted, then, in the terse advice from Aunt Betsey Trotwood as young David starts a new life: " 'Never,' said my aunt, 'be mean in anything; never be false; never be cruel. Avoid those three vices, Trot, and I can be hopeful of you' " (p. 236).

Another major concern of Carlyle and Dickens, in respect to the "condition of England question", was the failure of the natural aristocracy to live up to its heroic potential. In *David Copperfield* this sub-theme is developed through the story of Steerforth. Steerforth, like Carlyle's picture of Napoleon, turns out to be no hero, but early in the story he does inspire hero-worship—because of his generosity. Note the emphasis in David's speech to Mr. Peggotty: " 'Then, he's such a generous, fine, noble fellow,' said I, quite carried away by my favourite theme, 'that it's hardly possible to give him as much praise as he deserved. I am sure I can never feel thankful enough for the generosity with which he protected me, so much younger and lower in the school than himself' " (p. 150).

The reader has already been alerted to the real nature of Steerforth's generosity in the matter of David's seven shillings, and is prepared for young "Daisy's" later disappointment. Dickens, carefully delineating Steerforth for his readers, immediately after the character revelations of Traddles and Micawber which we have examined, closely parallels Carlyle's treatment of the aristocracy. In *Chartism* Carlyle had dismissed all hope of help from the upper class: "Where are they? —Preserving their Game!" Steerforth shows the same infelicity, an insensitivity which regards life as a game, the lower class not to be preserved but "ridden over rough-shod":

> "Why, there's a pretty wide separation between them and us," said Steerforth, with indifference. "They are not to be expected to be as sensitive as we are. Their delicacy is not to be shocked, or hurt very easily. They are wonderfully virtuous, I dare say. Some people contend for that, at least; and I am sure I don't want to contradict them. But they have not very fine natures; and they may be thankful that, like their coarse skins, they are not easily wounded." (p. 309)

The poignancy of David's beginning disappointment—and loss of hero-worship—is suggested: ". . . and when we parted, and I looked after him going so gallantly and airily homeward, I thought of his saying, 'Ride on over all obstacles and win the race!' and wished, for the first time, that he had some worthy race to run" (p. 450).

Elsewhere Dickens has Steerforth reject the role of a Carlylean hero as he speaks on the subject of Fame: " 'You romantic Daisy,' said Steerforth, laughing still more heartily, 'why should I trouble myself that a parcel of heavy handed fellows may gape and hold up their hands? Let them do it at some other man. There's fame for him, and he's welcome to it' " (p. 307). Hence the death scene has double significance: Steerforth as the symbol of the youthful potential for hero-worship ("I saw him lying with his head upon his arms, as I had often seen him lie at school") and as the symbol of Dickens' dead adult hope for a heroic aristocracy. In one moving scene Dickens rejected heroism in the Victorian upper class as dead, but retained confidence in the universal potential of the divine in men: ". . . no need to have said, 'Think of me at my best!' I had done that ever; and could I change now, looking on this sight?"

But that we might better understand the subtle meaning of the character of Steerforth, Dickens gives us Rosa Dartle. To help us see that Steerforth is no hero because he lacks the generosity which provokes true hero-worship, Miss Dartle repeats the Steerforth credo, first rebuking Copperfield for daring to present the cause of the injured Mr. Peggotty, then speaking as the voice of judgment to the crushed Emily: "The miserable vanity of these earthworms. . . . Your home!

Do you imagine that I bestow a thought on it, or suppose you could do any harm to that low place that money could not pay for, and handsomely? *Your* home! You were a part of the trade of your home, and were bought and sold like any other vendible thing your people dealt in" (p. 757). Here, in a fictional creation by Dickens, is the bitterness of Carlyle over "cash payment as the sole nexus between man and man."[19] Not "cash payment" but the recognition of the divine in all men was the reform Dickens urged upon all social classes as the spirit of revolt flamed in England in 1848.

Thus Forster's judgment that Dickens' own life is responsible for the message of *David Copperfield* seems as wide of the mark as the misconception of Carlyle concerning his protegé.[20] Amidst the autobiographical self-searching the resultant personal reform and virtue are associated with a concern for true heroes and the humanitarianism of hero-worship. The structure and characterization of *David Copperfield* shows this mutation of Carlyle's message. That the mutation was a turning point is evidenced by the even stronger pattern in Dickens' later novels. After *David Copperfield* Dickens no longer posed class against class, nor did he fail to find true heroes—and villains—at all social levels. In the light of the strong orientation toward Carlyle from 1844 to 1854, aware of the self-examination inherent in *David Copperfield,* and alerted by the dedication of *Hard Times* which closed this dark decade, we should concede to Dickens a philosophical reliance upon Carlyle at the pivotal moment in his career.

Forster, himself, seems to sense such an opinion in a passage which includes a character analysis of the mature Dickens and a reference to Carlyle:

> The saying in his letter to his youngest son that he was to do to others what he would that they should do to him, without being discouraged if they did not do it; and his saying to the Birmingham people that they were to attend to self-improvement not because it led to fortune, but because it was right; express a principle that at all times guided himself. . . . The one thing hateful to him was indifference. . . . There was nothing he more repeatedly told his children than that they were not to let indifference in others appear to justify it in themselves. . . . The rule in another form frequently appears in his letters; and it was enforced in many ways upon all who were dear to him. . . . It is also to be noted in the same spirit, that it was not the loud but the silent heroisms he most admired. . . .

It was for something higher than literature he valued the most original and powerful teacher of the age. "I would go at all times further to see Carlyle than any man alive." [21]

Still "thinking with" Carlyle, "the something higher than literature" became a role—derived from the teaching of his master—that marked the remainder of Dickens' career. Carlyle had suggested, in his lecture on *Heroes and Hero-Worship,* what might be accomplished by the English novelist in the turbulent 1840s:

> If *Hero* be taken to mean genuine, then I say the Hero as Man of Letters will be found discharging a function for us which is ever honourable, ever the highest; and was once well known to be the highest. He is uttering-forth, in such a way as he has, the inspired soul of him; all that a man, in any case, can do. I say inspired; for what we call "originality," "sincerity," "genius," the heroic quality we have no good name for, signifies that.
>
> . . . .
>
> Men of Letters are a Perpetual Priesthood, from age to age, teaching all men that a God is still present, in their life; that all "appearance," whatsoever we see in the world, is but as a vesture for the "Divine Idea of the World", for "that which lies at the bottom of Appearance." In the true Literary man there is thus ever, acknowledged or not by the world, a sacredness: He is the light of the world; the world's Priest; guiding it like a sacred Pillar of Fire, in its dark pilgrimage through the Waste of Time.[22]

At a time when England was in "its dark pilgrimage through the Waste of Time" Dickens addressed himself to the question of the role of the novelist in contemporary society. In *David Copperfield,* at the age of thirty-six, he summed up his experience and his training, to set the course for his remaining career as a writer. In doing so he was to influence his readers and his age, the novel form and the great body of Victorian novelists. Some—Charles Kingsley, Mrs. Gaskell, Charles Reade, for example—were such faithful imitators that they failed. Others—Thackeray and Eliot, for example—were turned away by distaste for his style. And as the century waned, still others found new causes, new literary modes, and a new understanding of man and his experience. But all—as George Ford has shown—were marked, inhibited, or at least aware that in Victorian England the most popular and powerful pen, when all England sought a hero, was employed in tales with "a purpose growing, not remotely, out of my experience."

The purpose, considering Carlyle's influence, could have been to serve as Heroic Man of Letters; the result, considering Dickens' influence, certainly was.

Notes

1. *Victorian Novelists* (Chicago, 1965), p. 22. Cecil concludes his chapter on Dickens with words which validate this essay: "The English, the kindly, individualistic, illogical, sentimental English, are, more than any other people, touched by impulsive benevolence, instinctive good nature, set a value on homely satisfactions. More than any other people they are repelled by the ruthless and impersonal—in thought or religion or administration or economics—by the ruthless and impersonal tyranny of church or class or state. Nor have they much perception of those purely intellectual values that Dickens' view of life overlooks. In fact they find expressed in him with all the eloquence of genius, their deepest feeling, their controlling convictions. He means something to them, therefore, that no other of their novelists mean. It is no wonder that to him, as to no other of their novelists, they have given their hearts."

2. *Dickens & His Readers* (New York, 1965), p. 233. This remark comes from the long concluding chapter of Ford's work (subtitled "Aspects of Novel-Criticism since 1836") in which he shows the amazing variety of interpretation of Dickens' work. Ford closes his survey with the warning, "to be suspicious of the critical arrogance which finds in one phase of Dickens' novels the whole of Dickens is an essential step toward synthesis."

3. Dickens in the Preface to 1869 edition of *David Copperfield*. All page references are to the Modern Library edition (New York: Random House, 1950).

4. "Dickens's Dark Novels, 1851–57," *Sewanee Review*, LI (1943), 398–409. Ford, however, points out that one reviewer *(Edinburgh Review, LXXXI, 1845, 183)* detects "darkness" as early as *The Chimes*.

5. *Novels of the Eighteen-Forties* (London, 1961), p. 13. Pertinent to our thesis are Tillotson's words: "One reason why the novel is particularly interesting in the eighteen-forties is that it was in process of becoming the dominant form. In the eighteen-forties critics began to say what they continued to say more forcibly for the next forty years or so, that the novel was the form of expression most suited to the age—."

6. Fifth lecture in Carlyle's series on *Heroes and Hero-Worship*, which brought the figure of the hero into contemporary times.

7. Tillotson (pp. 150–156) traces Carlylean influence on several novelists other than Dickens. Cf. Jack Lindsay, *Charles Dickens; a biographical and critical study* (London, 1950) and two articles, Mildred G. Christian, "Carlyle's Influence upon the Social Theory of Dickens," *Trollopian*, I (March 1947), 27–35, and (June 1947), 11–26.

8. Lindsay, pp. 202–204. Lindsay also sees *Chartism* as an influence on *Barnaby Rudge*, but denies Dickens' acceptance of Carlyle's' hero-worship, despite the new tone of sympathy with the aristocracy found in *Dombey and Son* (1848).

9. Perhaps *Past and Present*. John Forster, in *The Life of Charles Dickens*, ed. J. W. T. Ley (London, 1928), does not say so, but Lindsay (p. 253) does.

10. Forster, p. 839.

11. Quoted in ibid., p. 356.

12. *Charles Dickens*, p. 252.

13. T. Carlyle, *Works* (London, 1901), i, 96.

14. Edgar Johnson, in his *Charles Dickens* (New York, 1953), p. 800, finds this same decade of development running through *Dombey and Son, David Copperfield,* and *Bleak House,* to *Hard Times.* Professor Christian sees some acceptance, *circa* 1846, of Carlyle's "whole theory", but centers her analysis upon *Bleak House, Hard Times, Little Dorrit,* and *A Tale of Two Cities,* ii, 17.

15. *Works,* x, 206. Carlyle rejects "eye-service," the greedy grasping for wages.

16. *Works,* xx, 48–86. Of interest is the fact that, like Dickens, Carlyle records a personal visit to such a model prison.

17. From "The Hero as Divinity," *Heroes and Hero-Worship,* in *Works,* v, 10, but the same idea is presented in all major Carlylean works.

18. From "The Hero as King," ibid., p. 203.

19. "Chartism," *Works,* xxix, 132. Lindsay also notes this influence from Carlyle to Dickens, p. 203.

20. Forster says, ". . . Dickens' childish sufferings and the sense they burnt into him of the misery of loneliness and a craving for the joys of home, though they led to what was weakest in him, led also to what was greatest. . . ."

21. Forster, p. 839.

22. *Works,* v, 155, 157.

Politics and Society in *Felix Holt*

FRED C. THOMSON

Felix Holt, the Radical has seldom been considered altogether satisfying as a political novel. The rather mannered descriptions of electioneering and the heavy-handed didacticism of Felix's speeches suggest that George Eliot was ill at ease in the field of practical politics. Yet, properly understood, this neglected book is an important guide both to George Eliot's vision of English society and to the techniques of rendering it that she perfected in *Middlemarch*.

Despite the title (deliberately equivocal) it becomes readily apparent that *Felix Holt* is not a political novel as the genre is ordinarily understood. George Eliot was not attempting, like Disraeli, to disseminate a body of party principles; nor, like Trollope in *Phineas Finn*, to describe the vicissitudes of a career politician. Equally remote from her purposes was the strain of social protest to be found in the novels of Charles Kingsley and Mrs. Gaskell. She gives us no scarifying pictures of contaminated slums, inhuman working conditions, or lower-class degradation. The Sproxton colliers and the barflies at the Cross Keys are brutish and stupid, but there is none of the savor of real abandonment about them. Their ignorance and a kind of childish docility to evil counsel are emphasized above their squalor.

George Eliot repeatedly, almost wilfully, neglects her opportunities for outright political discussion or debate. To be sure, there are numerous passages (for instance the market-dinner at the Marquis of Granby) where the miscellaneous political views of the characters are exposed;

but the effect is more to expose the political ignorance of Trebians than to get at any real definition of principles. The most conspicuous issue of a political nature in the novel is bribery and corruption at elections, and that is made to touch as much on private as on public morality.[1] Only at the Duffield Nominations do we get anything like a straight-forward expression of George Eliot's political views, and then the spirit is hostile to practical politics. Not only does Felix, the titular hero, have no vote, he is not even interested in getting one. He is ambitious enough, but no part of his ambition is to become an elected representative of his class to what Carlyle called the "National Palaver." He is a Radical in an anti-political sense.

With her experience as an editor of the *Westminster Review*, George Eliot was surely well informed on the political currents of the age, but her mind habitually transmuted such ideas into broad humanitarian concepts with little correlation to legislative machinery. Believing that social reform was dependent on the healthy inner state of the individuals comprising the society, she was deeply skeptical of the wisdom of an extended suffrage while self-reform among the masses was so lagging. The veteran socialist agitator and free-thinker George Jacob Holyoake, a long-time friend of the Leweses, pointed out the deficiency of *Felix Holt* as a Radical document.

> Felix is a revolutionist from indignation. His social insurgency is based on resentment at injustice. Very noble is that form of dis-satisfaction, but political independence is not his inspiration. Free-dom, equality of public rights, are not in his mind. His disquiet is not owing to the political inability of his fellows to control their own fortunes. Content comes to Felix when the compassion of others ameliorates or extinguishes the social ills from which his fellows suf-fer. He is the Chartist of Positivism without a throb of indignation at political subjection. That may be Positivism, but it is not Radi-calism.[2]

If George Eliot's objective had been to depict in Felix a model political Radical, Holyoake's criticism would be unanswerable. He argued, however, from a wrong premise, giving insufficient weight to the irony in the title. Of course Felix is a Positivist, and a Tory Positivist at that.

Though it would be going too far to claim that George Eliot's political opinions were illiberal, they leaned distinctly towards the conservative side. In some thinly disguised autobiographical passages in the essay "Looking Backward," she tells us that she imbibed from her father, Robert Evans, much of his doughty conservatism.

> Nor can I be sorry, though myself given to meditative if not active innovation, that my father was a Tory who had not exactly a dislike to innovators and Dissenters, but a slight opinion of them as persons of ill-founded self-confidence; whence my young ears gathered many details concerning those who might perhaps have called themselves the more advanced thinkers in our nearest market-town, tending to convince me that their characters were quite as mixed as those of the thinkers behind them.[3]

This bent for "meditative if not active innovation" allowed her to hold the most advanced views in religion, philosophy, and science, while at the same time she cherished the established order in national institutions. Through Charles Bray, whom she met in 1841, she was introduced to some of the great liberal political and social movements of the time, but she never lost her "latent Conservative bias."[4] There is an interesting letter to John Sibree, Jr., in which George Eliot rejoices at the French Revolution of February 1848. But her conservatism soon comes to the fore. What is suitable to the conditions in France and the French national character would not be so in England. The English are "slow crawlers," fit at present only for the "slow progress of *political* reform," such as is permitted by the constitution. She has a horror of the brutal destructive violence, uninspired by higher motives of truth and justice, that she feels would characterize any insurrection of British laborers.[5]

In 1851 George Eliot became assistant editor for John Chapman of the *Westminster Review*, once a nursery of Philosophic Radicalism but which now announced a relatively conservative policy. She helped write the original version of the Prospectus prefacing the first number of the periodical under its new management.[6] One copy of this Prospectus was submitted for comment to John Stuart Mill, who after perusing it wrote Chapman "a long, half-sarcastic letter" criticizing the conservatism and generality of the stated policies.[7] Mill objected particularly to the assertions that "strength and durability are the result only of slow and peaceful development," and that "reform, to be salutary, must be graduated to the average moral and intellectual growth of a society."[8] These views, however, are quite consistent with

George Eliot's position in *Felix Holt,* written fifteen years later, and attest the conservatism of her politics, even when she was inhaling a "liberal air" in other intellectual areas. But her political principles were to receive their fullest exposition a year and a half after she had finished the novel in the "Address to Working Men, by Felix Holt," produced at the urging of her publisher, John Blackwood, an inveterate conservative.

Speaking to the workers newly enfranchised by the Reform Bill of 1867, Felix warns them against arrogant vaunting that they are "the future masters of the country," when instead they should bethink themselves solemnly and humbly of "our heavy responsibility; that is to say, the terrible risk we run of working mischief and missing good, as others have done before us." Political power, dangerously susceptible to abuse, is safely entrusted only to men possessing the indispensable qualifications of knowledge, ability, and honesty, without which no lasting good can be expected of the franchise. A society, he continues, is like the human body, a delicately poised system of parts—individuals and classes—whose health depends on the harmonious cooperation of these components. It is foolish to deny the existence of class distinctions, "as if everybody could have the same sort of work, or lead the same sort of life." Equally vain is the pretense that class interest is unreal. "It is clear that if any particular number of men get a particular benefit from any existing institution, they are likely to band together, in order to keep up that benefit and increase it, until it is perceived to be unfair and injurious to another large number, who get knowledge and strength enough to set up a resistance." Human nature being what it is, still tainted with selfishness, such resistance to injustice is itself in peril of becoming unjust, a mere "damaging convulsion" detonated by motives of greed and brutality. The working classes, embittered by a long history of political and economic repression, can least afford to forget that society is ligatured by all its members, all its classes. An individual, fast enmeshed as he is in the "fine widespread network of society," cannot pursue selfish interests without incurring harmful consequences to himself or his class. And no class can seek to eradicate or violently supplant another without disrupting the whole society.

> Now the only safe way by which society can be steadily improved and
> our worst evils reduced, is not by any attempt to do away directly

with the actually existing class distinctions and advantages . . .
but by the turning of Class Interests into Class Functions or duties.
What I mean is, that each class should be urged by the surrounding
conditions to perform its particular work under the strong pressure
of responsibility to the nation at large; that our public affairs should
be got into a state in which there should be no impunity for foolish
or faithless conduct.

Such an end will come to pass only with patience, forbearance, intelligence, and fortitude.

Recalling his part in the lamentable election riot of 1832, Felix
says the experience taught him the awfulness of disorder and the
futility of precipitating any change while the mass of the populace,
"the hideous margin of society," is yet unweaned from ignorance,
gross sensuality, and brutality. Disorder can inflict a mortal wound
on society, and the fundamental duty of the government is therefore
to prevent its occurrence and to enforce the laws. In their insistence
upon the maintenance of order, the governing classes are not simply
trying to protect a selfish tyrannic supremacy. They are exercising
their peculiar class function. Infuriating though it may be for the under-
privileged to behold the superabundance of wealth and comforts in
the ranks above them, frequently enjoyed by persons as stupid, coarse,
and selfish as the worst among themselves, they must realize that the
upper classes, by virtue of ancient heritage, are best qualified for the
stewardship of the national treasure of "knowledge, science, poetry,
refinement of thought, feeling, and manners, great memories, and the
interpretation of great records, which is carried on from the minds of
one generation to the minds of another." The unremitting task of
practical wisdom for the working man is "not to say, 'This is good, and
I will have it,' but to say, 'This is the less of two unavoidable evils,
and I will bear it.' " For people unaccustomed to the proper uses of
the precious cultural heritage to seize rashly the alluring prerogatives
of material wealth, refinement, and leisure, trampling down their
traditional custodians, would mean the debasement of the nation.
The lower classes must prepare themselves gradually and industriously
to become active sharers of "the common estate of society." The "Address" closes on a characteristic note of commodious generality. "I have
avoided touching on special questions. The best help towards judging
well on these is to approach them in the right temper, without vain
expectation, and with a resolution which is mixed with temperance."[9]

The exalted sentiments, the real compassion for working class misery and injustice notwithstanding, George Eliot's political principles are perhaps closer to Carlyle's in the *Latter-Day Pamphlets* than to John Stuart Mill's in *On Liberty*. History and the collective wisdom of the nation are on the side of the ruling classes. Human nature may be perfectible, but selfishness and meanness still predominate so that "however we insist that men might act better, we are forced, unless we are fanatical simpletons, to consider how they are likely to act." Until the vicious ignorance of the masses has been dispelled, political power is most safely left to those who have been traditionally invested with it. Sporadic corruption in high office is less to be feared than the insurrection of an insane rabble.

Such skepticism favors a conservative policy, but it cannot be said that George Eliot was attached to any organized party. Her political conservatism was not so much a basis for similar principles in other areas as it was an offshoot of the Positivist philosophy that actually controls the "Address to Working Men." The solidarity of mankind, the idea that the good of one is the good of all, that the unfailing law of consequences will punish any selfish deviation are at the heart of her message. Social and political change must be slow because the results of a mistaken course may be irreparable. Since the gradations by which great changes for good or ill are ultimately wrought are usually minute rather than spectacular, a society must keep ceaseless vigilance over the direction of its progress; for "they are comparatively few who see the small degrees by which . . . extremes are arrived at, or have the resolution and self-control to resist the little impulses by which they creep on surely towards a fatal end."

This concept of the "gradual operation of steady causes" is treated more lightly in the essay "A Political Molecule," first published in the *Impressions of Theophrastus Such* (1879). George Eliot here makes the point that even selfishness, so long as it does not violate the established order, can contribute to at least class welfare. She demonstrates how "a man often furthers larger ends than he is conscious of, and that while he is transacting his particular affairs with the narrow pertinacity of a respectable ant, he subserves an economy larger than any purpose of his own." The political molecule in this case is Spike, a cotton manufacturer whose professed Liberalism is a specious cloak for the narrowest self-interest. Spike had been in favor of the Reform Bill not because of any genuine sympathy for the unenfranchised multitudes

but because he saw that his business would profit from the representation of large trading towns in Parliament. He was for Corn Law Re-
peal not because it would help relieve famine and distress among the
poor but because he thought additional foreign markets for cotton
goods would thereby be opened up. Yet in advocating or opposing
certain legislation for the sake of his private prosperity he necessarily
acted for the weal of the cotton industry in general and of his class:
"A small mind trained to useful occupation for the satisfying of private
need becomes a representative of genuine class-needs. . . . Spike was
obliged to contemplate a general benefit, and thus became public-
spirited in spite of himself. Or rather, the nature of things transmuted
his active egoism into a demand for a public benefit."[10]

The ideas expounded in the "Address to Working Men" and "A
Political Molecule" permeate *Felix Holt.* But it is interesting and significant that these ideas emerge less effectively through the actions and
speeches of Felix himself than through characters opposed or contrasted to him, and through various symbolic features of the setting.

For the sake of playing on the ambiguity of the epithet, George
Eliot has aligned Felix with the Radicals, but he is plainly a misfit
in that political camp, as he would have been in the Tory, for which
his purely political beliefs better qualify him. He is above all a lay
Positivist, believing in the abstract principle of progress broadcast by
the Radicals yet holding with the Conservatives that the rate of in-
stitutional progress should never exceed that of human nature. His
Radicalism is of a root-and-branch order, which wants "to go to some
roots a good deal lower down than the franchise."[11] Better than persuade the Whig capitalist Garstin to establish a company school for
his employees' children, Felix aspires to get the men voluntarily to pool
savings from their drinking money to hire a schoolmaster. And at
Treby he carries on his educational crusade by teaching a small group
of local boys. His goal is the gradual development of a strong, wise,
and virtuous public opinion as the prerequisite for political power.
When the trades-union man at Duffield declares, "the greatest question
in the world is, how to give every man a man's share in what goes
on in life," Felix applauds; but he does not believe that the way to get
a man's share in life is by legislated nostrums, including a premature
franchise. Votes cannot help the workers if they are cast ignorantly
to elect time-serving rascals, "men who have no real opinions, but
who pilfer the words of every opinion, and turn them into a cant

which will serve their purpose at the moment; . . . men who know all the ins and outs of bribery, because there is not a cranny in their own souls where a bribe can't enter" (xxx, 241).[12]

Another immediate need is to develop among laborers and artisans a sense of class duties. Felix is proud of his lineage as a craftsman. "I have the blood of a line of handicraftsmen in my veins, and I want to stand up for the lot of the handicraftsman as a good lot, in which a man may be better trained to all the best functions of his nature than if he belonged to the grimacing set who have visiting-cards, and are proud to be thought richer than their neighbours" (xxvii, 180). Elsewhere he says, "If there's anything our people want convincing of, it is, that there's some dignity and happiness for a man other than changing his station" (xlv, 85). The moral deterioration of his father, he believes, can be partly attributed to his desertion of the class to which he was born. "My father was a weaver first of all. It would have been better for him if he had remained a weaver" (v, 114).

The ambivalence in Felix's position has the effect of alienating him from almost everyone. Too much of a gadfly to conscience to make anyone around him comfortable, he is regarded by Liberals and Conservatives, by traditionalists and levelers, by Churchmen and Dissenters as a sort of renegade or barbarian at odds with all the conventions of society. The dearth of camaraderie in Felix, his belligerent pedantry, his aloofness from the community life in Treby, to say nothing of the shadowiness of his background and motivations and the wooden dialogue, injure his effectiveness as a spokesman for George Eliot. Ardent as a polemicist, indomitable as a crusader, he fails to convince dramatically because the reader cannot fit him into the local context of organic social change, of which he emerges a calculated exponent, not a vital symbol.

Compared to the lofty moral idealism of Felix, the political Radicalism of Harold Transome may appear rather shallow and shabbily expedient. As a character, however, he is far more interesting. To call Harold, as several contemporary reviewers did, a cynical and nefarious politician is erroneous. He has aligned himself with the Radicals out of principle rather than opportunism. Belonging to a landed family traditionally of Tory persuasion, personally avid for reputation and honor in the county, he is well aware of the pejorative meaning Treby gentry attach to the word Radical. "It did not signify about your holding Radical opinions at Smyrna," his horrified mother tells him;

"but you seem not to imagine how your putting up as a Radical will affect your position here, and the position of your family. No one will visit you. And then—the sort of people who will support you! You really have no idea what an impression it conveys when you say you are a Radical. There are none of our equals who will not feel that you have disgraced yourself" (II, 67–68).

Every consideration of expediency would seem to militate against his decision; yet Harold sticks obstinately by it, convinced that the best interests of the country will be served by the Radical party. Holding that Toryism and Whiggery have lost their political identity and vitality, he believes that nothing is left "to men of sense and good family but to retard the national ruin by declaring themselves Radicals, and take the inevitable process of changing everything out of the hands of beggarly demagogues and purse-proud tradesmen" (II, 58). By disposition irregularly divided between rebellion and conformity, he likes to keep up the outward forms of convention but has no desire to stunt the growing Radical saplings in favor of the rotting Tory oaks.[13] His political downfall is therefore not the merited due of a mere charlatan. It is true that "the utmost enjoyment of his own advantages was the solvent that blended pride in his family and position, with the adhesion to changes that were to obliterate tradition and melt down enchased gold heirlooms into plating for the egg-spoons of 'the people' " (XLIII, 156).

But Harold is essentially honest, guilty of misjudgment rather than evil intent. Politically, as George Eliot sees it, he errs in believing that he thoroughly knows the condition of England after an absence of fifteen years. His Radicalism, as opposed to the root-and-branch moral radicalism of Felix, is superficial, confined to "rooting out abuses." He wants to accelerate reform artificially and prematurely, ingenuously crediting the masses with the intelligence to understand what is best for them. Morally Harold was wrong in winking at the lawyer Jermyn's bad character for the sake of securing him as an election agent, and then in conniving at the corrupt methods of Jermyn's hireling on the theory that if a man is to get into Parliament "he must not be too particular." By the law of consequences he assumes liability for his passive complicity.

Whether or not George Eliot so designed it, the Tories in *Felix Holt* and the social units of North Loamshire and Treby appear as symbols of organic change and the solidarity of mankind superior in

dramatic effect to the nominal hero. The Tories are represented chiefly
of course by the Debarry family.[14] Bluff, jovial Sir Maximus and his
hard-headed but finer-grained brother the Rev. Augustus are both excellent examples of those "political molecules" who almost in spite
of themselves contribute to wide public benefits. Sir Maximus, though
he flatters himself that he has the good of the country at heart, is
solidly dedicated to the interests of the landowning classes and is
opposed to any disturbance of the existing order and institutions. His
daughter Selina once asks why the Nonconformist movement in the
seventeenth century was condoned by the authorities:

> "But all those wrong things—why didn't government put them
> down?"
> "Ah, to be sure," fell in Sir Maximus, in a cordial tone of cor-
> roboration. (xiv, 290)

There is much that is faulty with what Sir Maximus stands for—
social inertia, neo-feudalism, rigid class barriers, cultural materialism,
monopolization of wealth, idleness, self-indulgence. He is the "long-
tailed saurian," a primeval creature too cumbersome to manage its
own bulk, attracting wasteful parasites, maintaining a manor that in
size and the amount of provisions therein consumed could rival an
entire village.

Nevertheless, by his very unprogressiveness Sir Maximus is a
valuable social component, retarding the destructive forces of hasty
change. The family, extending back in time to long before the English
Reformation, has its roots in ancient British traditions and is antago-
nistic to any rupture of their venerable continuity. If the saurian
is antediluvian, he has a warranted premonition of the extinction that
will come with the deluge, and is anxious to forestall that catastrophe
as long as possible. He is thus performing a valid class function, one
with which George Eliot sympathized.

In domestic life Sir Maximus is benevolent, generous, easy-going,
the worthy father of a worthy son; but when the safety of his class is
threatened, his instincts of self-preservation are swift and ruthless. He
cuts Harold Transome from his acquaintance the moment he hears of
his tergiversation. Despite his political treachery, Harold remains a
gentleman by birth (at least on his mother's side), and when it comes
to a showdown between a gentleman and a varlet Sir Maximus knows
whose part to take. Forgetting former grievances, he gallantly rescues

Harold when Jermyn reveals his paternity to the assemblage at the White Hart.

> "Leave the room, sir!" the Baronet said to Jermyn, in a voice of imperious scorn. "This is a meeting of gentlemen."
> "Come, Harold," he said, in the old friendly voice, "come away with me." (xLVII, 244)

Later he lends his prestige to suppress the scandal about Mrs. Transome in the Treby neighborhood.

The Rev. Augustus Debarry, "really a fine specimen of the old-fashioned aristocratic clergyman, preaching short sermons, understanding business, and acting liberally about his tithe" (III, 85)—*surtout point de zèle,* does for the Establishment what his brother does for the landed interests. Whereas Sir Maximus is concerned about the encroachments of manufacturers and parvenus, Augustus worries over the ominous ferment of once quiescent Dissent, a concomitant of creeping industrialism. Impervious to progressive influences, he efficiently protects sacred institutions and civil order. His grim hostility to the Independent preacher Mr. Lyon is based on reasons that in principle could hardly displease Felix himself.

> "Let me tell you, Phil, he's a crazy little firefly, that does a great deal of harm in my parish. He inflames the Dissenters' minds on politics. There's no end to the mischief done by these busy prating men. They make the ignorant multitude the judges of the largest questions, both political and religious, till we shall soon have no institution left that is not on a level with the comprehension of a huckster or a drayman. There can be nothing more retrograde—losing all the results of civilisation, all the lessons of Providence—letting the windlass run down after men have been turning at it painfully for generations. If the instructed are not to judge for the uninstructed, why, let us set Dick Stubbs to make our almanacs, and have a President of the Royal Society elected by universal suffrage." (xXIII, 122-123)

The rectory itself, like the Manor, symbolizes a surfeit of material wealth and secular comforts; it is also a symbol of what has proved best and sturdiest in the long history of British civilization.

> The Rectory was on the other side of the river, close to the church of which it was the fitting companion: a fine old brick-and-stone

house, with a great bow-window opening from the library on to the
deep-turfed lawn, one fat dog sleeping on the door-stone, another fat
dog waddling on the gravel, the autumn leaves duly swept away, the
lingering chrysanthemums cherished, tall trees stooping or soaring
in the most picturesque variety, and a Virginia creeper turning a
little rustic hut into a scarlet pavilion. It was one of those rectories
which are among the bulwarks of our venerable institutions—which
arrest disintegrating doubt, serve as a double embankment against
Popery and Dissent, and rally feminine instinct and affection to
reinforce the decisions of masculine thought. (xxiii, 120–121)

George Eliot's sympathy for these hidebound "molecules" is better
understood if one remembers the attitude of Dickens towards Sir
Leicester Dedlock of *Bleak House*. Like Sir Maximus Debarry, Sir
Leicester is a staunch conservative, loftily proud of his long ancestry,
yet capable on occasion of magnanimity.

His family is as old as the hills, and infinitely more respectable.
He has a general opinion that the world might get on without hills,
but would be done up without Dedlocks. He would on the whole admit Nature to be a good idea (a little low, perhaps, when not en-
closed with a park-fence), but an idea dependent for its execution on
your great county families. He is a gentleman of strict conscience,
disdainful of all littleness and meanness, and ready, on the shortest
notice, to die any death you may please to mention rather than give
occasion for the least impeachment of his integrity. He is an
honourable, obstinate, truthful, high-spirited, intensely prejudiced,
perfectly unreasonable man.[15]

Dickens gives his merits due credit but the portrait generally lingers
in a damp, musty gloom. The aristocratic world of Sir Leicester does
not idle in the afternoon sun of North Loamshire. It feebly expires in
a close shuttered room. "There is much good in it; there are many
good and true people in it; it has its appointed place. But the evil
of it is, that it is a world wrapped up in too much jeweller's cotton
and fine wool, and cannot hear the rushing of the larger worlds, and
cannot see them as they circle round the sun. It is a deadened world,
and its growth is sometimes un-healthy for want of air." Chesney
Wold decays in a leaden atmosphere of drizzle and mould. It resembles Transome Court more than Treby Manor in its disrepair
and haunted corridors. "The vases on the stone terrace in the foreground catch the rain all day; and the heavy drops fall, drip, upon

the broad flagged pavement, called, from old time, the Ghost's Walk, all night. On Sundays, the little church in the park is mouldy; the oaken pulpit breaks out into a cold sweat; and there is a general smell and taste as of the ancient Dedlocks in their graves." In the end, Sir Leicester "holds his shrunken state in the long drawing-room. . . . Closed in by night with broad screens, and illumined only in that part, the light of the drawing-room seems gradually contracting and dwindling until it shall be no more. A little more, in truth, and it will be all extinguished for Sir Leicester; and the damp door in the mausoleum which shuts so tight, and looks so obdurate, will have opened and relieved him." [16] What to Dickens, then, seemed an exhausted incubus to social and political progress was to George Eliot a useful counterbalance to the more subversive forces of radicalism.

Collective North Loamshire is in many ways a "political molecule," symbolic of organic change; and George Eliot's handling of the setting marks a definite stage in the development of her methods of social analysis. In *Adam Bede, The Mill on the Floss,* and *Silas Marner* she had closely studied the anatomy of town and rural life and manners. These stories are liberally sprinkled with minor characters representing the various trades, crafts, and professions, not to mention the subtle gradations within the land-owning and land-tilling classes. An excellent example of this kind is the account of the birthday celebration at Donnithorne Abbey, where every person is dined and entertained according to his station. Such social analysis is, however, even in the more complex world of *The Mill on the Floss,* relatively simple, unobtrusive, and incidental to other preoccupations.[17] George Eliot contented herself with careful observation of the accomplished fact of a certain class structure without searching into political and economic causes.

In *Felix Holt* the social system is not taken so comfortably for granted. The Introduction contains a brilliant survey of the agricultural, marketing, and manufacturing areas of the midlands, showing the encroachment of the Industrial Revolution on pastoral domain, its effects on the native resistance to change and sluggish political consciousness of the population, and on the redistribution of Orthodoxy and Dissent. The device of the coach-ride, so dear to Scott and Dickens, is resuscitated for a purpose that goes beyond picturesqueness and nostalgia. On its dawn-to-dusk odyssey from the Avon to the Trent, the coach becomes a symbol of organic progress, in contrast to the forced unnatural progress typified by the pneumatic railway. Mr. Sampson the coachman is himself a victim of industrialism.

> His view of life had originally been genial, and such as became a man who was well warmed within and without, and held a position of easy, undisputed authority; but the initiation of Railways had embittered him: he now, as in a perpetual vision, saw the ruined country strewn with shattered limbs, and regarded Mr. Huskisson's death as a proof of God's anger against Stephenson. "Why, every inn on the road would be shut up!" and at that word the coachman looked before him with the blank gaze of one who had driven his coach to the outermost edge of the universe, and saw his leaders plunging into the abyss. (i, 11)

The study is resumed in Chapter 3 with specific application to Treby Magna, where the peaceful social balances in the town had been upset towards the end of the eighteenth century by the advent of "new conditions, complicating its relation with the rest of the world, and gradually awakening in it that higher consciousness which is known to bring higher pains" (pp. 80–81). The difference of the analysis in these chapters is that whereas in George Eliot's earlier "English" novels the background material was woven unobtrusively into the stories, in *Felix Holt* it is a bit too conveniently marshalled and self-consciously displayed. By the time she wrote *Middlemarch*, George Eliot had regained her command of technique. Manipulating far more historical and sociological detail, she adroitly kneaded it into the stuff of her drama, occasionally consolidating some of it in a transitional paragraph or two, but never permitting it to usurp an entire chapter. It is this improved artistry that lends *Middlemarch* much of its extraordinary depth and richness as "A Study of Provincial Life."

Even so, the analysis of Treby is fine in its own right. Through the eighteenth century it had been a typical old-fashioned market town, specializing in "grazing, brewing, wool-packing, cheese-loading." The "new conditions" which have since arisen—the canal, the coal mines, the spa, the tape manufactory, and finally the Catholic and Reform agitations—have touched and awakened its political consciousness; they have not succeeded in hurrying it inordinately into a torrent of progressive change. The acceptance of innovation by native Trebians is painfully slow and circumspect, but left to themselves they preserve and perpetuate a genial community spirit, their morality kept healthy under the superintendance of public opinion. The disruptive elements—moral, economic, political—are not indigenous but intrude from the outside world. The Transome family declines rapidly with the accession of those "very distant connections" the Durfeys, and the genuine branch of the Transomes, uprooted from its hereditary estates, dies with the degraded Tommy Trounsem. Mrs. Transome, herself a newcomer to Treby forty years ago, suffers from a contagious moral debility, which could infect the whole society. Luckily Treby has sufficient antibodies to ward off her corruptive influence. Jermyn, too, with his uncertain parentage and his aura of illegitimacy, arrives "from a distance" and promptly attempts to undermine Treby traditions. He is chiefly responsible for the short-lived Bethesda Spa and indirectly for the odious tape manufactory, which is such an affront to the aristocratic pride of Sir Maximus. Morally Jermyn is corruptive in his liaison with Mrs. Transome, in his handling of the Bycliffe suit, and in his milking of the estate. In the end he is driven out without having seriously injured the community at large.

Harold, the son of Mrs. Transome and Jermyn, is another virtual *déraciné*. After fifteen years in Smyrna, he returns vainly imagining that he knows what the country needs, and embarks on a campaign which culminates in the fatal riot, itself incited by non-Trebians. "I'm an Oriental, you know," says Harold, and the term carries here overtones of a nomadic, alien character, one without a sense of English traditions and institutions. The breed is symbolized by Harold's prized servant, the polyglot Dominic,

> "one of those wonderful southern fellows that make one's life easy. He's of no country in particular. I don't know whether he's most of a Jew, a Greek, an Italian, or a Spaniard. He speaks five or six languages, one as well as another. He's cook, valet, major-domo, and secretary all in one; and what's more, he's an affectionate fellow—I can trust to his attachment. That's a sort of human specimen that doesn't grow here in England, I fancy." (II, 64)

Christian is another such mongrel type. Even Mr. Lyon and Esther are "intruders" and, in less sinister ways, disturbing to Treby—Esther by her ladylike airs, unbecoming to one of her supposed station, and Mr. Lyon by his Dissenting zeal and Radical pulpiteering. Both, however, are assimilated by the society because of their essential goodness of heart and discretion.

One sees in most of the native or soundly naturalized town and county folk motives of self- or class-interest working unintentionally for larger public benefits. There is scarcely one who understands the real political significance of Tory, Whig, Radical, or Reform. They profess their party allegiance and cast their votes with the haziest notions of principles involved. Until the agitation over Catholic Emancipation in 1829 they had dwelt in a snug tranquil provincial limbo and are now just beginning "to know the higher pains of a dim political consciousness" (III, 86). As yet party names and issues carry no more than vague connotations of honor or infamy, which impinge upon them emotionally rather than rationally. Reform is to them "a confused combination of rick-burners, trades-unions, Nottingham riots, and in general whatever required the calling-out of the yeomanry" (Introd., p. 10).

In personal relations, the breach between Churchmen and Dissenters is wider and more acrimonious than between Conservatives and Liberals. Mr. Pendrell will not employ Dissenters at his bank, and a "year ago he discharged Brother Bodkin, although he was a valuable servant" (v, 113). But the Tory farmers give Mr. Lingon a friendly cheer before his speech for Harold Transome. At the Tory inn, the Marquis of Granby, a minority from the opposite party, is good-humoredly welcomed to the dinner table. "A respectable old acquaintance turned Radical rather against his will, was rallied with even greater gusto than if his wife had had twins twice over. The best Trebian Tories were far too sweet-blooded to turn against such old friends, and to make no distinction between them and the Radical, Dissenting, Papistical, Deistical set with whom they never dined, and probably never saw except in their imagination" (xx, 72–73). Except among the aristocracy, political differences have not yet made deep cleavages in social relations.

So long as the Treby tradespeople and land-tillers go about their business, promoting what is best for their private interests in an orderly way, like Spike the political molecule, their political innocence is not very harmful. Though almost every shade of Conservatism and Liberalism is represented among the residents, the parish as a whole reacts gingerly to external progressive pressures. The Radical concentration is still at Duffield, the coal mines are two miles away at Sproxton, the commercialized Spa has failed, and only the tape manufactory has made a successful invasion as the vanguard of industrialism. This placid resistance to change, this gradual transition in mores, just keeping pace with individual enlightenment, is, George Eliot implies, the wisest course while self-reform and altruistic feeling remain undeveloped in the majority. Political awareness, if not bigoted political partisanship, is symptomatic of a spreading sense of community with the rest of the nation, and eventually with the human race. And the inhabitants of Treby, having already felt the "higher pains," whether they realize it or not are moving in the right direction. Already there is a glimmering of fraternalism in Mr. Nolan's remark, " 'It's all one web, sir. The prosperity of the country is one web' " (xx, 79).

Seen in this light, the title motto from Michael Drayton's *Polyolbion* truly embodies George Eliot's philosophy of organic change:

Upon the midlands now the industrious muse doth fall,
The shires which we the heart of England well may call.
. . . .
My native country thou, which so brave spirits hast bred,
If there be virtues yet remaining in thy earth,
Or any good of thine thou bred'st into my birth,
Accept it as thine own, whilst now I sing of thee,
Of all thy later brood unworthiest though I be.

Those midland shires "which we the heart of England well may call" were for her among the last jealous guardians of a hallowed continuity in British traditions.

Notes

1. The election, of which so much is made in Volumes I and II, is over and virtually forgotten in Volume III as the personal tragedy comes to a head. For an argument that the political element was not in fact a part of George Eliot's original plan for the novel, see my article, "The Genesis of *Felix Holt*," *PMLA*, LXXIV (1959), 576–584.

2. *Bygones Worth Remembering*, 2 vols. (London, 1905), I, 92.

3. *Impressions of Theophrastus Such* (Edinburgh and London, 1879), p. 40.

4. John W. Cross, ed., *George Eliot's Life as Related in Her Letters and Journals*, 3 vols. (Edinburgh and London, 1885), I, 5.

5. Gordon S. Haight, ed., *The George Eliot Letters*, 7 vols. (New Haven, 1954–1955), I, 252–255.

6. See Gordon S. Haight, *George Eliot and John Chapman* (New Haven, 1940), p. 32.

7. *George Eliot and John Chapman*, p. 34.

8. Hugh S. R. Elliot, ed., *The Letters of John Stuart Mill*, 2 vols. (London, 1910), I, 162–164.

9. *Blackwood's*, CIII (1868), 1–11 passim.

10. *Theophrastus Such*, pp. 138–139.

11. Quotations are from the first edition (3 vols.; Edinburgh and London: 1866), XXVI, 184. Subsequent references are to this edition and show chapter and page.

12. There is a symbolic parallel between the late Mr. Holt's Elixir and Cancer Cure and the legislative "Morrison's Pills" peddled by the political Radicals. Felix regards men like Harold Transome and Johnson as "quacks" who more or less cynically play upon the people's ignorance of the "nature of things" and their "vain expectations." " 'My father was ignorant,' said Felix bluntly. 'He knew neither the complication of the human system, nor the way in which drugs counteract each other. Ignorance is not so damnable as humbug, but when it prescribes pills it may happen to do more harm' " (V, 110).

13. "He meant to stand up for every change that the economical condition of the country required, and he had an angry contempt for men with coronets on their coaches, but too small a share of brains to see when they had better make a virtue of necessity. His respect was rather for men who had no coronets, but who achieved a just influence by furthering all measures which the common sense of the country, and the increasing self-assertion of the majority, peremptorily demanded. He could be such a man himself" (VIII, 203–204).

14. Regrettably little is said about the politics of Philip Debarry, who is a victorious candidate in the election, whose behavior, so far as we learn, is impeccable, and whom George Eliot is clearly glad to send to Parliament. He is described by the Rev. Mr. Lingon as "one of the new Conservatives," "a new-fashioned Tory"; that is, one of those men who were dissatisfied with the concessive, unstable, latitudinarian policies of Sir Robert Peel. These men, feeling the need for a sound and well articulated body of principles to underlie the Conservative party, later rallied under Disraeli as the "Young Englanders." The enthusiasm of many of their leaders had been kindled, it so happens, by the Church revival at Oxford. The subsequent conversion of Philip to Catholicism is therefore historically consistent with his politics. George Eliot does not specify his political tenets, but the combination of Catholicism and "new Conservatism" leads one to suspect that he was patterned to some extent after the benevolently feudalistic, alms-dispensing Catholic landlord Mr. Eustace Lyle in *Coningsby*. A frailer representative of the Debarrys than his father and uncle, Philip is subject to visitations of self-doubt, which enhance his appeal for George Eliot. Though the idea was left in embryonic condition, he seems partly designed to illustrate the type of personality on whom the Oxford Movement (incipient at the university when Philip was up in 1832) made its impact. George Eliot had read Newman's *Apologia* in 1864 with "absorbing interest." The book affected her "as the revelation of a life—how different in form from one's own, yet with how close a fellowship in its needs and burthens" (*The George Eliot Letters*, IV, 158–159).

15. *Bleak House*, New Oxford edition (London, n.d.), p. 9.

16. Ibid., pp. 8, 9, 874.

17. See the fine discussion by Claude T. Bissell, "Social Analysis in the Novels of George Eliot," *ELH*, XVIII (1951), 221–239.

The Last Chronicle of Barset:
Trollope's Comic Techniques

WILLIAM A. WEST

Behind much, if indeed not most, of the critical writing on Trollope, there lies the assumption that he is not a novelist of the first magnitude. Walpole was the first to be lengthily and harshly outspoken against him (1928); but even most of those favorably disposed toward him have withheld their full support. When Escott, who first wrote a full-length study (1913) and who is generally well disposed toward Trollope, speaks of the two greatest novelists of the day, he means Thackeray and Dickens;[1] and Bradford Booth, the critic of our own day probably most closely associated with the study of Trollope, finds the novelist deficient in those qualities that would put him in the front rank. Booth says, for instance, that *The Last Chronicle of Barset* is "Trollope's finest novel."[2] His admiration of that novel depends, however, exclusively on the portrayal in it of Josiah Crawley; considering the novel as a whole, his judgment is negative. And even in handling Crawley, Booth thinks Trollope fails, finally, because he refused to make him the tragic figure he had the potential to become: "In his facile resolution of the problems he had raised Trollope lost his chance to put Josiah Crawley beside Karamazov and Père Goriot and King Lear."[3]

The charge against Trollope that he is not really a serious novelist, which Booth, F. R. Leavis, and other contemporary critics make, goes back, of course, ultimately to Henry James. James, like Booth, was an uneasy admirer of Trollope. His well-known essay on the earlier novelist is by no means hostile; but James's own biases and practices as a novelist—largely antithetical to Trollope's—make it impossible for him to rank Trollope with "his three brilliant contemporaries," Thackeray, Dickens, and George Eliot.[4] He admired certain things about Trollope, especially his focus on the conscience of characters who are faced with grave moral dilemmas. But if James admired Trollope's matter, he was no admirer of his manner. He may have had good stories to tell, and in some measure they are well told; but he had those faults which James found grievous; and subsequent critics, from Escott to Booth, have echoed James's condemnation.

The technique that James most objected to was Trollope's intrusion into his novels as the commenting author speaking directly to the reader over the heads of his characters. "He took a suicidal satisfaction in reminding the reader that the story he was telling was only, after all, a make-believe. He habitually referred to the work in hand (in the course of that work) as a novel, and to himself as a novelist, and was fond of letting the reader know that this novelist could direct the course of events according to his pleasure."[5] James, of course, was committed to making the novel as dramatic as possible, to showing rather than telling, to removing from sight as nearly as possible any sense of the guiding hand of the novelist so that the reader would feel himself the observer of a realistically rendered drama. Trollope, needless to say, did not make himself invisible in the wings: as Ernest Baker puts it, in a Trollope novel "the showman is on duty all the time; Trollope did not think novels should be written like plays, with the barest minimum of stage signs."[6]

The kind of thing James and his followers object to could be illustrated easily by reference to any of Trollope's novels. James used passages from *Barchester Towers* to illustrate Trollope's practice at its most intrusive, and *Barchester Towers* has ever since been cited most frequently whenever a critic wishes to show Trollope intruding where he ought not to. But since I am more interested here in defending *The Last Chronicle of Barset,* a passage from it, illustrating Trollope's habit of speaking directly to the reader, will be given instead. The final paragraph of that novel is:

> And now, if the reader will allow me to seize him affectionately by the arm, we will together take our last farewell of Barset and of the towers of Barchester. I may not venture to say to him that, in this country, he and I together have wandered often through the country

lanes, and have ridden together over the too well-wooded fields, or have stood together in the cathedral nave listening to the peals of the organ, or have together sat at good men's tables, or have confronted together the angry pride of men who were not good. I may not boast that any beside myself have so realised the place, and the people, and the facts, as to make such reminiscences possible as those which I should attempt to evoke by an appeal to perfect fellowship. But to me Barset has been a real county, and its city a real city, and the spires and towers have been before my eyes, and the voices of the people are known to my ears, and the pavement of the city ways are familiar to my footsteps. To them all I now say farewell. That I have been induced to wander among them too long by my love of old friendships, and by the sweetness of old faces, is a fault for which I may perhaps be more readily forgiven, when I repeat, with some solemnity of assurance, the promise made in my title, that this shall be the last chronicle of Barset.

That is surely to take the curtain call oneself.

The other constant in criticism that is negative toward Trollope, or at least that begrudges him real magnitude, is the charge that his novels are poorly organized—that his plots are loose, full of irrelevant and distracting subplots.[7] Trollope himself admitted in his autobiography that handling of plot was not one of his strengths, but he waved aside the importance of plot, suggesting that if one could create characters, plot would take care of itself.[8] Plot was simply what one's characters did once they had been fully imagined.

Behind both these charges against Trollope's fictional techniques, however, lie critical assumptions which must be judged, finally, inappropriate in measuring Trollope's fiction. James's theory of the novel took as its explicit norm the drama; but it should be not only noted but emphasized that too many followers of James have allowed dramatic and tragic expectations to overlap, almost as if the drama and tragedy were synonymous terms. Bradford Booth, for instance, who feels called upon to apply James's aesthetic views to Trollope's novels, assuming that James must necessarily be the starting point of any discussion of the novel,[9] ends by condemning *The Last Chronicle of Barset* not because it is not dramatic enough but because it is not tragic enough: he is reduced to saying of it that, although the story of Josiah Crawley contains "the stuff of tragedy," Trollope failed "to meet his opportunity." The book does not reach the heights, says Booth, simply because "there is no tragedy."[10]

Other critics understand *The Last Chronicle* better than Mr. Booth because they allow the book to be the comedy it is. W. P. Ker, for instance, thinks, as Booth does, that *The Last Chronicle* is Trollope's best novel. It is, in his view, Trollope's most anxious and serious work, but it is not tragic. He speaks of Trollope's hero in it, Crawley, as "full of pride, selfwill, bitterness, contempt, and anger, unmistakeably true and courageous—all that was wanted for a tragic figure, if the author had been so inclined." But Ker allows Trollope to operate within the generic limitations of comedy and imposes no tragic demands on him. Trollope's works, Ker says, are comic, what he calls, following Fielding, "the comic epic in prose." That Trollope should have written comic works seems to him perfectly legitimate; though perhaps even here there is some condescension toward comedy and practitioners of the comic art: "he kept away from the tragic heights through a right understanding of his limitations and his proper scope, not through any want of sense or sensibility."[11]

That *The Last Chronicle of Barset* is both serious and anxious, as Ker puts it, does not, of course, mean that it cannot also be comic. Most of Trollope's novels are, in fact, comic, though one ranks them as comedies not because they are funny or amusing but because they contain overlapping narrative patterns that represent what Northrop Frye has called the Mythos of Spring: narrative patterns that have to do with the triumph of life forces over death, the return of spring after winter, the success of love and order after misunderstanding and chaos. According to this notion, *The Last Chronicle of Barset* must be called a comedy. Things turn out well in the end: the hero is restored, love triumphs. One could enumerate, in fact, a number of ways in which the workings of its plot, and the characters who figure in its unfolding, correspond to those narrative patterns and characters that seem most frequently to represent man's faith in and longing for a harmonious world order in which life is preserved and protected. Not all of the stock characters and situations of comedy are represented: as Frye reminds us, no single work represents the total *mythos* of comedy;[12] but enough are present to persuade us that the work is indeed comic. I shall return later to some of the comic patterns and characters that Trollope employs in *The Last Chronicle*. I am primarily interested, however, in defending those fictional techniques of Trollope's most often urged upon us as his chief faults—his authorial presence in the novels and the loose structure of his plots—on the grounds that they are demonstrably appropriate to comedy.

The presence in a novel of a benign narrator who stands in a sympathetic relationship to his creation can certainly be seen as an obvious fictional method of representing the reassuring comic view that things turn out well in this world because we are protected by kindly forces, forces that have to do with fertility, procreation, and the continuation of life. Such forces may be rendered abstractly, but more likely, since they are personal, friendly forces, they are represented in guises that man recognizes as like himself. The Greeks used fertility figures, like Priapus, or sometimes the Olympian deities to personify these forces friendly to man. Athene, although an obviously more advanced, more complicated figure than Priapus, is also such a personification as she appears in *The Odyssey.* There our comic expectations are aroused because the goddess makes her presence so continuously felt; and we know, from the beginning, that she has the power to achieve her benevolent intentions towards Odysseus. In the end, it is she who presides, amidst symbols of the earth's fruitfulness, over all those reunions whereby the family, in both the literal and the larger social sense, the institution most intimately associated with the procreation and protection of life, is reconstituted.

If the gods in tragedy are hidden, inexplicable, seemingly cruel (or at any rate capable of exacting justice that causes man's misery or death), the comic gods are gods of life: they are humane, associated with love, either of the lusty or the compassionate kind, and mercy. Such qualities need not, of course, be associated only with the gods or with supernatural figures. In some of Shakespeare's comedies, for instance, they are frequently represented by good women. Women like Hermione in *The Winter's Tale* or Portia in *The Merchant of Venice* may not be divine; but they are given qualities associated with benevolent deities, as well as the power to effect happy, comic endings.

In English comic novels of the eighteenth and nineteenth centuries, it is the narrator himself who best represents, by his manner of narration and by his occasional explicit appearances in the novels, speaking directly to the reader, the comic spirit, i.e., the forces that oversee and support comic actions. Trollope does not, of course, represent himself as a deity; but he shares the attributes of the comic gods nonetheless. The world he shows us is presumably like the real world; but in his representation of that world, he assures us that he is not only in command of it but that he is also friendly toward it. Therefore things do turn out well, as we have been encouraged to believe all along. For instance, in *The Last Chronicle,* Josiah Crawley, forced earlier to live in exile from the good opinion of the world around him, is eventually found innocent and, fully exonerated, is restored to membership in the community; in that sense, like the exiles, wanderers, and sufferers of other comic works, he returns "home" at the end. His reunion with the world is paralleled by the union of the novel's lovers, Grace Crawley and Major Grantley, who have been kept apart by the embarrassment attendant on her father's difficulties: Crawley's exile from the world, the result of his supposed guilt, causes Grace to separate herself from her lover because she does not want to bring the man she wishes to marry any disgrace. Once the father is returned to full membership in human society, Grace is released from her own exile and engages herself to and marries Grantley. The marriage that Trollope always provides at the end of his novels, itself an obvious metaphor of fruitful union, connects him most obviously with the original impulse of comedy to assure us of the ongoing of life through an eventual return to the rites and institutions associated with procreation.

Trollope is not so constantly or explicitly intrusive in his novels as one might expect, given James's criticism of him on that score.[13] He does tend to come forward from time to time, and one can almost always expect to hear directly from him in the last chapter when the comic dénouement is being unfolded. On the whole, however, as Hillis Miller points out, Trollope "speaks far less as a single person than does the moralizing narrator of *Vanity Fair* or the sermonizing narrator of *Adam Bede.*"[14] Still, his presence is more or less continuously felt, though just how, perhaps, has not yet been adequately described or analyzed. Primarily he makes himself felt by his style and his tone. He is famous for the evenness—the ordinariness—of his style, for maintaining a consistent "voice," always the same from first to last, from novel to novel. What that perhaps comes down to is the easy, confident flow of his sentences which provides his novels with an embracing medium which is itself reassuring, suggestive as it is of control, steadiness, regularity, measure.

If his style is even, untroubled for the most part by either metaphor or passion, and, being even, implicitly reassuring, it is also, more importantly, always warm, humane, kindly. It is difficult to discuss what one means by a sympathetic tone in specific terms, because it is impossible to cite any single passage to represent it. But the longer one listens to Trollope tell his story, the more reassured one is by the tone. The sympathy of the author for his characters accumulates like a subliminal aura of warmth and light. One does not need the rich testimony of *An Autobiography* to know that Trollope lived with his characters "in the full reality of established intimacy,"[15] so all-pervasive is his sympathy and understanding for them, manifesting itself in the way he describes their troubles, their doubts, their mistakes, their sufferings, their foibles, their joys. Even when Trollope is presenting situations that are in themselves unhappy, which end unhappily, his tone is compassionate. John Eames, for instance, in *The Last Chronicle of Barset,* is frustrated in his efforts to win the hand of Lily Dale and the novel ends with Lily having kept her vow never to marry any man, despite the obvious worth of Eames and his poignant devotion to her. But Trollope's representation of Eames's unhappiness is so accompanied by the narrator's obvious sympathy for the character that whatever Eames suffers is mitigated, in the very act of describing it, by the generosity of emotion that surrounds it and is finally quite inseparable from it.

Trollope's handling of the death of Mr. Harding is perhaps the best example of what seems to me his comic tone. The death of the old man, like the failure of the John Eames-Lily Dale romance, would seem to be a sad, not a comic note. But so easily and naturally does Trollope present the old man's decline and death that there is never any question that Trollope wishes to arouse the kind of passionate grief associated with tragic death; nor is there the slightest indication of a Dickensian invitation to shed a few sentimental tears. On the contrary: the death is presented as a kind of beautiful consummation; and surely there is no more splendid or moving instance of a comic sense of triumph and community in all of Trollope's work than the funeral of the old man to which come, in silent, ceremonial procession, many of Trollope's best characters from the Barchester series who unite to honor the deceased gentleman. Both Mr. Harding's mellow old age, enriched to the end by his life-long love of music, and the moving ritual of his funeral are finally strikingly affirmative of life itself. His death is, of course, a source of sorrow; but in Trollope's rendition of it, it seems equally a reason to celebrate, to feel how rich and full life is, to feel, further, that a success has been achieved: that a man has lived his life as it seemed fit to him to do so, and that life, by his own standards, must be adjudged a success.

Many of those who have attempted to locate and describe the ambience in which Trollope's fiction unfolds have paid more attention to his transcendent "views" which provide his novels with their consistent background than to what I would describe as the stylistic foreground which constantly creates and reinforces the ambience of any given novel, wishing to imply thereby that style always makes the transcendent background immanent. Those who have tried to piece together a consistent position for Trollope have succeeded in making it by this time a critical commonplace that Trollope is not a philosophical novelist in the way, say, that George Eliot is; by which one means, I gather, that Trollope's philosophical assumptions do indeed lie in the background, that they are transcendent rather than the subject of debate within the novel itself. Those critics who have spoken for Trollope's implicit and pervasive sense of life are agreed that he is essentially conservative, but his faith in an essentially fixed and orderly world is accompanied by a belief that, within certain limits, improvements in man's lot can be made.[16] But Trollope's conservatism, like that of his eighteenth-century predecessors in the practice of the comic novel, has deeper connections than those which bind it to recent intellectual traditions. His conservatism is related in fact to a tradition that is scarcely best described as an intellectual tradition at all, but instead simply to comedy itself, which, insofar as it has to do always with the conservation of life itself, by whatever means are available, may also be described as conservative. The comic view may perhaps best be described as an expression of faith—what Christopher Fry has described as "a narrow escape into faith"[17]—that life, beset and bewildered as it is within the confines of any given comic work, will survive and go on because the universe is sympathetic toward it, because there are forces that assure, ultimately, its continuation.

Such a faith is expressed by the course of actions which comedy describes; but it is also expressed by the first of those techniques employed by Trollope in telling his stories which I wish to defend against its detractors: the use of an authorial presence. If we are to feel that life itself is secure in the real world, the fictional world, which purports to tell us something about the world we live in, must also make us feel secure. It may simply remind us, in comedies of the most elemental kind, that as long as man has sexual powers, life will go on because procreation is endlessly assured by the simple fact of the fertility of the race. In more serious comedy, however, in what Meredith and others have considered high comedy, one is allowed to feel, further, that the world is sympathetic to the whole course of life, not just to its begetting; that there are, in addition to the acts of procreation, rituals and institutions that nurture life after it has begun. Only, perhaps, when one feels that his world is ultimately sympathetic can he feel secure enough to smile at, even to laugh at, the difficulties that inevitably beset man's life. But comedy itself is not funny. As Benjamin Lehmann has put it, "though we laugh at actions and utterances in comedy, we do not laugh at the comedy as a whole. For the comedy as a whole is a serious work, making an affirmation about life that chimes with our intuitive sense of how things are and with our deep human desire to have the necessary and agreeable prevail. . . . Never in comedy are we without love, and almost never without lovers. . . . It reassures us about life and its continuation. . . . We do not laugh at all this. We are delighted; we are content."[18]

Wayne Booth, speaking of *Tom Jones,* says that "our growing intimacy with Fielding's dramatic version of himself produces a kind of comic analogue of the true believer's reliance on a benign providence in real life."[19] Trollope may also be said to use himself, his own presence, as one of the devices appropriate to establishing the comic mood of his novels, a mood based upon trust in a benign controlling figure. When that tolerant, sympathetic narrator speaks to us, assuring us that things turn out well in this world of his and that life goes on despite obstacles to it, we feel ourselves made confident about life in general; and when he is not directly present, one continues to feel, by the evenness of his style and the friendliness of the narrative tone, that the characters moving before us exist in an ambience generally protective. "The poet," Aristotle said, "should speak as little as possible in his own person."[20] But Aristotle was concerned with tragic, not comic, effects. In comedy, on the contrary, some kindly, divine presence, or its surrogate, is needed if we are to be certain throughout that a comic ending is certain. Trollope is indeed a narrator whom one wishes to call, as C. B. Tinker has called him, "companionable."[21] What makes one most reluctant to have a Trollope novel end is, in fact, the sense of loss one feels when that good companion has departed.

If Trollope's presence in his novels is entirely consonant with the kinds of novels he wrote, namely comedies, so too is that other narrative technique of his, also much criticized, namely his use of large, loose plots; the two techniques are indeed so directly related to each other that one not only supports the other but makes it possible. The effect of Trollope's multiple plots is a constant dissipation of mood. One moves back and forth from one plot line to another, a movement which works against the accumulation or intensification of any one mood. That such a technique is appropriate to comedy is perhaps best established by first noticing how antithetical it is to tragedy. It is hard to imagine any effective tragic work that allows its audience's attention to shift constantly, or for prolonged periods of time, away from the events and characters of the main narrative line. Tragedy depends on intensity, and intensity, in turn, depends on concentration and rapidity. Aristotle first urged a unified action upon the tragedian as his ultimate technical aim, by which he meant there to be no irrelevant materials to the plot, no breaks in the mood appropriate to the tragic emotions. Shakespeare, as well as his contemporaries, violated some of Aristotle's strictures, but unity of mood and rapidity of pace remain characteristics of Elizabethan and Jacobean tragedy, too, even when subplots and other complexities were added to the classical idea. The use of subplots need not relax the concentration and pace necessary to tragic effect, as Shakespeare's tragedies illustrate, but multiple plots surely do: it is impossible to imagine a successful tragedy with a plot as complex as *A Midsummer Night's Dream.*

Tragedy, then, tends to proceed rapidly, even, as it approaches its climax, with a rush. It is preoccupied with a single action around which the work unifies and organizes itself. We need to feel that what we are watching proceeds inexorably, according to the laws of logic; and inexorability, the logic of events, is perhaps best seen and represented by a narrative that proceeds quickly, without distractions or irrelevancies, so that the beholder, or reader, apprehends clearly causal relationships, that one thing leads inevitably to the next. There must be no sense that there is room for escape.

Comic plots, on the other hand, tend to move back and forth, from one set of characters to another, from one story line to another, from place to place, even from time to time. That they should do so seems to me itself an expression of the comic point of view: if the world, whether real or fictional, is malleable, improvable, subject to the manipulation of sympathetic forces as it presumably is in comedy, then one must be assured that there is both time and room for such forces to operate. We must not be fixed, or trapped, in a plot so tightly or economically drawn that there is room for nothing but the cause-and-effect relationship of events. Northrop Frye has observed that "in striking contrast to tragedy, there can hardly be such a thing as inevitable comedy."[22]

The distinction between the inevitable plot of tragedy and its more fluid counterpart in comedy is paralleled and supported by yet another distinction that separates the two kinds of plots. Behind the logic of events in tragedy lies the belief in another kind of logic: the logic of a strict sense of justice according to which all errors are punished. In tragedy we are bound not only by the exact cause-and-effect relationship of events but by the unbending operation of moral laws. Tragic heroes tend to be well-intentioned, but they are caught up in events that establish their guilt and make mandatory their punishment. A comic plot, on the other hand, is not only more fluid, more episodic, it is also less bound by exact notions of justice. It may in fact be said to go beyond justice to mercy: the comic hero is successful, despite his faults of character and errors of judgment, because the world of comedy is presided over by forces that are themselves benign, merciful.

Aristotle, describing tragic aims and effects, contended that "of all plots and actions the episodic are the worst. I call a plot 'episodic' in which the episodes or acts succeed one another without probable or necessary sequence."[23] He even goes so far as to suggest what I am also urging: that a complex plot is essentially a feature of comic actions not tragic ones.[24] Trollope, appropriately enough for a comic writer, confessed that his own plots lacked inevitability, that they simply occurred to him as he proceeded. Speaking of *Phineas Finn,* for instance, he wrote: "As to the incidents of the story, the circumstances by which personages were to be affected, I knew nothing. They were created for the most part as they were described. I never could arrange a set of events before me. But the evil and the good of my puppets, and how the evil would always lead to evil, and the good produce good,—that was clear to me as are the stars on a summer night."[25]

Trollope does not, however, assume so melodramatic a view of man as that quotation from *An Autobiography* might lead one to believe. Melodrama assumes that good and evil are easily discernible and that good men and bad are quite separate categories. Such convenient categories simply do not exist in Trollope's fiction. All men, as Trollope shows them to us, combine strengths and weaknesses. Since all of them have some flaws, they would all, under a strict system of legalistic justice, of a kind that tends to operate in tragedy, rightly be subject to suffering and punishment. Their errors would inevitably lead to painful consequences. But in the more generous, more tolerant atmosphere of comedy, weak, fallible, sinful man may mercifully be forgiven, providing, of course, that he has strengths as well as weaknesses. The comic world is not judged according to fixed, rigid laws, represented fictionally by the workings of an inexorable, inevitable plot line, but instead remains open, malleable, merciful. If man is weak, full of error and waywardness, so too is he also good, or at least well-intentioned, worthy of preservation both as an individual and as a species. Comedy, unlike tragedy, does more than emphasize character above plot; it represents the triumph of character over plot, the escape of man from what would trap him, confine him to logic, strict justice, necessity. Northrop Frye has observed that "the action of comedy, like the action of the Christian Bible, moves from law to liberty."[26] It moves too from a system of strict justice, according to which man is punished according to his errors, toward an attitude of mercy in which man is forgiven because of his goodness, because of the goodness of life itself.

Surely comedies are nowhere more malleable, more open to the merciful manipulation of benevolent forces, than at the dénouement of the action. Then, some attitude toward the preceding actions and the characters who have figured in them is almost certain to become apparent: attitudes of either justice or mercy, praise or blame, punishment or forgiveness. Aristotle argued, again on behalf of tragedy, that "the unravelling of the Plot, not less than the complication, must arise out of the Plot itself; it must not be brought about by the *Deus ex·Machina.*"[27] That is to say, the inexorable laws of logic, like the strict application of justice, are to be observed at the end of a tragedy. But the dénouement of a comedy is not controlled by either law or logic. It is, instead, as open, as improbable even, as its action has been: never fixed or confined from its beginning, but episodic instead, improvised, it remains pervious to the intrusion of outside or divine intervention. Wylie Sypher, distinguishing between tragic and comic plots, says of tragedy that it "demands a law of necessity or destiny, and a finality that can be gained only by stressing a logic of 'plot' or 'unified action' with a beginning, middle, and end." Comedy, however, he goes on to say, "remains an 'improvisation' with a loose structure and a precarious logic that can tolerate every kind of 'improbability.' "[28]

Trollope frequently uses providential and improbable acts or discoveries within his novels to affect the comic ending: in *The Last Chronicle of Barset,* Eleanor Bold returns just in time to prove that Crawley is innocent. But it is Trollope himself, the narrator of the novel, who most often and most obviously functions as the deus ex machina. That he did so throughout his novel-writing career is demonstrated by reference to a late novel which shows that the author whose intrusions in the early *Barchester Towers* James objected to remained unreformed to the end. The concluding chapter of the much later *Ayala's Angel* begins as follows: "Now we have come to our last chapter, and it may be doubted whether any reader,—unless he be some one specially gifted with a genius for statistics,—will have perceived how very many people have been made happy by matrimony. If marriage be the proper ending for a novel,—the only ending, as this writer takes it to be, which is not discordant,—surely no tale was ever so properly ended, or with so full a concord, as this one." In *The Last Chronicle of Barset* the narrator also steps forward at the beginning of his final chapter to tell us that "It now only remains for me to gather together a few loose strings, and tie them together in a knot, so that my work may not become untwisted." In the process of tying the final "knots" —one of which is, of course, the matrimonial knot—our comic expectations are fully satisfied.

Bradford Booth, complaining against Trollope that he "never learned how to turn out a clean, bare narrative," maintains that his novels "have no particular form." What he goes on to say is particularly pertinent to my own argument because he brings together here for simultaneous consideration and condemnation those two techniques of fictional presentation which I wish to defend: "Plot is improvised around the characters. This spontaneous composition . . . promotes the relaxed ease of the informal essayist, and provides Trollope with a fine opportunity to indulge himself in humorous asides."[29] I wish, however, to approve what Booth disapproves and to insist that a loosely-structured plot and an intruding narrator are fictional modes of representing the comic point of view. Trollope's plots are indeed loose, improvised, but they are held together, not by the careful plotting appropriate to tragic expression but by the presence in them of the presiding, sympathetic narrator. It is, in fact, that very looseness of structure, as Booth suggests, that frees the voice of the author, that gives it room to speak and to affect the action. In short, the two modes I have been defending here as entirely consonant with comedy work together: the loose structure presents an image of a malleable world open to the influence of a benign, merciful being, namely the narrator himself.

That Trollope's fictional techniques—and, as a result, his novels as well—should have come to be viewed with hostility or condescension is perhaps not surprising given developments in the intellectual and spiritual climate of the nineteenth century. The belief in the reality of merciful forces that underlies comedy, operating in and above the world and ultimately sympathetic to life, was seriously challenged by counter views in Victorian times. The writings of Darwin, Malthus, as well as Marx and, later on, Freud, emphasized the existence of laws whose operation was deemed inexorable. Once again man was seen as subject to impersonal, even cruel laws from which there was no escape. The world came to seem neither so malleable nor so merciful as one had hoped or as comic novels had suggested. Other kinds of forces of the kind traditionally associated with tragedy, other deities began to loom larger, not only, of course, in men's minds but also in the imaginative literature that projected not only authors' hopes but also their fears and anxieties.

It is surely no accident that the so-called disappearance, or death of God and the disappearance of authors from the fictional worlds they created were almost simultaneous developments. They both express the same kind of loss. God's benign presence, felt as an actuality in the world, and the voice of the comic author, commenting kindly about his characters and seeing to it that things work out well in the end, died away about the same time. Once the old idea of a benign presider over the affairs of men was gone, the world seemed to grow inexplicable: what had seemed merciful was cruel; what had seemed open to man was perhaps closed. Man's sense of God's withdrawal, of the separation between God and man, led naturally to a new, or renewed, tragic sense of life. Northrop Frye speaks of "the sense of human remoteness and futility in relation to the divine order which is only one element among others in tragic visions of life, though an essential one in all." [30] The tragic mood that begins to be expressed in some of George Eliot's novels, like *The Mill on the Floss,* and then more fully by Hardy, James, and Conrad is accompanied and paralleled by a change in the role played by the author. He, like God, also withdraws: his characters, like men and women in the real world, must then not only act in darkness, but without the assurance that a benign being hovers over them who can be counted on to be merciful.

Trollope was the last of the chief exponents of the great comic tradition in the novel that began in the eighteenth century, and being last he came up against and was judged by novelists and critics whose fictional techniques and attitudes differed radically from his. James presumably found him not dramatic enough; but the real, the underlying charge against him has been that he is not tragic enough, hence not serious or not worthy of one's serious consideration. In point of fact, however, he is simply a different kind of artist from those who came immediately after him.

Nonetheless it is also true that within Trollope's fiction the comic point of view is directly challenged. All comic actions include, of course, difficulties. If there is nothing to overcome, there can obviously be no sense of triumph at the end of the action: if life is not threatened, we do not feel its resurgence at the dénouement. Insofar as that is true, most comedies could end tragically: they contain elements that, within another context, could easily lead to results antithetical to the comic spirit. There is, then, always within a comedy a conflict between comic and tragic aspects. Frye has observed "how frequently a comic dramatist tries to bring his actions as close to a catastrophic overthrow of the hero as he can get it, and then reverse the action as quickly as possible."[31] The same may be said of *The Last Chronicle,* too, when Crawley's misery becomes so acute that his wife fears he may even take his own life.

The specific threat to comedy in Trollope's novels is that strict legality which I have already described as appropriate to the logic of tragedy. From *The Warden* on, Trollope's most important heroes are threatened by law suits or the public exposure of hitherto hidden crimes against the letter of the law. In *The Warden* it is the remote, terrible voice of a newspaper appropriately called the *Jupiter* that measures Mr. Harding against its own exact sense of what is lawful and right, finds him guilty, and demands his punishment (i.e., his banishment from his position and his home). In *The Last Chronicle of Barset* Trollope's hero is threatened by a legal action, this time from both a secular and an ecclesiastical court, and his persecutors assume that he is guilty and that he must be punished, again by removal from his office. Outside the Barchester series the appearance of—one must call it the threat of—law suits, trials, and the like is an almost omnipresent feature of his fictional world.

If, then, the nineteenth century produced influential writers who insisted that there were laws from which there was to be no escape, so too does Trollope represent in his fiction the "Law" as something equally remote, equally impersonal, claiming the right to judge those accused of guilty practice according to measurements so exact and so unbending as almost to preclude the possibility of either rescue or mercy. If Mr. Harding, Lady Mason, Josiah Crawley, and Phineas Finn are not rescued by something outside themselves one fears all must be sacrificed because the instruments called upon to judge them are not responsive enough to their good qualities, to the innocence of their intentions, to be flexible in ways ultimately sympathetic to their cases.

Where the threat of punitive legalistic action is most oppressive, Trollope's comedies are darkest, most threatened by attitudes and standards basically antithetical to comedy. And surely *The Last Chronicle of Barset* must be placed among Trollope's most anxious works. Not only is its main hero accused by the world of being guilty of larceny, but the qualities of the hero himself are in many ways unlovable. He is proud, even overbearingly so, unable and unwilling to receive gifts from his well-wishers who want to share or soften his misery after he has been accused of theft. He disdains, in fact, the very gift which it is comedy's ultimate gift to bestow: the gift of sympathy, understanding, love. He wishes to stand perfectly alone, to be granted nothing but the most exact justice, accepting no penny that he has not earned, both literally and figuratively. Any attempt to encroach upon what seems to him his dignity provokes his anger and scorn. He is throughout, in fact, a character not only proud but irascible, a character difficult to remain sympathetic toward.

Nonetheless, he wins Trollope's mercy at the end, as he has clearly kept his sympathy throughout the novel. If one is to assent to the validity of a comic dénouement, the rescue of the hero, he needs to feel that mercy is properly granted, that its recipient is after all a worthy man, that the preservation of his life, or his reputation, is justified. The appearance of a deus ex machina does not, by itself, persuade us to rejoice about a happy, comic ending. For that, we have to want the exoneration of the hero.

The single most important episode for establishing Crawley's worth occurs, I believe, when he is most pressed by legal action and most convinced that a sentence of guilty will be passed against him.[32] Already summoned to stand trial at the next assizes, he receives a letter informing him that an ecclesiastical commission is also being appointed to take action against him should the civil court find him guilty. It is assumed, in that case, says the writer of the letter, that "the ecclesiastical judge would find himself obliged to visit [Crawley's offense] with the severer sentence of prolonged suspension, or even with deprivation" (p. 645).

Not only does Crawley think that both civil and ecclesiastical courts must find him guilty, but Trollope tells us that Crawley's faithful wife has decided that, strictly judged, her husband must be found guilty and that ruin is about to descend upon him and his family. Even Crawley himself, finally, "admitted to himself that in accordance with all law and all reason he must be regarded as a thief" (p. 648).

But Crawley, if guilty before legal, strict tribunals of men, also feels that, before a higher judge, a more merciful, more understanding one, one who would take his measure more fully, he would be found innocent.

> He might be guilty before the law, but he was not guilty before God. There had never been a thought of theft in his mind, or a desire to steal in his heart. . . . In spite of his aberrations of intellect, if there were any such, his ministrations in his parish were good. . . . Had he not been very diligent among his people, striving with all his might to lessen the ignorance of the ignorant, and to gild with godliness the learning of the instructed? Had he not been patient, enduring, instant, and in all things amenable to the laws and regulations laid down by the Church for his guidance in his duties as a parish clergyman? (p. 649)

While pitying himself and arguing his case, as it were, before that other judge whom he imagines more understanding than those men who will actually judge him, he has been walking toward Hoggle End, where the brickmakers, his poorest, most miserable parishioners, live. It begins to rain as he proceeds, but so absorbed is he by his own thoughts of his innocence that he fails to notice his outer circumstances until he encounters an old worker from the brickfields. There where they meet, at the very nadir of Crawley's fortunes—beset by legal actions that are sure to find him guilty, convinced that he will be ruined, outcast from the church and the society of good men, assaulted from within and from without, finally even by the rain—he receives a message that makes possible the beginning of his recovery. "There ain't nowt a man can't bear if he'll only be dogged," Giles, the brickworker, says. "It's dogged as does it. It ain't thinking about it" (p. 652). The words become a kind of recurring refrain in the novel, echoing in Crawley's mind repeatedly; and for anyone widely read in Trollope's fictional world, they are words that come to seem especially characteristic of his sense of human worth. They are also words at the heart of comedy itself: for comic figures, male or female, are dogged, they persevere, they either outlast or outwit their adversaries. They endure as life itself, according to comedy, also endures.

Crawley's descent into the miserable world of the brickmakers who live at Hoggle End is itself emblematic of the whole action of the novel: one may even describe it as an archetypal comic action. The walk to Hoggle End, like the novel and like comedy itself, may be described as a descent, a fall not unlike a tragic fall. But the fall of a comic hero produces only a ritual death, not a real one; and instead of being an end, it is instead a beginning, the beginning of those processes that have to do with resurrection, return, reunion. The descents into the underworld of the dead in *The Odyssey* and *The Aeneid* are accompanied by visions of prophecies regarding the future: which assumes, of course, that there is a future to be looked forward to. Likewise in *The Last Chronicle* we are assured at the bottom of the descent that there is a future, that if one will be dogged, one will come through one's troubles after all.

Comedy has always been associated with low characters. If one is a follower of Aristotle, one is asked to believe that comedy shows us to be worse, or less, than we are or should be, an attitude toward comedy that helps explain, probably, the general condescension toward it. I wish to suggest, however, that comedy's connection with low characters, like comic descents into lower worlds, simply affirms the crucial role played by elemental forces in the continuation and preservation of life into the future.

Crawley's descent is accomplished at several levels. He declines first in the eyes of others, only gradually losing confidence in his own technical innocence. His most desperate sense of his own situation, however, the point where he is most stripped, most unprotected, comes at the end of his walk in the rain toward Hoggle End. During a miserable rain that soaks him, but which must finally be recognized as itself a symbol of elemental fertility, he encounters a low figure, a figure so low, in fact that he is, appropriately, covered with mire and mud, and he emanates a steamy moisture. It is he who gives the crude but reassuring message that doggedness does it, that "thinking" has nothing to do with survival, that man does come through if only he will endure. Trollope renders the point in the trappings that most graphically represent it.

It is, then, at the bottom of his fall, at the point where he seems, in the eyes of the world as well as in his own, most guilty, most divorced from all expectations of rescue or exoneration, that Crawley discovers what is certainly one of the grounds for sympathy toward man in general: his capacity to endure. That capacity is obviously on the side of life itself, as Trollope's handling of romantic difficulties demonstrates again and again: his lovers are always separated by what seem at least formidable, if not insurmountable, problems. But his romantic heroes—and especially his heroines—almost always hold out; they are dogged, to use again that characteristically Trollopian word, they persevere. And in the end, of course, they succeed: marriage is the reward of their persistence. Crawley, too, holds out, sustained primarily by his belief in his own innocence and by the message he has received from the "underworld." And in the end, he too succeeds in outlasting his difficulties: he is exonerated, forgiven, returned to his family and to his position. His position, both professional and metaphorical, is even elevated.

It may also be argued that only when he accepts the words of Giles the brickworker does Crawley become himself consonant with the comic spirit; i.e., only when he is willing to heed the advice of another does he admit and accept the need of outside sympathy and assistance, making possible thereby the comic rescue. The proud, stern man who has refused all offers of help, or accepted them only grudgingly, demonstrates finally that he is not self-sufficient after all. The basis of his trouble is in a sense symbolically rendered by the issue over the missing check which leads to the accusation of theft against him. The check has come to him from the Arabins, friends and well-wishers whose efforts to assist him are constantly rebuffed by Crawley because he thinks them condescending. The check that causes all the trouble is passed between Arabin and Crawley in an envelope that Mrs. Arabin, the former Eleanor Bold, has prepared to relieve the financial distress of Crawley, who is, even at the novel's outset, threatened with legal action by his creditors. Mrs. Arabin later blames herself for having put the check whose theft is charged against Crawley into the same envelope with other money for the beleaguered clergyman without letting her husband and Crawley know about it since their ignorance of how it reached Crawley causes all the mischief. But the person who causes Mrs. Arabin's error is Crawley himself and his attitude toward the sympathy of others. Mrs. Arabin eventually explains to John Eames that Crawley had come to her husband, the dean, for financial assistance, but he had come "with so much reluctance that his spirit had given way while he was waiting in the dean's library, and he had wished to depart without accepting what the dean was quite willing to bestow upon him. From this cause it had come to pass there had been no time for explanatory words, even between the dean and his wife" (p. 738).

It is Crawley, then, who is at fault behind the series of errors that get him into trouble; and his error is perhaps best seen as his refusal to accept his fallibility, as his exalted sense of himself that precludes not only receiving the sympathy and assistance of others but finally even the friendly communication with his fellow man. Crawley has a debt which he hates and refuses to acknowledge, a debt which may be said to be the universal debt owed by all men to their kind: a recognition of the human need for help and understanding based upon the apprehension of our incompleteness and weakness.

Crawley, though a man of God by profession, is essentially a man of pride, certain of his worth and innocence. Finally, belatedly, he discovers that he has something to learn, something to take, from another, from even so low a figure as Giles Hoggett. From that point rescue becomes possible, not only because Crawley has demonstrated and must go on demonstrating his worth and his strength, his ability to endure and his confidence in his own intentional innocence, but also because he has acknowledged the need for assistance. There must be, perhaps Trollope suggests by his demonstration of the principle, not only a kindly deity to rescue befuddled mankind, but a disposition on the side of mankind to want and to feel the need for outside assistance.

The Last Chronicle of Barset is indeed, as all readers and critics of it have felt, Trollope at his darkest. But however completely Trollope could render the obstacles that beset a proud, overbearing man, and however completely he could acknowledge the reality of laws that, strictly observed, must find such men not only fallible but guilty, his own faith in ultimate mercy, in that kind of final sympathy that looks favorably upon man's intentional innocence and his power of endurance, along with his recognition of weakness and need, obviously remains intact. That he continued to believe so when other writers no longer shared his faith and hence looked askance upon his novels should not lead us to conclude that he is therefore a lesser artist than they. One cannot argue, of course, that authors like Hardy, James, and Conrad are less sympathetic, less understanding towards their characters than is Trollope. One can only say that their characters are doomed nonetheless to impersonal fatalities, to inexorable laws, that drive or destroy them. Trollope believes in the reality of that kind of law, too, as the presence of lawyers and trials and legal actions in his novels testifies; but there is in his fictional world not only reason for mercy but still room for it to operate. Men may be found guilty by strict legal standards; but they also will be found to represent goodness and innocence and the perennial capacity of life to endure and to renew itself, to resurrect itself from the depths of death-like despair and confusion. If it needs an occasional helping hand, a deus ex machina, Trollope demonstrates again and again his own conviction that such help will be forthcoming, because the world is finally sympathetic towards life, because there remains, even in a law-ridden world, a chance for mercy.

Notes

1. T. H. S. Escott, *Anthony Trollope: His Work, Associates and Literary Originals* (London, 1913), p. 151.

2. *Anthony Trollope: Aspects of His Life and Art* (Bloomington, 1958), p. 161.

3. Ibid., p. 56.

4. "Anthony Trollope," *Partial Portraits* (London, 1888), p. 104.

5. Ibid., p. 116.

6. Ernest A. Baker, "Trollope," *The History of the English Novel,* viii (New York, 1937), p. 137.

7. For criticism that attacks Trollope on account of his plots, see Hugh Walpole, *Anthony Trollope,* English Men of Letters (New York, 1928), p. 33; Bradford A. Booth, "Trollope's *Orley Farm:* Artistry *Manqué,*" in *From Jane Austen to Joseph Conrad,* ed. Robert C. Rathburn and Martin Steinmann, Jr. (Minneapolis, 1958), p. 158; and again Booth's *Anthony Trollope,* p. 163.

8. *An Autobiography* (London, 1950), pp. 126, 175, 232.

9. Booth, *Anthony Trollope*, pp. ix–x and 204.

10. Ibid., p. 56.

11. "Anthony Trollope," *On Modern Literature: Lectures and Addresses* (Oxford, 1955), pp. 143–144. See also William Cadbury, "Determinants of Trollope's Forms," *PMLA*, LXXVIII (1963), 326–332. Cadbury, taking his lead from Northrop Frye, also asks that one demand of Trollope's fiction only what is generically appropriate to it, though Cadbury's notion of the genres appropriate to an understanding of Trollope's work is slightly different from mine.

12. Northrop Frye, *Anatomy of Criticism: Four Essays* (Princeton, 1957), p. 171.

13. Booth feels, in fact, that the intrusions of the narrator grow more infrequent in Trollope's later fiction. See his *Anthony Trollope*, p. 178.

14. J. Hillis Miller, *The Form of Victorian Fiction* (Notre Dame, 1968), p. 86.

15. *An Autobiography*, p. 233.

16. Both Escott's *Anthony Trollope* and Booth's *Anthony Trollope* are helpful in locating what may be described as Trollope's philosophical position. See, as well, C. J. Vincent, "Trollope: A Victorian Augustan," *Queen's Quarterly*, LII (1945), 415-428.

17. "Comedy," *Vogue* (January 1951), p. 137.

18. "Comedy and Laughter," *Five Gayley Lectures*, in *University of California Publications, English Studies,* (Berkeley, 1954), p. 82.

19. *The Rhetoric of Fiction* (Chicago, 1961), p. 217.

20. *On the Art of Poetry*, trans, S. H. Butcher, The Library of Liberal Arts, VI (New York, 1948), p. 33.

21. "Trollope," *Essays in Retrospect* (New Haven, 1948), p. 116.

22. *Anatomy of Criticism*, p. 170.

23. *On the Art of Poetry*, p. 14.

24. Speaking of the kind of tragedy which he considers inferior, "in the second rank," he writes that "it has a double thread of Plot, and also an opposite catastrophe for the good and for the bad. It is accounted the best because of the weakness of the spectators; for the poet is guided in what he writes by the wishes of his audience. The pleasure, however, thence derived is not the true tragic pleasure. It is proper rather to Comedy, where those who, in the piece, are the deadliest enemies . . . quit the stage as friends at the close, and no one slays or is slain" (p. 17).

25. *An Autobiography*, p. 320.

26. *Anatomy of Criticism*, p. 181.

27. *On the Art of Poetry*, p. 20.

28. "The Meanings of Comedy," in *Comedy* (New York, 1956), pp. 218-219.

29. *Anthony Trollope*, pp. 121, 211.

30. *Anatomy of Criticism*, p. 147.

31. Ibid., p. 178.

32. *The Last Chronicle of Barset*, The Penguin English Library (Harmondsworth, Middlesex, 1967), Chap. 61. Subsequent quotations from the novel are taken from this edition and are cited parenthetically.

Ancestral Voices
in *Jude the Obscure*

J. O. BAILEY

Hardy spoke with scornful irony of reviewers who suspected *Jude the Obscure* to be autobiographical: "Some paragraphists knowingly assured the public that the book was an honest autobiography."[1] In reply to a letter he declared that "there is not a scrap of personal detail in it."[2] When he visited the Masefields, he spoke of Jude as "that fictitious person. If there ever was such a person."[3] Yet Hardy's critics have continued to surmise that, as Rutland says, "there is more to be seen of [Hardy's] own inner life . . . in *Jude the Obscure* than in any other novel."[4] Weber says that in *Jude* Hardy's "subjective identification of himself with his characters became more pronounced than ever."[5]

Hardy had several reasons for denying that he drew the novel from his own experiences. He was so shy that he did not like to be touched and would shrink from a friendly hand, so secretive that after tearing pages from his notebooks and burning thousands of letters, he instructed his executors to tear out and burn more, and so sensitive to criticism that when *Jude* was reviewed under the headings of "Jude the Obscene"[6] and "Hardy the Degenerate"[7] he stopped writing novels. *Jude* echoes incidents in Hardy's long-concealed love affair with Tryphena Sparks and in his secret affection for Mrs. Arthur Henniker. The novel also does not tell Hardy's life-story precisely. He was not, like Jude, an orphan, and was not subject to lapses into drunkenness and sensuality; he did not die in poverty in Christminster.

[143]

Jude, not a novelist, a poet, a musician (though sensitive to music), or a dancing man, had no apprenticeship in London and did not become a club-man or a diner-out in elegant society.

Yet Hardy's Preface suggests a personal background: "The scheme was jotted down in 1890, from notes made in 1887 and onward, some of the circumstances being suggested by the death of a woman in the former year. The scenes were revisited in October, 1892; the narrative was written in outline in 1892 and the spring of 1893, and at full length, as it now appears, from August, 1893, onward into the next year." *The Early Life* presents the "notes made in 1887," but dated in Hardy's notebook April 28, 1888: "A short story of a young man— 'who could not go to Oxford'—His struggles and ultimate failure. Suicide [Probably the germ of *Jude the Obscure*]. There is something [in this] the world ought to be shown, and I am the one to show it to them—though I was not altogether hindered going, at least to Cambridge, and could have gone up easily at five-and-twenty."[8]

In his progress from an idea for a short story to *Jude,* a milestone seems to be the death of a woman in 1890. She was Hardy's cousin Tryphena Sparks, to whom he had been engaged in the late 1860s. An obstacle to their marriage was the risk in marrying a cousin, in a family already intermarried. His including Tryphena perhaps suggested the treatment of heredity in his story of an ambitious young man. When the plan began to involve his family, apparently Hardy decided to include material from the reminiscences of his paternal grandmother, Mary Head Hardy, whose birthplace was Fawley. He recorded his visit to this village: "At Great Fawley, Berks. Entered a ploughed vale which might be called the Valley of Brown Melancholy. . . . I can see only the dead here, and am scarcely conscious of the happy children at play."[9] The statement suggests that Hardy, with Mary Head in mind, explored the graveyards and church records of Fawley and nearby Chaddleworth.

Brooding over his family (including Tryphena's) Hardy saw its decline due to the processes of heredity. He wrote of the Hardys: "They had all the characteristics of an old family of spent social energies. . . . At the birth of the subject of this biography the family had declined, so far as its Dorset representatives were concerned, from whatever importance it once might have been able to claim there."[10] Recording a trip to Evershot, Hardy wrote: "The decline and fall of the Hardys much in evidence hereabout. An instance: Becky S.'s mother's sister married one of the Hardys of this branch, who was considered to have bemeaned himself by the marriage. . . . So we go down, down, down."[11] Since Hardy and his wife Emma had no child and his brother Henry and his sisters Mary and Kate did not even marry, Hardy saw himself as the end of the line, a fact lamented in the poem "She, I, and They," where his ancestors "repine / That we should be the last / Of stocks once unsurpassed, / And unable to keep up their sturdy line."

It seems that these ancestors had brought about the decline through intermarriages and illegitimacies. The facts Hardy discovered so dismayed him that he omitted names from the pedigrees he drew up. His autobiography almost omits his paternal grandmother, Mary Head Hardy, who lived until January 9, 1857, when he was nearly seventeen, slept in the bedroom next to his, and told tales of her life that provided several scenes in the novels and poems. He referred to her briefly in connection with *Jude:* on a trip in June 1923 he and his wife Florence "paused also at Fawley, that pleasant Berkshire village described in the same novel under the name of Marygreen. Here some of Hardy's ancestors were buried, and he searched fruitlessly for their graves in the little churchyard. His father's mother, the gentle, kindly grandmother who lived with the family at Bockhampton during Hardy's childhood, had spent the first thirteen years of her life here as an orphan child, named Mary Head, and her memories of Fawley were so poignant that she never cared to return to the place after she had left it as a young girl. The surname of Jude was taken from this place." [12] The autobiography makes only one other allusion to this grandmother. Hardy visited "Reading, a town which had come into the life of Hardy's paternal grandmother, who had lived here awhile."[13] But the poem "One We Knew," subscribed "M. H. 1772-1857," indictates that from her he learned old songs, dances, ballads, customs, tragedies, and tales of French Revolutionary times and of Napoleon. The poem pictures her by the fireside, where "She would dwell on such dead themes, not as one who remembers, / But rather as one who sees."

Parish records suggest what was poignant in Mary Head Hardy's memories. Her father, James Head, had married Mary Hopson, but James died in May 1772, four months before his daughter Mary's birth. Mary Hopson Head did not remarry, but seven years later she bore a second child, William, baptized on April 25, 1779.[14] William died on May 2, 1779, and his mother soon after; she was buried on May 8. Her death left Mary Head an orphan at the age of six and a half. The records of Fawley and Chaddleworth note many illegitimate births and mention members of the Head family, including: "Baptized John Stroude the natural son of Anne Head, March the 16th, 1752," and "Baptiz'd Mary the daughter of John Street & of one Lydia, whom he calls his wife tho' not lawfully married, as the said Lydia had as well . . . a husband living at least for anything she knew to the contrary . . . Dec. 12th 1779." Irregularities in these tiny villages include even incest. On July 2, 1820, Jesse, son of William Darling and Susan Goddard, "his wife's sister," was baptized. Hardy was interested in his grandmother's background long before he thought of *Jude.* Its Preface says that he "revisited" Fawley in 1892. The autobiography says nothing of the first visit, but apparently it was in 1864. A sketch of Fawley Church, drawn and dated by Hardy in this year, is in the Firestone Library, Princeton.

These facts suggest that Hardy began *Jude* as a story of the Head family. Through the first forty pages of the manuscript[15] the surname of the characters that became Jude and Sue is Head. Jude was first called Jack, suggesting James Head, the father of Hardy's grandmother. Here and there his surname is Hopeson which suggests both Jude's idealism and Mary Hopson, the maiden name of Mary Head's mother. Hardy then called the village Fawn Green. In these pages he may have intended to base the story upon the poignant events of Mary Head's girlhood. We do not know what these events were, and possibly Hardy knew only in fragments. A love-triangle is suggested in his poem "Family Portraits," in which his ancestors' portraits come to life:

> Three picture-drawn people came down from their frames,
> And dumbly in lippings they told me their names,
>   Full well though I knew.
>
> The first was a maiden of mild wistful tone,
>   Gone silent for years,
> The next a dark woman in former time known.
> . . . .
> The third was a sad man—a man of much gloom.

These three "set about acting some drama obscure, / The women and

he, / . . . . Till I saw 'twas their own lifetime's tragic amour, / Whose
course begot me." But before the story is clear, the poet says:

> . . . fear fell upon me like frost, of some hurt
>   If they entered anew
> On the orbits they smartly had swept when expert
> In the law-lacking passions of life,—of some hurt
> To their souls—and thus mine—which I fain would avert.
>   So, in sweat cold as dew,
>
> "Why wake up all this?" I cried out. "Now, so late!
>   Let old ghosts be laid!"
> And they stiffened, drew back to their frames and numb state,
> Gibbering: "Thus are your own ways to shape, know too late!"

The poet, grieving that he did not get a clear picture of his "blood's
tendance foreknown," has tried in vain to analyze "the drift of their
drama," for "therein lay my own." If the "drama, obscure" concerns
Mary Head and is echoed in *Jude,* Hardy pieced it out with scraps of
his own drama. As he changed plans, he changed the name Mary
Head to Susanna Florence Mary Bridehead, in which Mary——head
is still part of the name. He changed Jack Head or Hopeson to Jude
Fawley, and the village from Fawn Green to Marygreen.

Perhaps Hardy included events from his mother's side of the
family, to which his cousin Tryphena belonged. In poignance Mary
Head's girlhood resembles that of Jemima, Hardy's mother, and her
mother, Betty Hand. Though Betty did not live in the Hardy house-
hold and though she died on May 27, 1847, before Hardy was seven
years old, his biography has much to say of her literary tastes, excellent memory, and "clandestine" marriage to a man whom her
father so disapproved that he disowned her. When her husband died
in 1822, Betty was left with "several children" (seven) and no money.
Hardy says that "she was at her wit's end to maintain herself and
her family, if ever widow was." Thus Jemima "saw during girlhood
and young womanhood some very stressful experiences of which she
could never speak in her maturer years without pain." [16] As she grew
up, Jemima did sewing and cooking: "She resolved to be a cook in
a London club-house," and she was a cook in London for the family
of Charles Fox-Strangways. [17]

Hardy's account does not name her "very stressful experiences."

We may look first at Betty's village, Melbury Osmund, with a population in 1861 of 329. There, as in Fawley, members of the same
family married one another. Betty's mother, Hardy's great-grandmother,
was Maria Childs, and the Childses frequently intermarried: in 1790
Thomas Childs married Hannah Childs; in 1792 Edmund Childs married Frances Childs; in 1813 Thomas Childs married Sarah Childs;
in 1816 Edmund Childs married Elizabeth Childs, and so on. The
records list illegitimate births: on October 17, 1830, Jemima Woods,
daughter of Charlotte Childs, was baptized; on July 29, 1827, Caroline
Childs, "base-born daughter of Charlotte Bird," was baptized; on
January 20, Ann, daughter of Mary Childs, "Single woman," was
baptized, and so on.

Hardy was mistaken in calling Betty's marriage to a man her
father disapproved "clandestine." Betty's father, John Swetman, was a
well-to-do yeoman; George Hand, whom Betty married, is described
in the parish registers as a "Servant." Since the banns for the marriage
of George Hand and Betty Swetman were read in the Melbury Osmund Church on December 9, 16, and 23, 1804, John Swetman knew
of the coming marriage, but did not forbid it; it took place in the
church on December 27. On January 4, 1805, eight days later, Betty
gave birth to her eldest daughter, Maria, who grew up to marry James
Sparks and become the mother of Tryphena, Hardy's cousin. Maria's
sister Jemima, Hardy's mother, was born in 1813. She married Hardy's
father on December 22, 1839, and Hardy was born on June 2, 1840,
a little more than five months later. Hardy, who read parish records
for his pedigrees, knew these facts, though he did not publish them;
but it seems that he was for a moment tempted to do so. In an unpublished note for his autobiography, a paragraph about Jemima
opens: "Thomas Hardy, the third child, was rather fragile, and pre-
cocious to a degree." [18] If this note concerns Jemima's "very stressful
experiences during . . . young womanhood," nothing certain is known
of the two previous children. Lois Deacon, who discovered most of the
facts about Hardy's love affair with Tryphena Sparks, has surmised
that one of the children was Rebecca, born on September 26, 1829,
when Jemima was sixteen, and that Jemima gave Rebecca to her
older, married sister, Maria Sparks, to bring up as Maria's child. [19]
Miss Deacon has also theorized from suggestions in Hardy's poetry
that Tryphena was Rebecca's illegitimate daughter, not her sister,
likewise brought up as Maria Sparks's daughter. According to these

surmises, Tryphena would be Hardy's niece, rather than his cousin. Whatever the facts concerning Betty, Jemima, Rebecca, and Tryphena, Hardy probably knew them, but deliberately left them out of his pedigrees. In the pedigree photographed from Hardy's manuscript and published in Evelyn Hardy's *Thomas Hardy,* he traced his ancestry back into the seventeenth century, but in listing his grandmother Betty's seven children, listed only Martha, Christopher, and Jemima, with blank spaces for the other four. Why did he omit Maria, Henery [sic], William, and Mary? He certainly knew his Aunt Maria, presumably the mother of Tryphena.

As in "Family Portraits" Hardy feared that the eddying bloodstreams in his ancestry came to a stagnant end in himself. In the poems "Heredity" and "The Pedigree," the poet broods at midnight over the mazes and tangles in his heritage, concluding that the traits of his begetters fatally determined what he is:

> Said I then, sunk in tone,
> "I am merest mimicker and counterfeit!—
> Though thinking, *I am I,*
> *And what I do I do myself alone.*"

In *Jude,* he presents both Jude and Sue as similarly products of their parents' temperamental conflicts. The novel opens with Jude an orphan about the age of Mary Head when her mother died. Jude's father had so mistreated Jude's mother that she drowned herself. This does not seem to parallel anything in the lives of James and Mary Hopson Head, but this Mary, shortly before her death, bore a bastard son that died within a week, an event echoed in the novel: Jude and Sue had three bastard children, the third one born dead. Similarly Sue's father and mother quarrelled, her mother died, and her father taught Sue to hate her mother's family, possibly paralleling hostilities between the Hands and the Swetmans, Hardy's maternal ancestors.

These facts suggest that Hardy at first intended to treat some obscure drama in the lives of his ancestors, a little later saw himself as the victim of inherited tendencies, and then identified himself with these ancestors and worked his own experiences into the novel. Hardy was an architect, novelist, and poet, not a stone-cutter, as Jude was, but his father was a mason and builder. Though the novel begins after the orphan Jude has arrived in Marygreen, his aunt says, "He come from Mellstock, down in South Wessex, about a year ago."[20]

Mellstock is Hardy's name for Stinsford parish, where he was born. The autobiography presents the bookishness of Hardy's grandmother Betty and his mother Jemima.[21] Jude's aunt says of Jude, "The boy is crazy for books, that he is. It runs in our family rather" (I, ii). Hardy was so frail as a boy that "Until his fifth or sixth year his parents hardly supposed he would survive to grow up,"[22] and the aunt speaks of Jude as a "poor or'nary child" and says to him, "there never was any sprawl on thy side of the family, and never will be!" (I, ii). In discussing his own lack of "sprawl" as a boy, Hardy pictured himself: "He was lying on his back in the sun, thinking how useless he was, and covered his face with his straw hat. The sun's rays streamed through the interstices of the straw, the lining having disappeared. Reflecting on his experiences of the world so far as he had got, he came to the conclusion that he did not wish to grow up. . . . He did not want at all to be a man, or to possess things."[23] The boy Jude, after being scolded, "pulled his straw hat over his face and peered through the interstices of the plaiting at the white brightness, vaguely reflecting. Growing up brought responsibilities, he found. . . . As you got older . . . you were seized with a sort of shuddering. . . . If he could only prevent himself growing up! He did not want to be a man" (I, ii).[24] Hardy wrote of himself: "that he was a child till he was sixteen, a youth till he was five-and-twenty, and a young man till he was nearly fifty."[25] He described the boy Jude likewise as "an ancient man in some phases of thought, much younger than his years in others" (I, iv). Hardy's bedroom in his youth was something like an attic with a sloping ceiling, where he would arise before day to study by candlelight. Similarly, after encountering Arabella, "Jude Fawley was pausing in his bedroom with the sloping ceiling, looking at the books on the table, and then back at the black mark on the plaster above them, made by the smoke of his lamp in past months" (I, vii). The day after he first kissed her, he revisited the spot: "Jude looked on the ground and sighed. He looked closely, and could just discern in the damp dust the imprints of their feet as they had stood locked in each other's arms" (I, vii). Hardy described this experience as if his own in the first stanza of "Four Footprints." When an apprentice to the architect John Hicks, he was sent to various dilapidated churches to supervise repairs. His *Architectural Notebook* is full of heads and capitals of Stinsford Church and other village churches. Similarly, while Jude was an apprentice, he "occupied his spare half-hours in copying the heads and capitals in his parish church" and a little later became "handy at restoring the dilapidated masonries of several village churches roundabout" (I, v). Jude delighted in "deciphering 'the Latin inscriptions on 15th-century brasses and tombs,' a favourite pastime of Hardy's, who had a predilection for medieval Latin."[26] His poems "The Memorial Brass" and "The Inscription" reflect this activity.

A central theme in *Jude* is Jude's effort to enter Christminster (that is, Oxford) as a student, and when that fails, to enter the Church as a licentiate, and finally his becoming an agnostic, though continuing to read and quote the Bible. Hardy wrote of himself: "As a child, to be a parson had been his dream."[27] Edmund Blunden's biography of Hardy adds: "His mother hoped at one time . . . to obtain for him a presentation to Christ's Hospital, London,—this would have been about the year 1848,—but, the Governor through whom this admission should have come happening to die, the opportunity was lost."[28] Hardy said of himself at about sixteen years old that he "had sometimes, too, wished to enter the Church; but he cheerfully agreed to go to Mr. Hicks's" as an architectural apprentice.[29] Frank Pinion, in his *Hardy Companion,* adds that "It has long been held, though no evidence has yet appeared, that [Hardy] applied for admission to Salisbury Theological College, and was rejected."[30] (This seems a reference to a statement by Dr. Elsie Smith, Librarian of Salisbury Cathedral, that she had documentary evidence Hardy had sought to enter the Church, but was rejected. When I asked her about this, she said she had the evidence, though she did not show it to me, since she planned to write an article about it.) In a letter to an unnamed correspondent from Oxford, Hardy stated again: "when I was young, I had a wish to enter the Church."[31] At about twenty-one he wavered. He asked his friend Horace Moule whether to throw up architecture and try to get into a university. Moule advised him to go on with architecture. The autobiography comments: "It may be permissible to ponder whether Hardy's career might have been altogether different if Moule's opinion had been the contrary one. . . . [Hardy's] father never absolutely refusing to advance him money in a good cause. Having every instinct of a scholar he might have ended his life as a Don."[32] He continued to ponder religion even after reading Darwin. In 1865, he recorded in his notebook: "Worked at J. H. Newman's *Apologia.* . . . A great desire to be convinced by him, because Moule likes him so much." [33] In the same year, he "formed the idea of combining poetry and the Church—towards which he had long had a leaning—and wrote to a friend in Cambridge for particulars as to matriculation at that University . . . his idea being that of a curacy in a country village." [34]

Hardy's effort to get into (presumably) Salisbury Theological College and his rejection seem the basis for Jude's letter to the heads of the colleges at Christminster, and the snobbish reply from T. Tetuphenay: "I venture to think that you will have a much better chance of success in life by remaining in your own sphere and sticking to your trade than by adopting any other course" (II, vi). Jude's reading as he pondered a career in the Church included Newman. As he wandered over Christminster, he dreamed of "modern divines . . . among whom the most real . . . were the founders of the religious school called Tractarian" (II, i). After being defeated in his aim to enter the University, like Hardy, he chose an humbler aim, to enter the Church as a licentiate and aspire to no more than a curacy. "What better place to pursue his studies than a cathedral-city such as Melchester?"—that is, Salisbury. [35]

Hardy abandoned becoming a curate because he found, "after some theological study, that he could hardly take the step with honour while holding the views which on examination he found himself to hold." [36] These views were agnostic, based upon reading in scientific and rationalistic works, especially those of Darwin, Huxley, and J. S. Mill. Jude, likewise, under the influence of Sue, who frequently quotes Mill, comes to the agnostic position he describes to a street crowd in Christminster: "Eight or nine years ago, when I came here first, I had a neat stock of fixed opinions, but they dropped away one by one; and the further I get the less sure I am. I doubt if I have anything more for my present rule of life than following inclinations which do me and nobody else any harm" (VI, i). This is Hardy's final position, stated in the last sentence of his Preface to *Winter Words:* "I also repeat what I have often stated, that no harmonious philosophy is attempted in these pages, or in any bygone pages of mine, for that matter."

Other incidents in Hardy's life are echoed in Jude's. When Emma Gifford introduced Hardy to her father, Gifford called Hardy a "churl" and refused to bless his daughter's choice. Emma married Hardy in something like an elopement. She went from her home in Cornwall to London; there she met Hardy, and they were married "at St. Peter's, Elgin Avenue, Paddington, by her uncle Dr. E. Hamilton Gifford."[37] Of this, Hardy wrote to his brother Henry: "There were only Emma and I, her uncle who married us, and her brother; my landlady's daughter signed the book as one witness."[38] Presumably Emma's brother gave her away. When Sue is to marry Phillotson, she writes to Jude: "Jude, will you give me away? I have nobody else who could do it so conveniently as you . . . even if my father were friendly enough to be willing, which he isn't" (III, vii).

In Part V of *Jude*, Jude and Sue move constantly from place to place, "sometimes . . . at Sandbourne, sometimes . . . at Casterbridge, sometimes as far down as Exonbury, sometimes at Stoke-Barehills. Later still he was at Kennetbridge" (v, vii) and so on. This constant moving shortly after their union resembles the moving of Hardy and Emma in their early married life. They lived at several places in London, and then in Swanage, Yeovil, Sturminster Newton, London again, Weymouth, London again, Wimborne, and Dorchester, until they moved into Max Gate in 1885.

Other parallels suggest that Hardy looked in the mirror, so to speak, as he wrote *Jude*. He portrayed himself as a boy as either ecstatic in response to music or somberly meditative. Jude's face as a boy wore "the fixity of a thoughtful child's who has felt the pricks of life somewhat before his time" (I, i). A photograph of Hardy at the age of thirty shows him with a full black beard. Jude is described as "a young man with a black beard" (III, iii).

Hardy's methods of study and the books studied are Jude's. From childhood onward, Hardy read the Bible, after his early teenage years reading it in Latin, Greek, and some Hebrew. Similarly, Jude knew the Bible, while drunk recited the Nicene Creed in Latin, and died reciting a passage from Job. Hardy described his methods of study at the age of sixteen to twenty: "In the long summer days he would even rise at four and begin [before going to Hicks's office for a day's work]. In these circumstances he got through a moderately good number of the usual classical pages—several books of the *Aeneid*, some Horace and Ovid, etc.; and in fact grew so familiar with his authors that in his walks to and from the town he often caught himself soliloquizing in Latin."[39] "When young Tom Hardy became old enough to take his studies seriously, he taught himself Homer by using Clarke's edition of the *Iliad*, just as Jude Fawley 'dabbled in Clarke's Homer.' "[40]

Hardy "acquired a copy of Griesbach's edition of the New Testament in Greek. . . . In *Jude the Obscure* young Fawley obtains 'by post from a second-hand bookseller' a copy of the 'New Testament in the Greek . . . Griesbach's text.' "[41] Hardy even used his old notes on the *Iliad* to describe Jude's reading. In Hardy's copy of the *Iliad*, signed and dated 1858, the inside front cover lists his favorite passages as follows:

> "Speech of Phoenix, 9, 434–601.
> Fight of Hector and Ajax 14, 388–432.
> Appearance of Achilles unarmed 18, 202–26.
> Heavenly armour for A(chilles) 18, 468–612.
> Funeral games in honour of Patroclus 23, 700.

Beneath is written 'Left off. Bockhampton 1860.' "[42] Jude, walking home one evening, soliloquizes about his plans for study: "I have read two books of the *Iliad*, besides being pretty familiar with passages such as the speech of Phoenix in the ninth book, the fight of Hector and Ajax in the fourteenth, the appearance of Achilles unarmed and his heavenly armour in the eighteenth, and the funeral games in the twenty-third" (I, vi)—exactly Hardy's list. In addition, Jude and Sue quote and discuss ideas from modern books that Hardy owned and often quoted: Gibbon, Shelley, Browning, Swinburne, J. S. Mill, etc.[43]

In temperament Jude resembles Hardy. Though agnostic, Hardy continued all his life to read the Bible daily, quote from it, and attend church. He laid numerous scenes in his novels and poems in a church or churchyard. Evelyn Hardy's biography points out that *Jude* contains no fewer than eleven such scenes.[44] In the concluding portion of *Jude*, when Sue, wild with grief, retreats from free-thinking into orthodoxy, she quotes to Jude "Charity seeketh not her own," from I Corinthians 13. Jude, now agnostic, says to her: "In that chapter we are at one, ever beloved darling. . . . Its verses will stand fast when all the rest that you call religion has passed away" (VI, iv). This is the chapter from which Hardy most frequently quoted. When, in the poem "Surview," he sought to evaluate his life, he judged himself against its verses. Jude, like Hardy, loved church music. Weber says that " 'the great waves of pedal music' which 'tumbled round the choir' of [Christminster] Cathedral affected Jude precisely as the organ music had affected Thomas Hardy on June 22, 1875, when he listened to it in Wimborne Minster."[45]

Hardy and Jude shared not only a humanitarian feeling for animals, but an imaginative kinship with them. When crossing a eweleaze as a child, Hardy "went on hands and knees and pretended to eat grass in order to see what the sheep would do. Presently he looked up and found them gathered around in a close ring, gazing at him with astonished faces."[46] When the child Jude was employed by Farmer Troutham to scare birds from his grainfield, "A magic thread of fellowfeeling united his own life with theirs." He said, "Poor little dears! . . . You *shall* have some dinner—you shall. There is enough for us all" (I, ii). When he has to kill his pig, he proposes a swift death to save the pig from suffering. Arabella, to prevent the meat from being bloody, cries, "He ought to be eight or ten minutes dying, at least," and Jude replies, "He shall not be half a minute if I can help it" (I, x). Hardy was so interested in having pigs killed painlessly that he joined the Wessex Saddleback Pig Society and wrote to its chairman: "I add a suggestion that the question of slaughtering . . . should be among the matters that the society takes up, with a view to causing as little suffering as possible to an animal so intelligent. . . . I am not aware if the stupid custom still prevails of having pork well bled."[47] Cruelty to horses enraged both Jude and Hardy. Jude was horrified when a cab-driver in Christminster whose horse failed to stop at the exact point "began to kick the animal in the belly. 'If that can be done,' said Jude, 'at college gates in the most religious and educational city in the world, what shall we say as to how far we've got?' " (VI, i). In letters and in poems like "Horses Aboard" and *The Dynasts* Hardy protested the use of horses in war. Both Jude and Hardy imagined that even trees suffer when mutilated. As a boy, Jude "could scarcely bear to see trees cut down or lopped, from a fancy that it hurt them; and late pruning, when the sap was up and the tree bled profusely, had been a positive grief to him in his infancy" (I, ii). Hardy's novels and poems are sprinkled with this fancy. The paragraph opening *Under the Greenwood Tree* reads: "At the passing of the breeze the fir-trees sob and moan no less distinctly than they rock; the holly whistles as it battles with itself; the ash hisses amid its quiverings; the beech rustles while its flat boughs rise and fall." Such poems as "Yell'ham-Wood's Story" and "The Pine Planters" repeat the idea.

Both Hardy and Jude protested the class system. Hardy's first unpublished novel, *The Poor Man and the Lady,* was destroyed, except for fragments, but he wrote of it: "The story was, in fact, a sweeping dramatic satire of the squirearchy and nobility, London society, the vulgarity of the middle class, modern Christianity, church restoration, and political and domestic morals in general."[48] When Jude returned to Christminster for the last time, he harangued a crowd gathered for Remembrance Day, saying that the class system had caused his failure. A man, he said, must "be as cold-blooded as a fish and as selfish as a pig to have a really good chance of being one of his country's worthies" (VI, i). On his death bed Jude said of himself and Sue: "Our ideas were fifty years too soon to be any good to us" (VI, x). In various poems Hardy stated this idea with obvious application to himself, as in "Mute Opinion." There "spokesmen" for society, in "pulpit, press, and song" ignore the silent, thoughtful "large-eyed few." But as the years pass, history is "outwrought / Not as the loud had spoken, / But as the mute had thought."

Besides reflecting himself in Jude, Hardy drew upon people he had met and stories he had heard. He got the idea for young Jude's studying Latin while driving a baker's cart when he met "a youth like Jude who drove the bread-cart of a widow, a baker . . . and carried on his studies at the same time, to the serious risk of other drivers in the lanes; which youth asked him to lend him his Latin grammar."[49] In a note made in 1882 he wrote about a man who had taken his degree and been ordained. "But he drank. He worked with the labourers . . . in the yarn barton. After a rollick as they worked he would suddenly stop, down his implement, and mounting a log or trestle, preach an excellent sermon to them; then go on cursing and swearing as before."[50] Similarly Jude, after he had been refused admission to a college, went to a tavern, got drunk, and to show off before some Christminster undergraduates recited the Nicene Creed in Latin.

The names in *Jude* seem significant. The surname Fawley, the name of the village where Mary Head grew up, points to Hardy's ancestors. To suggest the theme Hardy may have invented the name Jude to stand for the Hebraism of Arnold's *Culture and Anarchy*. It contrasts Jude's attitude toward life through the first half of the novel with Sue's Hellenism. Sue's names suggest various relationships to Hardy's life. She wrote Jude some notes signed Sue, but others signed Susanna Florence Mary Bridehead. Hardy calls attention to a symbolic meaning of the name Susanna, derived from Latin, Greek, and Hebrew, with the meaning "lily." When Sue is ready for her second marriage to Phillotson, "She had never in her life looked so much like the lily her name connoted as she did in that pallid morning light" (VI, V). Sue's second name Florence suggests Hardy's friend Florence Henniker, whom he met on May 19, 1893, perhaps at about the time he was changing his heroine's name from Mary Head to Sue Bridehead. (Mr. Purdy says: "Mrs. Hardy is my authority for the statement that Sue Bridehead was in part drawn from Mrs. Henniker."[51]) Hardy wrote to a friend on November 20, 1895: "Sue is a type of woman which has always had an attraction for me, but the difficulty of drawing the type has kept me from attempting it till now."[52] The phrase "till now" may mean May of 1893, when Hardy met Florence Henniker. Her letters to Hardy were destroyed, but since she preserved most of Hardy's letters, we may infer from them a temperament reflected in Sue. Hardy's diary for May 19, the day he met her, speaks of her as "A charming, *intuitive* woman apparently."[53] When she took up residence at Southsea in Portsmouth, "Letters began to fly back and forth between Max Gate and Southsea."[54] Hardy and Florence met at various places, as at Winchester, apparently about once a week. In October he began his collaboration, working with her (a novelist) on a story called "The Spectre of the Real." His letters to her, especially in the years 1893 through 1896, though they say nothing improper, are emotionally warm. Possibly, as Hardy says in one of his poems, she did not know the extent of her elderly friend's attraction to her. "Wessex Heights," written in 1896, says: "Yet my love for her in its fulness she herself even did not know; / Well, time cures hearts of tenderness, and now I can let her go." He did not exactly "let her go" in 1896, but his letters after that date are less ardent; they continued until her death in 1923. As Hardy said, his poems are more autobiographical than his novels. Purdy, calling Mrs. Henniker "a woman of warm sympathies and unfailing charm," lists twelve of Hardy's poems to or about her.[55]

According to the Preface *Jude* was written "at full length, as it now appears, from August, 1893, onward into the next year," the period of Hardy's warmest feeling for Florence Henniker. He found in her, according to Frank Pinion, Sue's "Shelleyan qualities."[56] One of her traits that we find in Sue is her compassion for animals and birds. Hardy wrote to her on September 28, 1898: "Those Americans who come here think of taking a house, & 700 acres of shooting . . . not to shoot over, but *to keep the birds from being shot.*"[57] As this tone appears over and over in the letters, we may be sure of her sympathy. When Sue's pet pigeons were sold at auction to a poulterer, she could not bear to think of their being slaughtered for food. Like some outraged schoolgirl she went to the poulterer's shop, opened the cage, and ran. Jude, already destitute, had to pay the poulterer.

Mary Head, Hardy's grandmother, is represented in Sue's two last names, Mary Bridehead. Since we know of Mary Head as a girl only that her memories were "poignant," I can only surmise what traits of Mary Head entered into Sue. Probably her memories provided a basis for the story of Sue's parents.

Tryphena is *not* one of Sue's names. The name does not appear in Hardy's autobiography or in any letter I have seen. It appears in no novel (except as Phena for the name of a chicken in *Tess*, Chapter ix), and only Phena appears in the title of one poem, "Thoughts of Phena." Yet there is much evidence that Tryphena Sparks was the unnamed woman of Hardy's Preface who died in 1890, and that Hardy had Tryphena in mind when creating Sue. The relations between the cousins Jude and Sue seem to echo the relations between Hardy and his cousin Tryphena.[58] Because of the history of intermarriages in both families and strong suggestions in Hardy's poems that seem to treat Tryphena,[59] we may feel certain that both her parents and Hardy's discouraged the courtship. Their arguments were probably those of Jude's aunt, that it would be "stark madness" for Jude to be more than civil to Sue (ii, vi). As a result of his aunt's arguments, Jude reasoned: "It was not well for cousins to fall in love . . . in a family like his own, where marriage usually meant a tragic sadness, marriage with a blood-relation would duplicate the adverse conditions, and a tragic sadness might be intensified to a tragic horror" (ii, ii).

Demonstrable facts about Tryphena include: Born in Puddletown, about three miles from Hardy's birthplace, on March 20, 1851, she was still a child when he went away to London in 1862. She went to school at Athelhampton, near Puddletown, where at the age of twelve she became a monitor. When Hardy returned home in 1867, she was attractive at sixteen. In the months following, they became engaged. Evidence for their long-concealed engagement, in addition to that recently uncovered by Miss Deacon, is an unpublished manuscript [60] by Miss Irene Willis, friend of the second Mrs. Hardy and lawyer for the trustees of the Hardy Estate. The manuscript does not give the name, but speaks of Hardy's engagement to a local girl. More specifically, Miss Willis wrote to Miss Deacon on June 25, 1960, that Florence Hardy told her Hardy was almost engaged to a Dorset girl when he met Emma Gifford in 1870, and later on becoming engaged to Emma took back the ring he had given or intended to give the local girl.[61] Where much is disputed in Miss Deacon's inferences, Hardy's quasi-engagement to Tryphena seems beyond question a fact.

From November 1866 until January or February 1868 Tryphena was a pupil-teacher in the Puddletown Elementary School. Then she left Puddletown and enrolled, in 1869, in Stockwell College in London. Completing her work here in the autumn of 1871, she became head-mistress in the Plymouth Public Free School. Hardy saw her from time to time until they parted in 1872 or 1873, Hardy to marry Emma Gifford in 1874, and Tryphena to marry Charles Gale in 1877. In the poem "Thoughts of Phena" Hardy calls her his "lost prize," but indicates that he no longer has the letters or other tokens (presumably including photographs) she had sent or given him. Tryphena died on March 17, 1890. In the following summer Hardy and his brother Henry visited her grave, laid a wreath on it, and called at Gale's house.

In addition to these facts, Deacon and Coleman have surmised that Tryphena bore Hardy a son who was successfully concealed, was brought up by Tryphena's brother Nathaniel in Bristol, and died in late adolescence or early manhood, and that when in London, Tryphena became intimate with Hardy's friend Horace Moule, who did not know that Tryphena was engaged to Hardy. Evidence for these surmises lies chiefly in the contested identification of some photographs and the interpretation of two poems, "Midnight on the Great Western" and "Standing by the Mantelpiece."

Much in Hardy's pen-portrait of Sue seems based upon Tryphena. Both she and Sue were slender and volatile, with dark hair and eyes. In the poem "The Wind's Prophecy" Hardy speaks of the "ebon locks" of a girl in London, evidently Tryphena. Sue has "vivacious dark eyes and hair" (II, iv). Both Jude and Phillotson treasured photographs of Sue as a child and as a young woman. The photographs in Tryphena's album, of her at about the age of twelve and as a young woman in London, suggest Sue.[62] Somewhat like Tryphena at Puddletown, Sue was an assistant teacher in Phillotson's elementary school before she went to a Training College. Sue's college was not in London, but was one in Melchester (Salisbury), which Hardy's sisters Mary and Kate had attended. But it is significant that in June 1891, when

Hardy was making notes for *Jude,* he visited Stockwell College in London, which Tryphena had attended.[63] He describes the discipline at Sue's college, her plainness of dress while there, and the prohibition of flowers, ornaments, or finery. When Jude visits her she appears in "a murrey-coloured gown with a little lace collar. It was made quite plain. . . . Her hair . . . was now twisted up tightly, and she had altogether the air of a woman clipped and pruned by severe discipline" (III, i). Dress of this sort was required at Tryphena's Stockwell College.

I mentioned Sue's pet pigeons in connection with Mrs. Henniker. Multiple sources for the same scene may overlap. While living in Plymouth, Tryphena kept caged birds, a fact to which Hardy refers in the poem "Her Love-Birds."[64]

Sue confesses to Jude that for a while in London she had lived in a Platonic companionship with a Christminster undergraduate who had died. She says: "We shared a sitting-room for fifteen months; and he became a leader-writer for one of the great London dailies; till he was taken ill and had to go abroad. . . . He came home merely to die" (III, iv). Possibly this story echoes the alleged relationship of Tryphena and Horace Moule, who had been an undergraduate at both Oxford and Cambridge, who wrote for the *Saturday Review* and other journals, and who committed suicide in 1873.

Tryphena's daughter Eleanor told Miss Deacon that when Hardy and his brother Henry visited Gale's house, Henry said to the daughter that she was just like her mother and kissed her. At this Hardy turned away as if hurt. Eleanor, as an old woman, is reported to have said: "Because I was exactly like her and we belonged to him. Of course he was hurt."[65] Hardy's poem "To a Motherless Child" treats this incident, and the substance of the poem appears in *Jude.* There, Jude "projected his mind into the future, and saw [Sue] with children more or less in her own likeness around her. But the consolation of regarding them as a continuation of her identity was denied to him . . . by the wilfulness of Nature in not allowing issue from one parent alone" (III, viii).

Besides creating Sue from traits in Mary Head, Florence Henniker, and Tryphena, Hardy attributed to her some of his own feelings. After living in furnished houses during his early married life, he commented: "The worst of taking a furnished house is that the articles in the room are saturated with the thoughts and glances of others."[66] Sue, when she goes to live with Phillotson in Old Grove's

Place, says: "Such houses are very well to visit, but not to live in—I feel crushed into the earth by the weight of so many previous lives there spent" (IV, i).

Having read many books Hardy had read, Sue expressed some of his typical views. Hardy wrote of J. S. Mill's *On Liberty* that "we students of that date knew [it] almost by heart."[67] In discussions with Jude and Phillotson, Sue quoted Mill, as she also quoted from Hardy's favorite poem by Shelley, "Epipsychidion." In her pagan phase she argued against medievalism, saying that "The medievalism of Christminster must go, be sloughed off, or Christminster itself will have to go" (III, iv). Hardy expressed this idea in the poem "A Cathedral Façade at Midnight," in which "Reason's movement" is "making meaningless / The coded creeds of old-time godliness." When Sue asked Phillotson to release her to go with Jude, she said: "Domestic laws should be made according to temperaments, which should be classified. If people are at all peculiar in character they have to suffer from the very rules that produce comfort in others" (IV, iii). Hardy stated this opinion in a letter to the Paris *L'Ermitage* in August 1893: "I would have society divided into *groups of temperaments,* with a different code of observances for each group."[68] After the death of her children, Sue meditated: "that the First Cause worked automatically like a somnambulist, and not reflectively like a sage" (VI, iii). This idea is basic in *The Dynasts,* where the Immanent Will "works unconsciously . . . / Eternal artistries in Circumstance, / . . . wrought by rapt aesthetic rote."[69]

Hardy transferred to Sue some of his own experiences. In 1870, when he was trying to get started as a novelist, Emma Gifford helped him. He sent her chapters of *Desperate Remedies,* interlined and altered, and she made fair copies for the printer. When Phillotson agreed to let Sue go, he turned to writing a book on *The Roman Antiquities of Wessex,* and Sue volunteered: "If you will send me some of the manuscript to copy . . . I will do it with so much pleasure" (IV, iv). When Hardy was desperately ill in 1881 and Emma sat with him watching a gorgeous sunset Hardy could not rise up to see, a caller, Maggie Macmillan, "conceived the kind idea of reflecting the sun into my face by a looking glass. The incident was made use of in *Jude the Obscure* as a plan adopted by Sue when the schoolteacher was ill."[70]

Other characters in the novel seem drawn from observation. Hardy identified the model for Arabella. On March 1, 1888, he wrote in his notebook: "Youthful recollection of four village beauties: . . . Rachel H———, and her rich colour, and vanity, and frailty, and clever artificial dimple-making. [She is probably in some respects the original of Arabella in *Jude the Obscure*.]" [71] But Rachel is only "in some respects" Arabella. Jude's reflections about the wreck of his marriage to Arabella and her excursion into piety and hymn-singing suggest Hardy's assessment of his wife Emma in the 1890s, when she had become stout, snobbish, and childishly pious. The following sentence from Jude's meditations might have been written of Emma: "Their lives were ruined, he thought; ruined by the fundamental error of their matrimonial union: that of having based a permanent contract on a temporary feeling which had no necessary connection with affinities that alone render a life-long comradeship tolerable" (I, xi). Emma did all she could to prevent the publication of *Jude*, even taking a trip to London to plead with Dr. Garnett of the British Museum to interfere.

The son of Jude and Arabella offers a puzzle. Jude and Sue call him Little Father Time. Some critics have said that "Father Time is surely a thinly veiled persona for Hardy himself." [72] Some of the child's meditations do reflect Hardy's attitudes. When Father Time says, "I ought not to be born, ought I?" (VI, i), we think of Hardy's poem "The Unborn," and when he looks with dismay at flowers and says, "I should like the flowers very, very much, if I didn't keep on thinking they'd be all withered in a few days!" (V, v), we think of Hardy's poem "To Flowers from Italy in Winter." The doctor who says of Father Time's suicide "it is the beginning of the coming universal wish not to live" (VI, ii) reflects Hardy's reading of Schopenhauer. But Father Time is not a picture of Hardy as a boy, who was, except in certain moods, an ecstatic fiddler at country dances, religious, trusting, and a zealous bookworm. As Hardy has three poems, "Midnight on the Great Western," "The Boy's Dream," and "Boys Then and Now," besides the travelling boy of "Wessex Heights," all picturing a frail, meditative boy, it seems reasonable that Father Time must have been an actual boy that Hardy observed. We simply do not know who the boy was.

The Widow Edlin, reminiscing of the old days when a marriage meant junketing and merrymaking, suggests some reminiscence by Hardy's grandmother, born Mary Head of Fawley. The name Edlin is an actual one. Dozens of Edlins lie under the gravestones in the villages of Fawley and Chaddleworth, but nothing identifies any one as the widow of the novel.

The name Phillotson may suggest Philistine in Matthew Arnold's sense, but the man is generous and liberal-minded, possibly Hardy's comment upon the strictures of Arnold's definition. Hardy wrote that some of Arnold's pronouncements "may well be questioned." [73] Weber points out that "Richard Phillotson shares Hardy's knowledge of Bernardin de St. Pierre and his familiarity with Shelley's poetry." [74] For instance, Phillotson describes Sue's character as "Shelleyan" and says that Jude and Sue "remind me of Laon and Cythna" (IV, iv). In this sense Phillotson's character reflects an aspect of Hardy's.

Perhaps Hardy denied that Jude was autobiographical for fear that reviewers would interpret everything in it as literal fact. Clearly he put much of his bloodstream, so to speak, into the novel. Yet he was dissatisfied with the result. He wrote to a friend on November 20, 1895: "Alas, what a miserable accomplishment it is, when I compare it with what I meant to make it!—*e.g.* Sue and her heathen gods set against Jude's reading the Greek testament; Christminster academical, Christminster in the slums; Jude the saint, Jude the sinner; Sue the Pagan, Sue the saint; marriage, no marriage; &c., &c." [75] Perhaps he was dismayed because he could not in this novel exhaust all his experiences or, as a reformer, convince his readers of all he felt to be true.

Notes

1. Florence Emily Hardy, *The Later Years of Thomas Hardy* (New York, 1930), p. 44. (This book and *The Early Life* are autobiographical, written in the third person and published as by Hardy's wife.)

2. Ibid., p. 196.

3. Ibid., p. 233.

4. William R. Rutland, *Thomas Hardy: A Study of His Writings and Their Background* (New York, 1962), p. 246.

5. Carl J. Weber, *Hardy of Wessex*, 2nd ed. (New York and London, 1965), p. 200.

6. In the *Pall Mall Gazette*, November 12, 1895.

7. In the New York *World*, November 13, 1895.

8. Florence Emily Hardy, *The Early Life of Thomas Hardy* (New York, 1928), pp. 272-273. The brackets are Hardy's.

9. *Later Years,* p. 13.

10. *Early Life,* pp. 5, 6.

11. Ibid., p. 281. In this statement Hardy is typically evasive. The comment seems to refer to his father and mother. "Becky S." seems to stand for Rebecca Sparks, daughter of Mrs. Maria Sparks, older sister of Jemima, Hardy's mother.

12. *Later Years,* p. 231.

13. Ibid., p. 54.

14. The records do not name a father.

15. In the Fitzwilliam Museum, Cambridge, England.

16. *Early Life,* p. 9.

17. F. R. Southerington, *The Early Hardys* (Mount Durand, St. Peter Port, Guernsey, 1968), p. 32.

18. Ibid., p. 33.

19. Lois Deacon and Terry Coleman, *Providence and Mr. Hardy* (London, 1966), pp. 204–205.

20. Thomas Hardy, *Jude the Obscure,* Part I, Chapter ii. I have used the Mellstock edition of *The Works of Thomas Hardy* (London, 1920), in which *Jude* is Volumes V and VI; but because *Jude* is published in many editions, I am referring to it by part and chapter, noted hereafter in parenthesis as (I, ii).

21. *Early Life,* p. 8.

22. Ibid., p. 20.

23. Ibid., pp. 19–20.

24. An almost exactly similar scene appears in I, iv. Hardy's poem "Childhood Among the Ferns" re-presents the scene with application to himself.

25. *Early Life,* p. 42.

26. Evelyn Hardy, *Thomas Hardy: A Critical Biography* (London, 1954), p. 249.

27. *Later Years,* p. 176.

28. *Thomas Hardy* (London, 1942), pp. 8–9.

29. *Early Life,* p. 35.

30. London and New York, 1968, p. 361.

31. *Later Years,* p. 246.

32. *Early Life,* p. 44.

33. Ibid., pp. 63–64.

34. Ibid., p. 66. The friend was probably Horace Moule.

35. Pinion, p. 329.

36. *Early Life,* p. 66.

37. Ibid., pp. 132–133.

38. Evelyn Hardy, p. 143.

39. *Early Life,* p. 36.

40. Weber, 2nd ed., p. 201.

41. Ibid.; *Jude,* I, vii.

42. Rutland, pp. 21–22.

43. Carl J. Weber, in his *Hardy of Wessex* (1st ed.; New York, 1940, pp. 240–246) lists passages Hardy quoted.

44. Page 109.

45. Weber, 2nd ed., p. 202.

46. *Later Years,* p. 263.

47. Letter of August 23, 1919, in the Dorset County Museum.

48. *Early Life*, p. 81.

49. *Later Years*, p. 44.

50. *Early Life*, pp. 188, 189.

51. Richard Little Purdy, *Thomas Hardy: A Bibliographical Study* (London, 1954, 1968), p. 345.

52. *Later Years*, p. 42.

53. Ibid., p. 18.

54. Weber, 2nd ed., p. 197.

55. Purdy, pp. 344–346. The poems are "A Broken Appointment," "A Thunderstorm in Town," "At an Inn," "In Death Divided," "He Wonders about Himself," "The Coming of the End," "The Month's Calendar," "Last Love-Word," "Alike and Unlike," "The Recalcitrants," "Come Not; Yet Come," and "The Division."

56. Pinion, p. 247.

57. In the Dorset County Museum.

58. For the story of Tryphena Sparks, see Deacon and Coleman, *Providence and Mr. Hardy*. In reading this book, it is important to distinguish fact from surmise. In Hardy's manuscript, "Thoughts of Phena" was titled "T——a, at News of her death. (Died 1890)." See Purdy, p. 102.

59. For instance, "At the Wicket Gate."

60. In the Colby College Library, Waterville, Maine.

61. Deacon and Coleman, p. 218.

62. The photographs are reproduced in Lois Deacon, *Tryphena and Thomas Hardy* (Beaminster, Dorset, 1962), frontispiece and p. 15.

63. *Early Life*, p. 310.

64. See also Deacon and Coleman, pp. 82–83.

65. Ibid., p. 65.

66. *Later Years*, pp. 17–18.

67. Ibid., pp. 118–119.

68. Ibid., p. 23.

69. Fore Scene.

70. *Early Life*, p. 191; see *Jude*, IV, vi.

71. Ibid., p. 270. The brackets are Hardy's.

72. For instance, Walter K. Gordon, "Father Time's Suicide Note in *Jude the Obscure*," *Nineteenth-Century Fiction*, XXII (1967), 298.

73. *Early Life*, p. 175.

74. Weber, 2nd ed., p. 202.

75. *Later Years*, p. 42.

Nostromo:
The Theology of Revolution

DOUGALD McMILLAN

Joseph Conrad's *Nostromo* is one of his intricate novels. It reflects both his full maturity and the growing complexity and subtlety of the English novel in the first part of the twentieth century. A "tale of the seaboard," it contains enough of the obvious elements of exotic adventure to be satisfying to the American businessman who enraged Conrad by asking him, "When are you going to spin some more yarns about the sea?" [1] and then propitiated him by commissioning a 100,000-word novel that turned out to be *Nostromo.* It also contains more than enough exacting investigation of character to belie the man's assessment of Conrad as only a writer of sea stories. It is particularly rich in the themes of personal morality which have attracted critics like Robert Penn Warren and Albert Guerard. Almost all the elements which occur in Conrad's greatest works can be found in this novel. Like *Lord Jim* and *The Nigger of the Narcissus* it asserts the sacredness of the human community. Like *Heart of Darkness* it tests the values we espouse so glibly by showing what happens when men are placed in isolation. It depicts again personal estrangement like that described so poignantly in "Amy Forster." It deals with the problem of self-knowledge personified in "The Secret Sharer" and also the burden of responsibility for others which animates *Victory.* In this novel Conrad lays bare for the first time in his work the motives behind political revolutions—a major theme in both *The Secret Agent* and *Under Western Eyes.* Finally it rivals even *Lord Jim* and *Heart of Darkness* in its treatment of guilt and redemption, the most persistent of all the themes in Conrad.

Technically, *Nostromo* also bears most of the trademarks which we associate with Conrad. Events come to us through "narrative filters"—those narrators like Captain Mitchell and Don Martin Decoud whose perspectives allow us to see events only in a certain light. As nearly always in Conrad, the chronology of events is involuted to bring us to what Conrad called "The Truth" of the novel, by the surest if not the easiest and most direct route. The book is also full of the irony of events and statement which gives all Conrad's work a sense of the deepest kind of sophistication. The descriptions of nature, realistic but also reflecting and foreshadowing the action of the novel, are also characteristic. And of course, we can see in *Nostromo* the trait for which readers return again to Conrad's books without ever quite realizing why: his willingness to speak freely of the great abstractions like "truth," "courage," and "fidelity" and the ability to use them without cheapening them.

To be a compendium of all the essential elements of Conrad, the novel seems to lack only Marlow, the narrator of *Heart of Darkness, Victory,* and *Lord Jim.* In scope, though, *Nostromo* is a departure from Conrad's other novels. In the author's note to *The Secret Agent* he refers to *Nostromo* as "an intensive creative effort on what I suppose will remain my largest canvas." [2] Unlike most of his works (even the other political novels like *The Secret Agent* and *Under Western Eyes),* it does not focus primarily upon the fate of one character. The events in the book revolve around Nostromo, but the story is of the fate of all the people of Costaguana. There are no less than fifteen major characters, most of whom have a past life which plays a significant part in the novel. In addition, there is the political history of Costaguana itself, remarkably complete and detailed but never summarized chronologically.

More than in any other of Conrad's novels the reader needs some familiar pattern beneath the complex surface of events and details to help him see the structure of the novel. Both Dorothy Van Ghent [3] and Claire Rosenfield [4] have pointed out that Nostromo's acts follow the pattern of "the myth of the hero" as detailed in Joseph Campbell's *The Hero with a Thousand Faces.* [5] Miss Van Ghent goes on to compare the novel with the Irish Fairy tale of Con-Edda, while Miss Rosenfield finds the folk legend of "The King and the Corpse" most instructive. Costaguana does labor under a curse like those of the old legends, and

Nostromo is clearly the hero who undertakes a quest and undergoes an ordeal to save the people. But to see only the similarities of his actions to the large patterns of nearly all heroes is to perceive only a vague outline where Conrad has provided a distinct and remarkably intricate pattern to give form to his novel. The guilt and redemption which dominate the book are worked out specifically in terms of Christian myth and theology. To overlook this is to miss one of the most central sources of unity in the novel.[6]

The silver of the San Tomé mine from which the curse upon the land emanates is a vastly powerful but ambiguous force. It has the potential to make Costaguana a kind of paradise, but on the other hand it is a strong temptation that drives men to cruelty and barbarism. There is no neutral point in the struggle between the two tendencies inherent in the mine. Like Eden, Costaguana must be a successful paradise or its inhabitants must be under a curse. It has not been a paradise since the first Europeans set foot there in search of treasure.

In the beginning of *Nostromo* the curse of the mine rests only upon the Gould family in the form of an unworked concession.[7] But when Charles Gould and his wife Emilia decide to make the mine operative, they, like Adam and Eve, extend the curse to all of Costaguana. The dual nature of the mine's potential and the parallels with Eden are made quite specific in the physical description of the mine. It is a lush mountain garden with a pure waterfall later "dammed up above" (p. 117) to make sluices for working the mine. Don Pepe, the overseer, calls it "the very paradise of snakes" (p. 116). The allusion to Eden becomes unmistakable when Don Carlos Gould says to his wife, "It is no longer a paradise of snakes. We have brought mankind into it, and we cannot turn our backs on them to go and begin a new life elsewhere . . ." (p. 232). But it is she who feels the responsibility for extending the curse beyond herself and more than Don Carlos seeks to ease the suffering it has brought. When she and her husband began their plans to make the mine operative, they thought they were making the cause of "an absurd moral disaster" into a "serious and moral success" (p. 73), but the problem remains with them only on a much larger scale.

When the curse of the silver manifests itself in the form of the greed that leads to the Monterist revolution, Mrs. Gould's compassionate instincts come into conflict with her husband's attitudes. As Decoud explains in his letter to his sister, "Don Carlos's mission is to preserve unstained the fair name of his mine . . ." (p. 272). His idea of a "moral success" is law and order above all else. "Haunted" by the "fixed" idea "of justice" (p. 422), he will do anything to keep the mine out of the hands of the corrupt Monterists. He is prepared, if necessary, to blow up the mine, out of the territory of the republic (p. 407), an action that will bring political reprisal and misery to Sulaco. So strong is his passion for justice that even his wife is not exempt from it. He is even willing to "bring heaven down piteously upon a loved head" (p. 422). Mrs. Gould's mission is "to save him from the effects of that cold and overmastering passion" (p. 272). This is only possible through the agency of Nostromo. Unless he is successful in keeping the most recent shipment of silver out of the hands of the Monterist revolutionaries and securing aid against them, her compassion cannot win out over her husband's rigid demands for justice.

Nostromo thus becomes the agent of mercy protecting vulnerable humanity caught between the opposed forces of corruption and stern justice. To save the mine and abort the revolution, Nostromo must take the curse of the silver, "The curse of death" (p. 288) as he calls it, upon himself. Like Christ who undoes the curse brought upon the world by Adam and Eve, he performs an act of vicarious atonement.

The specific curse with which Nostromo is burdened as a direct result of his efforts to save Sulaco is not exclusively brought on by his own guilt. It originates from his involvement with other people. In choosing to go to sea with the lighter of silver rather than bring a priest for the dying Teresa Viola, Nostromo abandons her to death without confession. She dies believing that he has "deprived her of Paradise" (p. 297). In her despair she is the first to speak of the curse that will fall on him. In choosing to complete the salvation of Sulaco by bearing a message to the friendly general, Barrios, rather than returning to the Great Isabel, he leaves Martin Decoud to perish alone. Decoud might have survived, but he lacks the faith to wait even a few days for Nostromo's return. The manner of these two deaths and Nostromo's part in them are the direct cause of the curse under which he labors. He realizes in thinking how his fate has come upon him, "the part he had played himself. First a woman, then a man, abandoned each in their last extremity, for the sake of this accursed treasure. It was paid for by a soul lost and by a vanished life" (p. 561).

By his later actions Nostromo assumes the guilt for both a failure to confess and a lack of faith. In his case they are combined in an act of secrecy which determines that he shall die like a thief. He has only to have enough faith in the reliability of other men to tell them what has happened to Decoud and the silver and he will avoid all the suspicion and guilt with which he is later surrounded, but he chooses instead to keep silent.

Nostromo returns from taking the silver out into the Golfo Placido to a scene dominated by confessions about the silver. The first person he encounters is Dr. Monygham, who is already infamous for one false confession and is in the process of making another. The body of Hirsch, the ox-hide merchant who has been killed because he "confessed everything" (p. 504), dangles in the background during their conversation, casting its large shadow over two living men. Both duty and love demand that Nostromo also make a kind of confession—that he give an account of his acts to Captain Mitchell out of duty and to Giorgio Viola out of friendship and a sense of community. But from his first waking moments on shore, the idea of betrayal destroys in him all faith in other men and works to prevent this confession.

Certainly Nostromo has been used by the Europeans and undoubtedly Decoud does betray him later, but the cries of betrayal which he makes at this point are founded more upon his own vanity than upon real grievances. Because there is no one to welcome him and applaud his great exploit publicly, he comes to see all those who have depended upon his great fidelity as enemies and betrayers. This mistrust aroused in him by the wound to his vanity leads him to reject mentally the idea of revealing the fate of the silver to Captain Mitchell or to old Viola (pp. 468-469).

While Nostromo's mistrust begins mentally, his first real opportunity to share his knowledge of the silver comes when he meets Dr. Monygham in the custom-house and his mistrust rapidly becomes centered in the doctor. Though Monygham thinks to himself, "I must take him into my confidence completely," and does so, Nostromo makes no reciprocal gesture of faith. Instead he succumbs to the temptation to use Monygham's former weakness as a betrayer who has confessed to a conspiracy that did not exist as justification for his own distrust of other people. He expands his assessment of Monygham first to the San Tomé oligarchy, "You fine people are all alike. All dangerous. All betrayers . . ." (p. 508). Later at Viola's, he includes everyone in his judgment. "There was no one to understand; no one he could take into the confidence of Decoud's fate, of his own, into the secret of the silver. That doctor was an enemy of the people —a tempter . . ." (p. 525).[8]

The attitude of secrecy established in the encounter with Monygham grows like an ever more binding spell cast upon him by the silver. Aboard the ship bringing Barrios back to Sulaco he is again given an opportunity to confess the secret of the silver but again he remains silent, "under the influence of some indefinable form of resentment and distrust" (p. 551). He thinks to himself that he will let Decoud tell the story "from his own lips" but even as this thought is going through his mind, Decoud is already dead. Nostromo's silence and lack of faith have assured that he will become a figure of guilt.

The nature of the curse of secrecy and the power it has over Nostromo may be seen in his near attempt at confession to Giselle. Softened by her love, he struggles against the spell of the silver which he feels like a "weight as of chains upon his limbs, a pressure as of a cold hand upon his lips" (p. 602). As he is able to confess that he has a treasure gotten "like a thief," he feels that he has "struck a blow for his freedom" (p. 603). But when he forbids her to ask where it is hidden, we see that his confession is incomplete, that "He had not regained his freedom" (p. 605).

In one sense Nostromo's sin of secrecy is Adam's sin of possessing forbidden knowledge. Though the knowledge of the silver is not in itself damning, Nostromo makes it so by turning it into a guilty secret in defiance of love and duty. In the scene in the custom-house when Nostromo makes his decision to keep his secret, he is presented as a guiltless Adam who becomes more and more Satanic as he becomes more committed to secrecy. At the beginning the emphasis is upon his innocence.

> Nostromo woke . . . from his lair in the long grass. He stood knee-deep among the whispering undulations of the green blades, with the lost air of a man just born into the world. Handsome, robust, and supple, he threw back his head, flung his arms open, and stretched himself with a slow twist of the waist and a leisurely growling yawn of white teeth; as natural and free from evil in the moment of waking as a magnificent and unconscious wild beast. (p. 458)

From the reference to him as a beast in a "lair," his serpentine movements and the "lost air" about him we may see his potential for evil but at this point it remains only a potential.

As he begins to experience the vanity which sets his mind against his fellow men, he is described in terms suggesting both Adam and Satan: "Nostromo tasted the dust and ashes of the fruit of life into which he had bitten deeply in his hunger for praise" (p. 464). The fruit he eats suggests the forbidden fruit of Adam,[9] but the taste is that of the dust and ashes which Satan is condemned to eat for his part in corrupting man. After he has met Monygham who further wounds his vanity by assuming the silver lost, his feelings are described in terms suggestive of Satan's fall. "The sense of betrayal and ruin floated upon his sombre indifference as upon a sluggish sea of pitch" (p. 477). The mind of the previously innocent and incorruptible Nostromo has now become a kind of hell. In the necessity to come to grips with Monygham's plan to tell Sotillo that the silver is on the Great Isabel, he gives way to "hissing vehemence" (p. 514). And finally, as he commits the first act of deceit to keep the silver a secret by offering the counterplan to tell that the silver has been lost in the sea, the process is complete: Monygham calls him a "Devil of a man!" (p. 516).

While Nostromo is depicted as Adam succumbing to temptation and assuming the characteristics of Satan, another undercurrent of suggestion keeps us aware that in assuming this sin he is atoning vicariously for all of Costaguana. His unexpected return to shore when "everything seemed lost in Sulaco" (p. 465) is looked on as a miracle of rebirth bringing deliverance. Giorgio Viola experiences it as "a return to life" (p. 481). Monygham calls it a "marvelous" reappearance (p. 476). To him "Nostromo's return was providential. He did not think of him humanely, as of a fellow-creature just escaped from the jaws of death. The capataz for him was the only possible messenger to Cayta, the very man" (p. 483). He says again later that Nostromo is "the only man" (p. 509). Nostromo, himself, alludes to his accomplishment in saving the silver, saying, "if that silver turned up this moment. . . . That . . . would be a greater miracle than any saint could perform" (p. 486). And he speaks of his arrival with Barrios as a "return in triumph" (p. 510).

Despite the new hope that Nostromo's awakening brings to Sulaco, he himself experiences it as a kind of death. After we see him depicted first as lying "as if dead," "still as a corpse" (p. 459) watched over by a vulture, we are told that for him awakening "was more like the end of things. The necessity of living concealed somehow, for

God knows how long . . . made everything that had gone before for years appear vain and foolish, like a flattering dream come suddenly to an end" (p. 462). As his old innocent life passes away and he feels "the burden of sacrilegious guilt descend upon his shoulders" (p. 470), Nostromo undergoes a kind of passion which parallels his assumption of the qualities of Satan. In the sky the cloud bank is like "a floating mantle stained with blood" (p. 457). In the ocean below the blood red of the sky is mingled strikingly with the water. In this atmosphere he experiences the "bitterness approaching that of death itself" (p. 466) which overcomes him at the thought of his betrayal as physical thirst. "His mouth was dry . . . with heavy sleep and extremely anxious thinking. . . ." And he tries to reject the very praise for which he longs. "He tried to spit before him—'Tfui'—and muttered a curse upon the selfishness of all the rich people" (p. 464). As he makes the mental decision that he can trust no one, an owl lets out an "appalling cry—'Ya-acabo! Ya-acabo!' (It is finished! It is finished!)" (p. 468). Nostromo thinks that this cry is a sign that Teresa is dead and that the "unseen powers which he had offended by refusing to bring a priest to a dying woman were lifting up their voice against him" (p. 468), but he does not realize that it signifies the finality with which the curse he earned by the act has been settled upon himself.

Though Nostromo has assumed the guilt of others and suffered for it symbolically in the scene in the custom-house, the guilt with which the novel is charged is not purged until the end of the book. Before the curse can be removed permanently, Nostromo must find absolution, and those for whom the sacrifice is made must demonstrate their belief so that the vicarious atonement can be effective.

At his physical death Nostromo retains the role of sacrificial victim. He is shot while "weighted down with silver" (p. 607). His wrongdoing is thus exposed, but he makes sure that no one shares with him the guilt of the knowledge of the treasure's hiding place. His first words to Mrs. Gould after she is summoned to his side are an attempt to ensure that Giselle will not be thought guilty. "She is innocent," he says, "She is innocent. It is I alone" (p. 622). If he has not bought the golden crown for her brow or taken her to that paradise with a palace on a fertile hill crowned with olive trees, vineyards, and corn that he dreams of for her (p. 604), he has at least kept her free from guilt in the eyes of others.

Nostromo's own sins are absolved by acts of confession and faith which parallel and counteract the events by which he assumed guilt.[10] His request (carried out by Dr. Monygham) to have Mrs. Gould brought to him brings someone to perform an office of confession like that denied to Teresa Viola. When she arrives "cloaked and monastically hooded" (p. 622), Mrs. Gould hears him confess that he is "Nostromo the thief" (p. 623).

This confession undoes half of the guilt. Mrs. Gould is the kind and gracious lady whose presence throughout the novel we experience as a constant force for good. When she responds to Nostromo's offer to tell her where the treasure is by saying "No capataz . . . no one misses it now. Let it be lost forever" (p. 624), we feel that Nostromo has been forgiven and that the curse attached to the silver has been allowed to go out of the world. This impression is strengthened later when she silences Dr. Monygham's question about Nostromo's relationship to the treasure with "He told me nothing" (p. 625).

Despite all this Mrs. Gould's response to Nostromo is ambiguous and insufficient to clear the air of all guilt. Her dismissal of his rescue of the silver is only one of many such dismissals, each of which Nostromo has regarded as a betrayal. Nostromo might have divulged his secret to Monygham, Viola, Captain Mitchell, and Don Carlos Gould and saved himself, but each of them encouraged his silence by assuming the silver lost and Nostromo incapable of retrieving it. Only moments before, Nostromo has reproached Don Carlos for saying, "It was nothing of importance. Let it go" (p. 624). He reacts to her words by closing his eyes, saying "no word" and, making "no movement." This may be construed as a sign of relief from his burden, but it may also be seen as an indication of complete despair.

However we read Nostromo's response to the pardon bestowed on him by Mrs. Gould, it is clear that his absolution is incomplete, for she still believes him a thrall to the silver. Although she has heard him declare his love for Giselle and his faith in her and say that he could have torn himself away from the treasure for her (p. 623), she nonetheless says to Giselle, "Console yourself, child. Very soon he would have forgotten you for his treasure" (p. 626). In her eyes he has found forgiveness for taking the silver but not for the faithlessness it aroused in him. The guilt associated with Decoud's death is not yet purged, and even as he is confessing to Mrs. Gould, Nostromo denounces Don Martin as a betrayer.

The act of faith necessary to make salvation complete comes

from Dr. Monygham. He accepts Mrs. Gould's assertion that Nostromo told her nothing as absolute pardon for Nostromo. As soon as she speaks, the light of the "temperamental enmity to Nostromo" goes out of his eyes (p. 625). Paradoxically, however, he does not give up his belief that Nostromo has somehow saved the silver that was lost. He alone believes that Nostromo has performed the "miracle greater than any saint could perform" and yet affirms his innocence. His act of faith not only completes Nostromo's absolution but provides the belief in the act of sacrifice that makes it effective.

It is significant that Monygham's forgiveness and faith come first when he has no cause for them. It is thus the counteraction not only to Decoud's suicide and the long series of failures to ask about the silver, but also to Nostromo's secrecy itself. In the custom-house Nostromo holds Dr. Monygham strictly accountable for his past, and thus begins the chain of events that leads to the dishonorable death. Monygham, in contrast, extends his forgiveness in spite of even more tangible evidence of Nostromo's guilt.

It is typically Conradian irony that the essential act of faith in the novel comes from the man most swathed in scepticism and cynicism. Conrad extends the irony of events even further by the manner of its expression. Monygham's belief in Nostromo's ability to save the silver is revealed in the sentence. "He did not believe her" (p. 626). Monygham's role is not, however, so strange as it at first appears. His faith in the power of redemption is born of the knowledge of his own guilty past. He is able to forgive because he has himself known guilt and overcome it and is thus prepared to believe others capable of the same regeneration.

Even in the earlier scene where revealing his plans for the false confession costs him the confidence of Nostromo, Monygham is, without knowing it, affirming Nostromo's power to save the silver. The story he proposes to tell Sotillo is precisely the truth and in marked contrast to the fatal confession of Hirsch which fosters the belief that the silver is lost; the confession he finally does make asserts that the silver has been saved and therefore leads to life. Not only does it save his own life, it also buys the time that keeps Sotillo from slaughtering the members of the Gould entourage. The penalty for failure to believe is death, as the fates of the otherwise innocent Hirsch and Decoud illustrate. But belief, even though coupled with guilt as in Dr. Monygham's case, brings salvation.

Nostromo has earlier denounced Monygham in political gather-
ings and to the last refuses all medical aid from him, but ultimately
Monygham's belief in Nostromo buys pardon. Nostromo's last conscious moments are spent with the blood-thirsty little Communist
photographer. The little man asks him if Monygham is "really a
dangerous enemy of the people" (p. 627). Nostromo responds by
"directing at the weird figure perched by his bedside a glance of enig-
matic and mocking scorn" (p. 627). While it suited his purposes in the
past to denounce Monygham, when he must answer to his deathbed
he can only express contempt for the petty little materialist who has
believed his lie about the doctor. As is frequently the case in Conrad,
this is a paradoxical and negative statement of a positive attitude, but
it is nevertheless the pardon necessary to bring a sense of reciprocal
acceptance and completion to the relationship between Nostromo and
Monygham. Immediately following Nostromo's scene with the photographer, Dr. Monygham sees "the glitter of the moon upon the gulf
and the high black shape of the Great Isabel sending a shaft of light
afar from under the canopy of clouds" (p. 628). The "ray of hope"
through the "rift in the appalling darkness" formerly denied by a God
who "looked wrathfully" on his creatures (p. 92) shines down at last
on Dr. Monygham.

The guilt in the novel is purged only because Monygham has
broken the impasse of absolute judgment with an act of grace that
leads to faith. Unlike the inexperienced scepticism of Decoud, the
vanity of Nostromo, and the idealism of Don Carlos, Dr. Monygham's
self-knowledge bought by bitter experience teaches him not to hold
men forever responsible for their past actions or for their deviations
from perfect models—real or abstract. The failure of the other characters
to extend a similar kind of grace to their fellowmen leads inevitably
to separation, which brings suffering.

The fate of Decoud, "the apostle of separatism," is the best example of the disastrous results of dwelling ungenerously on human
imperfection. His newspaper, called ironically, the *Porvenir* (the Future)
is devoted primarily to excoriating publicly the past wrongdoing of
the Montero brothers—an activity he calls "a sort of intellectual
death" (p. 199). He is therefore one of the first targets for their revenge
should their revolution succeed. As he explains to Antonia, "—Haven't I
written that he was taking the guests' overcoats and changing plates
in Paris at our Legation in the intervals of spying on our refugees

there . . . ? He will wash out that sacred truth in blood. In my blood!" (p. 199). Though his one admitted aim is "not to be separate from Antonia" (p. 238), the necessity to protect himself leads him to become the author of both the plan to separate the smaller load of silver from the mine and the one to separate the Occidental Republic from the rest of Costaguana. (Significantly, Dr. Monygham is opposed to both plans.) Finally his scepticism leads to the ultimate separation, his suicide "from solitude and want of faith in himself and others" (p. 555).

By the end of the novel Nostromo has atoned for the separation of the silver. And on the personal level both Nostromo and Decoud have been forgiven for the infidelities which separated them from the women who loved them. The growing intimacy between Mrs. Gould and Dr. Monygham, while not a substitute for her early love for Charles, is at least a relief from loneliness. The two of them are in some measure brought together when he becomes "a familiar of the house. Everlastingly there" (p. 538).

In the political sphere, however, separation born of strict judgment remains a burden on the land. Captain Mitchell speaks glowingly of the "regeneration" of Sulaco, but the true nature of the Occidental Republic may be seen in the proposed monument to the counter-revolution which established it. There is to be "a marble shaft commemorative of Separation, with angels of peace at the four corners, and a bronze Justice holding an even balance, all gilt, on the top. . . . Names are to be engraved all round the base" (p. 539). Obviously a monument to abstractions, it contains no real human figures. What human deeds it acknowledges are to be accounted for strictly by a list.

The reality of the republic is much different. " 'Will there never be any Peace? Will there be no rest?' Mrs. Gould whispered. . . . 'There is no peace and rest in the development of material interests.' " Dr. Monygham replies: "They have their law and their justice. But it is founded on expediency, and is inhuman . . . , the time approaches when all that the Gould Concession stands for shall weigh as heavily upon the people as the barbarism, cruelty, and misrule of a few years back" (p. 571). Later Mrs. Gould envisions the San Tomé mountain "hanging over the Campo, over the whole land, feared, hated, wealthy, more soulless than any tyrant, more pitiless and autocratic than the worst government, ready to crush innumerable lives in the expansion of its greatness" (p. 583). The curse of "poverty, misery and starvation" (p. 521) spoken over Nostromo by Teresa may have been lifted from him personally, but politically it hangs over his people.

Against this persistent oppression there remains only the hope that the harsh judgment which separated one part of Costaguana from the bounty of the mine can be reversed. There are rumors of a popular revolution for national unity to be led by Hernandez, the pardoned criminal, and in the circle around Mrs. Gould there is talk of an act of annexation. Antonia Avellanos expresses the hope when she asks, "How can we abandon, groaning under oppression, those who have been our countrymen only a few years ago, who are our countrymen now? . . . There is a remedy." "Annex the rest of Costaguana to the order and prosperity of Sulaco," snaps Dr. Monygham. "There is no other remedy" (p. 569). These rumors and the hopes of this little band around Mrs. Gould give the only indication of any relief from the oppression of political separation.

Some of what they hope for may be seen in the devotion to Garibaldi shared by Mrs. Gould and Giorgio Viola. The old Italian is himself the embodiment of the principles of Garibaldi. He cannot understand the ways of Divine Justice (p. 32) but he lives simply in dedication to the Garibaldist revolutions for Italian unity and independence for Uruguay. These were revolutions based not upon strict accountability (Garibaldi refused to keep accounts) and separation but upon their leader's "divine force of faith" (p. 34) that inspired a band of men who "wanted nothing" but "suffered for the love of all humanity" (p. 35). This dedication has engendered in Viola a "soldier-like standard of faithfulness and duty, as if the world were a battle-field where men had to fight for the sake of universal love and brother-hood instead of a more or less large share of booty" (p. 347). Viola retains his faith in spite of the fact that the revolution for which he fought was later betrayed by politicians. His little inn, Albergo D'Italia Uno, is a simple memorial "more in memory of those who have died than for the country stolen from us soldiers of liberty by the craft of that accursed Piedmontese race of kings and ministers" (p. 137). Italy as he would have had it is gone, and Viola has seen ample evidence that men are unworthy of the sacrifices made for them, but still he has not lost his "energy of feeling" and "personal quality of conviction" (p. 35). It is he who keeps the light that exposes the darkness of Nostromo (that other man of the people), just as the lithograph of

Garibaldi looks "dimly" down on Decoud, "the man with no faith in anything except the truth of his own sensations" (p. 254).

Conrad demands from his readers the same faith based on extension of grace that is demanded of his characters. If we believe that either the popular revolution or imperialist expansion will change Costaguana, we do so in the face of vast evidence to the contrary. The history of Costaguana as it is given in the book, from the earliest Conquistadores through the reign of Guzman Bento and the Ribierist experiment down to the most recent attempted coup in Santa Marta, gives no reason to expect salvation from either end of the political spectrum. And yet if Conrad has been successful and if we respond to the prodding he gives in his author's note, we see Antonia Avellanos as a figure modeled on "the standard-bearer of a faith to which we all were born, but which she alone knew how to hold aloft with an unflinching hope!" (p. 8). We do somehow disregard all the history which Conrad has shown us in such detail and suspend our judgment of men enough to hope at least that Costaguana can be reunified and the benefits of the mine extended to all. The faith demanded is not, however, merely optimism. It contains the awareness that all humanity is involved in a "desperate affair." Like Linda's cry—"Never Gian Batista"—with which the novel ends, it is a mixture of anguish at the impossibility of human perfection, unquestioning pardon for imperfection, and affirmation of a spirit of love that binds us together in spite of the infidelities we commit.

The presence of a theological structure unifying *Nostromo* not only helps us to order the threads of the plot, it also suggests a relationship between Conrad and the reader somewhat different from the one we are accustomed to thinking about. Encouraged by the dramatic presence of his famous narrators, Conrad's readers have for the most part been content to see themselves as listeners to a story. Their job has been the familiar one of judging character, weighing motives, responding to description, and following the action. To be sure most of them have felt the need to participate actively in the telling to evaluate testimony and correct the biases of the various points of view. But even in this complex process readers have involved themselves primarily in a transaction with the personae of the stories. Conrad's presence, except in the degree that he is equated with his narrators, is not felt. But as soon as the words we read begin to have suggestions about a larger structure of which the characters of the novels are themselves unaware a new element is present. When, for example, we read a phrase like "a very devil of a man" not as Dr. Monygham commenting idly on Nostromo's tenacity, but also as Conrad inviting us to share his knowledge of the order behind these events, we realize that we are more than listeners to a story related by the personae that inhabit Costaguana. We are dealing directly with the more complex literary mind of Joseph Conrad. From time to time as in the playful double entendre that allows us to read "damned up above" in "dammed up above" we get a relieving glance at the kind of sophisticated and sometimes humorous relationship Conrad has to his material. The feeling of discovery and the relief of the humor are in themselves important parts of the pleasure of the novel, but like most of the other elements of Conrad's technique they also serve the purpose of involving us more directly by fostering a sense of participation on a level of understanding shared only between us and the author. By making us his accomplices in discovery and by letting us smile with him in the playful superiority of our knowledge, Conrad forestalls our criticism of what he has to tell us and gains a kind of acceptance few novelists enjoy.

The kind of involvement implied by this reading of *Nostromo* extends as well to much of Conrad's other fiction. Many of his stories and novels employ Christian parallels like Nostromo's progression from Adam to devil. In "An Outpost of Progress," for example, events recapitulate man's "progress" through the roles of Adam and Eve, Cain and Abel, and Christ and Judas. In "Amy Forster" the rejected young alien Yanko dies in an atmosphere of cries and symbols strongly suggestive of the crucifixion.

Other works employ the parallel less prominently but still are based upon a structure of secularized Christian elements. Freedom gained through the sacrifice of innocents is the essence of *Under Western Eyes, The Secret Agent,* and *Victory.* But more specific than these elements so common in literature is Conrad's preoccupation with questions of faith and grace. Not only *Nostromo* but several of his most important novels turn upon the acceptance of some extraordinary central character in the face of evidence that would normally preclude that acceptance. This is what makes Marlow so important in *Heart of Darkness* and *Lord Jim.* More than a device for giving credibility to the tale, more even than an intelligence to help us evaluate character by complex standards, Marlow is an active participant in a drama of belief. In spite of all that he knows about them, he comes finally to affirm his faith in Kurtz and Lord Jim. The "true lie" which he tells about each of them is an act of grace like that of Monygham toward Nostromo; it is also an act of faith in a man whose life and suffering have far exceeded the normal. *Chance* is animated by the necessity for faith on the part of both Captain Anthony and his bride Flora de Barral that one can be loved even when imperfect and when the love is unmerited. The unexpected incident which ends the unnatural separation between them is ascribed by the narrator to "chance, fate, providence, call it what you will!" He might as easily have spoken of it as an act of prevenient grace, for this theological concept is far nearer the center of the novel than the philosophical concept of random circumstance. Indeed, the echoes of this theme are seldom absent from Conrad's later works and to them it adds a dimension like the one explored here in *Nostromo.*

This aspect of Conrad confirms his position as one of the first of the moderns, the forerunner of Joyce and Eliot rather than the technically superior contemporary of Hardy. In manipulating a parallel between the present action and the religious structures and in involving the reader as a mind that must actively perceive patterns beyond the overt action, Conrad made innovations in the British novel as great as those Yeats made in poetry. All this is not to say of course that those elements of setting, plot, character, and narration for which Conrad has been so frequently praised do not remain a major part of his attraction. It is only to say that along with them, often providing the unity for his complex actions, there is often another structure to which we should respond. To see this structure and its implications in *Nostromo* is to approach a little closer to the heart of Conrad.

Notes

1. Frederick R. Karl, *A Reader's Guide to Joseph Conrad* (New York, 1960), p. 146.

2. Joseph Conrad, *The Secret Agent,* Anchor edition (New York, 1953), p. 8.

3. In her Introduction to the 1961 Rinehart edition of *Nostromo.*

4. In *Paradise of Snakes: An Archetypal Analysis of Conrad's Political Novels* (Chicago, 1967).

5. Miss Rosenfield describes the patterns as follows: "the hero must undertake

a night-sea journey into an ambiguous region either in the dark interior of the earth or below the waters of the sea. This is a symbolic death that occurs so that he may encounter the forces of evil, the monsters that blight the world of natural cycle; he descends, so to speak, into the belly of the whale or into the mouth of the dragon. In overcoming the monster which is death, he experiences the peace of paradise and a knowledge of the unity of existence. But he must be reborn in order to bring his special truth back to a fallen world, in order to redeem mankind. On a personal level, the ritual quest symbolizes the journey into the self, into the dark interior landscape of the dream which approximates the still waters of the womb. After conquering the dragon that is the Ego, the individual is reborn better able to endure the continual flux of life because he has gained a new knowledge of the self, a new sense of identity" (p. 65).

6. Miss Rosenfield, for example, concludes that "Nostromo is essentially two imperfectly integrated stories, each with its particular hero [Nostromo and Decoud], each with felt life of its own" (p. 44). The integration of Decoud's fate with Nostromo's depends upon an understanding of the importance of the Christian element of faith and grace.

7. Joseph Conrad, *Nostromo,* Modern Library edition (New York, 1951). All references are to this edition and are shown parenthetically in my text.

8. As this reference to Monygham in a diabolical role indicates, the patterns in the novel are much more complex than this article can indicate. Superimposition, inversion, and ironic modulation occur throughout the novel. For example, see the ironic crucifixion and resurrection of Monygham on pages 416–417.

9. Adam, of course, tastes of the fruit of knowledge of Good and Evil, not the Tree of Life. Conrad's departure from the account in Genesis indicated that Nostromo is leaving the sheltered existence of his magnificent reputation and entering for the first time the realm of complete human experience including wrongdoing and retribution.

James Joyce
and the Power of the Word

WELDON THORNTON

In his *De Anima* Aristotle, "maestro di color che sanno," refers to the mind as the "form of forms." When Stephen Dedalus ruminates this in the second episode of *Ulysses,* his observation sounds dangerously like a parody of the master's intention: "Thought is the thought of thought." What Stephen's reflection suggests, and what Aristotle would have been appalled to learn, is that for twentieth-century thinkers the regressive form of his statement has carried more paradigmatic force than its content. We regard John Locke as one of the first "modern" philosophers partly because he redirected philosophy's quest from knowing the world to knowing the mind. This regressive shift of emphasis from the object of knowledge to the organ of knowledge is a hallmark of the modern. One of the results of man's ever-increasing self-awareness is our turning the bright light of analysis into those dim corners that were the assumptions, the givens, of our less introspective predecessors. One way this increasing self-scrutiny has shown itself is in our interest in language, the medium of our thoughts. Here again John Locke made his contribution, for he devoted a book of his *Essays* to words and language; but only within the past century has there been any intensive analysis of the medium, and the scientific study of languages (i.e., structural linguistics) is a child of the last few decades. It is inevitable and good that we should come to analyze the medium of our thoughts, but here, as in other regressive studies, there is some danger of reductionism, of our becoming so fascinated with the analysis of the medium that we lose our perspective and forget to ask what it is a medium of.

Of all modern writers none has shown so much interest in language, the medium of his art, as James Joyce. Other writers have worked as hard at developing their own style, and have used language with complete skill, but for no other has the medium of language assumed the importance it did for Joyce. But hard as it is to overestimate the importance of language for Joyce, it is possible to misunderstand it. For example, several critics have argued that for Joyce language is not simply the medium through which we see reality, but is the reality, and others have said that language itself is his major theme.[1] But I cannot agree that Joyce ever *identifies* language either with reality or with the principle of meaning; nor is language per se his theme. Joyce remains aware that meaning is a principle or capacity, and language is a medium, and that every uttered statement, whether offhand comment or structured work of art, involves a blending of principle and medium. He is also aware that reality is partly a raw material independent of the observer or the medium, and that no matter how fully or subtly our language informs reality, its power to manipulate reality is limited.[2]

Joyce does know of course that though meaning and reality and language are not identical, they are inextricably related, and his works constantly testify to this. He also knows that the power of language in forming our picture of reality is so great that one who remains unaware of it may be manipulated and victimized by language, for one's conception of reality, or even of himself, can be distorted by it. My purpose in this essay is to clarify Joyce's views about the relationships between meaning, reality, and language. I wish to show that while Joyce was conscious of how fully language informs our view of reality and of how dependent our expression of meaning is on the medium, he never reductionistically identifies the medium with reality or with meaning. First I will explore some concrete ways in which Joyce shows our language's influence on our view of reality in the opening pages of *A Portrait of the Artist*. Then, focusing on the naming power of language and on analogies between the artist and the priest, and the artist and God, I will show the implications of Joyce's view of language for his theory of meaning.

I

The subject of *A Portrait of the Artist* is the formation of Stephen's soul, and in the early pages of the novel Joyce gives us a relatively clear view of how language enters into that genesis and development. Here more than anywhere else in Joyce's works we have a chance to observe the individual mind feeling its way into the structures of language and reality. We have an opportunity to view almost in their atomic components the various facets, powers, valences of language before they are blended into an unanalyzable compound. From the opening pages of the novel we can infer some ideas about language which may help us to understand better Joyce's later novels and his aesthetic theory. Even by the later chapters of *A Portrait,* the interrelationships between language and reality have become so complex that it is almost impossible to separate them, and Joyce's focus has shifted from these concerns to more general aesthetic and philosophic ones.

One of Joyce's purposes in the first chapter of *A Portrait of the Artist* is to show the simplicity and falseness of the idea that language is a translucent, inert medium through which a static, objective reality is observed. Four ways that Joyce illustrates the interrelationship of language and reality in the early pages of *A Portrait* are: the structure of syntax blends with the structure of reality and offers possibilities which reality itself may not suggest or sanction; through language we have the power to name or fix our experiences; our mental associations are frequently determined by language rather than reality; and language itself, the medium, becomes the subject of some of our value judgments, even while we think we are directing these judgments toward reality. Let us look more closely at each of these.

On the opening page of *A Portrait,* Stephen hears the song about the wild rose that blossoms on the little green place. When he repeats the song, it becomes "O, the green wothe botheth." [3] In substituting *green* for *wild,* Joyce is illustrating, simply and amusingly, how the structure of syntax may influence our picture of the structure of reality. Syntactically the "green rose" is perfectly acceptable; it is an ordinary juxtaposition of adjective with noun. But we know there is no such thing as a green rose in reality. Stephen's locution hints to us, though not to him, that we are dealing with two different but related (or at least relatable) structures, the structure of reality (where a green rose is unacceptable) and the structure of language (where a green rose is as acceptable as a wild rose or a red rose). Joyce's point here is not that the structures of language and reality are identical or of equal metaphysical status, but that the structures of language, having their own nature and their own logic, give the imagination a means by which to play over reality, to explore possibilities about it beyond the ken of our experience, and to come to know reality partly by measuring it against what it might conceivably be, but is not. Language is seen as a potential vehicle of the imagination, an extender of our view of reality into directions which first-hand experience and common sense might never suggest. The person with an active imagination, the potential artist, finds in all the permutations and combinations implicit in syntax a ready, even enticing, vehicle for exploring the possibilities of reality. He may if he likes join any modifier with any noun, and let his imagination toy not just with green roses, but with the "cruel, crawling foam," or with "perfumes as green as fields." Some of these combinations, while not at first sanctioned by common sense, might prove to be interesting and fruitful, and might even result in a new, broader awareness of reality. Others, however, would be completely unsanctioned by reality and perhaps even repugnant to the imagination, and any attempt to live in terms of them would be fruitless or destructive. But since Stephen is essentially romantic, his native inclination is to trust the imagination and accept its creations uncritically, and he must learn later that not all that the imagination can conceive and language can embody is stable enough to build on. He shows his latent awareness of this problem early in the novel when he thinks "Lavender and cream and pink roses were beautiful to think of. Perhaps a wild rose might be like those colours and he remembered the song about the wild rose blossoms on the little green place. But you could not have a green rose. But perhaps somewhere in the world you could" (p. 12).

Language also has the power to pin down, to fix, our experiences. This naming power of language comes into the novel in several ways—in Stephen's amusement that Nasty Roche (itself quite a name) calls the Friday pudding "dog-in-the-blanket," and in his puzzlement when Nasty asks Stephen his name and then says "What kind of a name is that?" (p. 9). One interesting illustration of the naming power of language occurs when Stephen writes in the flyleaf of his geography book:

                    Stephen Dedalus
                    Class of Elements
                Clongowes Wood College
                        Sallins
                    County Kildare
                        Ireland
                        Europe
                      The World
                     The Universe

Stephen is using language to try to fix his own identity and his place
in the whole scheme of things. He begins with his name, and, moving
outward through concentric circles, maps his world as fully as he can
through language. His ability to name things does not imply his total
comprehension of them, but it does transfer them from the chaos of
the completely unknown into the more ordered realm of the named.
Having carried this naming process as far as he can, Stephen wonders
"What was after the universe? Nothing. But was there anything round
the universe to show where it stopped before the nothing place began?"
(p. 16). Here Joyce illustrates the puzzlement and frustration felt
when thought runs to the limits of language. Stephen's circumlocution
"nothing place" helps him to think his problems through, but it is
less helpful than a *name* for the "nothing place" would be. Stephen
does not understand what "universe" means, but having a word to
name the idea permits partial understanding and mutes frustration.

   Struggling with the problem of what lies beyond the universe,
Stephen thinks

> It was very big to think about everything and everywhere. Only God
> could do that. He tried to think what a big thought that must be
> but he could think only of God. God was God's name just as his
> name was Stephen. *Dieu* was the French for God and that was God's
> name too; and when anyone prayed to God and said *Dieu* then God
> knew at once that it was a French person that was praying. But
> though there were different names for God in all the different lan-
> guages in the world and God understood what all the people who
> prayed said in their different languages still God remained always
> the same God and God's real name was God. (p. 16)

Stephen alleviates his puzzlement over "the nothing place" beyond the universe by calling in another name, God, which must mean little more to him than "the nothing place" does. Joyce tells us "It made him very tired to think that way. It made him feel his head very big" (p. 16). Stephen's thoughts about God's name in French, and his conclusion that His real name is God, also illustrate that although *God* and *Dieu* are equally "correct" names for God, the innate human tendency is to feel that the names we use are the *real names.* (This tendency is partly responsible for our making language itself the object of our value judgments, as we shall see more fully below.)

Later Joyce again suggests the power of words to lead us into reality when he says "Words which he [Stephen] did not understand he said over and over to himself till he had learned them by heart: and through them he had glimpses of the real world about him" (p. 62). Doubtless Stephen's clear distinction between words and the "real world" oversimplifies, for at this time he sees words as mere counters, bearing a one-to-one relationship to aspects of reality. Later in the novel Stephen ceases to be the passive applier of individual words and becomes the active manipulator or creator of phrases, sentences, even of a whole poem. This more complex use of the word to fix experiences and formulate reality deserves fuller discussion later. But whether we regard the distinction between words and reality simply or complexly, Joyce wishes us to see that the two are not identical.

Another important way that language influences our view of reality, one widely recognized since the days of John Locke and Laurence Sterne, is that our mental associations are often influenced more by linguistic affinities than by "real" affinities. Joyce illustrates this in Stephen's train of thought about his belt. Standing beside the playing field, Stephen "kept his hands in the side-pockets of his belted grey suit. That was a belt around his pocket. And belt was also to give a fellow a belt. One day a fellow had said to Cantwell: 'I'd give you such a belt in a second'" (p. 9). This simple chain of thoughts suggests one important way that our map of reality is influenced, almost dictated, by language rather than reality. Each of us comes to his own individual view of the world largely through the associative links which our language permits or encourages. Not that every speaker of a given language sees the world identically. Every language provides its users a complex body of possible associations not available to speakers of another language, but the particular associations that become func-

tional will vary widely from one individual to another. Some people
are by nature more responsive to linguistic hints than others, so that
the degree to which homographs, homonyms, rhymes, etc. form someone's map of reality varies considerably from person to person. Also
the particular associative links which are formed are often the product
of chance or accident. The result is that even among speakers of the
same language, linguistic associations may produce very different maps
of reality.

In Joyce's example, Stephen, on the basis of a homonym, forms a
link between a piece of cloth or leather worn about one's waist and a
blow given. Clearly these two things have no "natural" connection,
but for Stephen they will always be more or less connected because
they are thus associated in his mind. When he thinks of the belt he
wears, the other belt, the sort you give to someone, will always be
lurking in the back of his mind. Such associations will determine the
flow of his mind regardless of whether reality sanctions these connections or not. His mind will also inevitably be more responsive to any
possible "natural" connections traceable between objects thus associ-
atively linked. Since the fertile mind, especially the metaphorically
oriented literary mind, seeks for analogues among all parts of reality,
we can see how important such linguistic affinities can be in forming a
world picture.

Joyce also illustrates in the first chapter of *A Portrait* that the
medium of language becomes so subtly intertwined with what it depicts that we come unawares to make value judgments about the
medium itself. (We saw an example of this earlier in Stephen's thoughts
about *God* and *Dieu.*) Nor is this true only when we are reading and
evaluating literature, where part of our judgment is consciously directed
at how the artist uses his medium; it is true even of our most pragmatic
statements. Immediately after he thinks about someone saying that
he would give Cantwell a belt, Stephen remembers that Cantwell
had answered "Go and fight your match. Give Cecil Thunder a belt.
I'd like to see you. He'd give you a toe in the rump for yourself,"
and then he thinks "That was not a nice expression. His mother had
told him not to speak with the rough boys in the college" (p. 9). We
should note that Stephen's judgment about what Cantwell said is
directed not at the thought he expressed (Stephen would probably
agree with Cecil Thunder's giving the bully a toe in the rump), but
at the expression Cantwell used. Stephen is really responding to the
medium—language—rather than to the content of the remark, so that

Joyce once more illustrates how difficult, almost impossible, it is to separate the two.[4] The same point is suggested again when Stephen thinks

> And there were nice sentences in Doctor Cornwall's Spelling Book. They were . . . only sentences to learn the spelling from.
>
> > *Wolsey died in Leicester Abbey*
> > *Where the abbots buried him.*
> > *Canker is a disease of plants,*
> > *Cancer one of animals.*
>
> It would be nice to lie on the hearthrug before the fire, leaning his head upon his hands, and think on those sentences. (p. 10)

Stephen's enjoyment of the sentences clearly stems more from their qualities of sound and rhythm than from their content.

Stephen's reaction to the word "suck" (p. 11) might be regarded as another similar example, but it is really more complicated, involving both a value judgment directed at language and an association. When Stephen hears Simon Moonan called "McGlade's suck," he says that "Suck was a queer word," and he also says "the sound was ugly" (p. 11), but his value judgment about the sound derives from associations with the unpleasant experience in the Wicklow Hotel lavatory.

As I have already indicated, it is difficult, even in these relatively simple passages early in *A Portrait,* to isolate the effects of language on Stephen's conception of reality in their atomic components, and this becomes increasingly harder as the development of Stephen's soul becomes more complex. Stephen's reflections about a phrase from Hugh Miller's *The Testimony of the Rocks* (1869) illustrate this. After thinking "A day of dappled seaborne clouds,"[5] Stephen reflects:

> The phrase and the day and the scene harmonized in a chord. Words. Was it their colours? He allowed them to glow and fade, hue after hue: sunrise gold, the russet and green of apple orchards, azure of waves, the greyfringed fleece of clouds. No, it was not their colours: it was the poise and balance of the period itself. Did he then love the rhythmic rise and fall of words better than their associations of legend and colour? Or was it that, being as weak of sight as he was shy of mind, he drew less pleasure from the reflection of the glowing

sensible world through the prism of a language manycoloured and richly storied than from the contemplation of an inner world of individual emotions mirrored perfectly in a lucid supple periodic prose? (pp. 166–167)

All four facets of language which we isolated in the opening pages of the novel are here explicitly or implicitly. In addition, Joyce complicates the theme of language and ties it in effectively with one of the novel's largest themes—the reconciliation of the inner, subjective world and the outer, objective world—in the distinction this passage suggests between the contents or connotations of individual words, associated by Stephen with the outer world, and the rhythm of "the period itself," associated with the inner. The main point for our purposes, however, is that Joyce's handling of language here consistently depicts it as a medium intimately related with, but not identical with, reality. Stephen learns about reality through it, fixes his experiences with it, even begins to realize potentialities latent in reality by means of it. Each of these implies, even necessitates, our recognizing that however subtly language and reality may blend and interpenetrate, they cannot simply be identified.

II

We have seen that words such as *universe* or *God* serve to name and to pin down experiences, and we saw young Stephen using such words to explore the real world about him. This power of individual words is also present in phrases, such as "A day of dappled seaborne clouds." Such a phrase is another species of the word, serving the same function as a single word, but on a larger, more complex scale. More important for Stephen, however, than these words and phrases of others' manufacture are the phrases, sentences, and the poem he himself creates to map his own view of reality. Stephen's creating a complex sentence or a poem gathers and gives form to his diverse experiences, and enables him to unify, to comprehend, to rise above the mere having of these experiences. By the end of the novel Stephen has moved from being a pawn of his language and an applier of handed-down labels to being a manipulator of language and a creator of complex "words" to map reality.

For Joyce, then, a phrase, a sentence, or a work of art can be considered a kind of complex word. Just as individual words pin down

aspects of reality, so can these larger elements of language comprehend and express correspondingly larger and more complex portions
of reality. As we shall see more fully later, in every such use of the
"word," two powers or potentialities are at work, one within the speaker
or artist, and the other within the crude reality he is trying to form and
comprehend. Within the artist we have the imagination; within reality
we have a potentiality for meaning. The medium of language provides the vehicle for fulfilling these two potentialities in a "word"
having both a subjective and an objective dimension.

If Stephen's increasingly complex sentences and his poem are
sophisticated examples of the word, there are still more sophisticated
examples beyond them. Just as a sentence interprets a portion of reality, so, in a larger way, does a style. The styles of Bacon, of Swift, of
Carlyle select and interpret reality from a distinct vantage point embodied in that style as it is in nothing else. Their style is the complex
word by which they fix and articulate their view of life, so that when
we read them, we see life from their perspective. But just as any style
has particular capacities, it also has particular limitations. Even the
styles of Newman or Milton, supple and comprehensive as they may
be, are selective and incomplete, for they fail to do justice to the aspects of life highlighted by the styles of Charles Lamb or James
Thurber. However sublime or sophisticated, a style can only give us a
limited vantage point on reality.

In these respects, there is little difference between literary styles
and what we might call literary modes, such as naturalism or symbolism. These modes, while broader, deeper, and more inclusive than
particular styles, may be seen as still more comprehensive examples
of the word. They too use the medium of language to express an
interpretation of life. Writers who fall within the naturalist or sym-
bolist camps may show considerable diversity, but we call them
naturalists or symbolists because they share underlying similarities of
world view that manifest themselves in their writing. Even symbolism
and naturalism necessarily take something less than the whole of life
as their domain (though their practitioners typically deny this); they
necessarily present it with some bias, and they are less than complete.

But while these styles and modes usually encompass many individual works of literature, we should recognize that an author can,
if he sets out to, make one individual work, one novel, a more comprehensive "word" than any style or mode. This fact helps us to under-

stand some features of Joyce's epic creations, *Ulysses* and *Finnegans Wake.* Unwilling to have his great works mere examples of one style or mode, Joyce sought in both books, by different means, to transcend the limitations of a single style, even a single literary mode. In *Ulysses* Joyce writes in a variety of styles, pointedly showing the limitations and imperfections of each. He also intentionally makes his novel the most fully naturalistic and the most fully symbolic novel ever written, in an attempt to reconcile and transcend the two major nineteenth-century literary modes. He further strives to set *Ulysses* above other novels by being as encyclopedic as possible, by incorporating as many patterns and cycles of man's activity as he can, and by incorporating some of the most comprehensive earlier literary works into his own by extensive allusion and by blending their major patterns into those of *Ulysses.* In *Finnegans Wake,* though a variety of styles still can be felt, Joyce achieves something closer to a single style, one radically different, and more generic, than any previous style. While it apparently does not attempt to join and transcend specific, recognizable literary modes, *Finnegans Wake* is even more encyclopedic than *Ulysses.* Its scope is the whole of human experience (at least western experience), and Joyce uses an archetypal method to achieve it. He develops his belief, embryonically present in *Ulysses,* that each man's life recapitulates the life-pattern of all men, and that the patterns of all human relationships are contained in the basic familial relationships, those of father and son, brother and brother, etc. However various his devices, Joyce's aim in both these novels is to make them as comprehensive examples of the Word as they can be.

All the levels of expression we have considered, from the single verbal item to *Finnegans Wake,* have in common that they are examples of the power of the Word. I have already suggested that this involves the imagination of the artist, the potential for meaning in reality, and the medium of language. A fuller understanding of what this implies for Joyce's ideas on reality, meaning, and language can be gained from examination of the analogies between the artist and the priest, and the artist and God, analogies frequently hinted at by Stephen Dedalus and by Joyce himself. But before we look into the aesthetic and philosophical implications of these analogies, we should consider how they pertain to Stephen's situation in the dramatic context of *A Portrait* and *Ulysses.*

We said that Stephen at the end of *A Portrait* had grown from a mere applier of linguistic labels to a creator of complex "words," including his villanelle. But not all of the edifice his imagination has built is solid, for, as he comes to realize, it rests on unstable foundations. The Stephen of *Ulysses* is soberer and maturer than was the Stephen of *A Portrait.* He has realized the superficiality of his earlier attitude and the depth of certain questions he had never before recognized. He is plagued by a host of new problems, and he sees no answers to them. The most important thing that has happened to Stephen in the intervening months is the death of his mother. Her death has given him first-hand knowledge of the undeniable domain of physical nature and the transience of each person's life, including his own. It has shown him the naivete and exuberance of his earlier optimism, held without any awareness of the power and terror of death. It has shown him that he is not a world to himself, that his own happiness and meaning in life are qualified by his relations with others and by his physical being. It has also shown him that no mere act of imagination can lift one above the claims of the physical world. His happiness and self-satisfaction are not destroyed simply by his grief for his mother, but also by his realization that the world view he had earlier found fulfilling was so purely subjective and baseless. He sees now that he was naively disregarding concrete reality and was trying to elevate the wishes of his own soul to the level of substantial fact.[6]

In addition to being shocked by his mother's death and doubtful about the powers of the imagination, Stephen is frustrated by his failure as an artist. At the end of *A Portrait* he seemed well on the way to forging in the smithy of his soul the uncreated conscience of his race, but he returns from his flight not an eagle or a hawklike man, but a lapwing. His despondency and self-doubt stem partly from his realization of the inadequacy of his earlier, romantic attitude. In typical romantic fashion, Stephen had erected his world upon the foundation stone of *self,* and it has simply proved incapable of supporting it.[7] But because of the sensitivity and depth of his mind, Stephen's malaise goes deeper than any ordinary counterreaction to romanticism. Though aware of the inadequacy of his earlier stance, he does not succumb to the materialism that is often the complement to naive romanticism.[8] He cannot accept Mulligan's simple verdict that his mother's death is a beastly thing and nothing else. But he also cannot continue to be idealistic or aspire to be an artist if his ideals and aims are purely subjective and solipsistic. What is the point of trying to create art if each man's work is merely the expression of his own fancy and self-indulgence, if there are separate, private meanings, but no Meaning—separate words, but no Word?

In these terms Stephen's search for a father in *Ulysses* is a search for some underlying principle which will give worth and validity to his artistic endeavor. His failure to be an artist grows not out of any mental dullness or incapacity with language or lack of sympathy and imagination, but out of his lack of a viable metaphysic on which to base his art. Stephen is especially sensitive to this lack because of the earlier collapse of what he had thought to be a stable, solid world view in *A Portrait*.

The answer Stephen is seeking is perhaps closer than he realizes, for it seems to be implicit in the power of the Word and in the analogies between the artist and the priest and the artist and God, analogies which Joyce himself apparently accepted and which Stephen several times suggests. From quite early in his career, Joyce saw analogies between the practice of art and a religious calling. He expresses this in various ways, such as his choice of religious terms to describe aesthetic phenomena (epiphany, epiclesis, eucharistic moment) and in his belief that being an artist involves a true dedication and calling. The analogy appears more explicitly in certain passages in the letters, essays, and novels, though even there it is presented piecemeal and suggestively rather than fully and systematically.

One of the earliest and clearest such references is in a letter Joyce wrote to Constantine Curran about some of the early *Dubliners* stories in 1904. There Joyce said, "I am writing a series of epicleti—ten—for a paper. I have written one. I call the series *Dubliners* to betray the soul of that hemiplegia or paralysis which many consider a city."[9] Ellmann explains that *epicleti* (an error for Latin *epiclesis* or Greek *epicleseis*) refers to "an invocation still found in the mass of the Roman ritual, in which the Holy Ghost is besought to transform the host into the body and blood of Christ."[10] Though the analogy is not very precisely indicated, Joyce is suggesting that his stories function in some way analogous to the mass. A somewhat clearer statement is recorded by Stanislaus Joyce, to whom Joyce said "Don't you think . . . there is a certain resemblance between the mystery of the Mass and what I am trying to do? I mean that I am trying in my poems to give people some kind of intellectual pleasure or enjoyment by converting the bread of everyday life into something that has a permanent artistic life of its own . . . for their mental, moral, and spiritual uplift. . . ."[11] The same analogy is expressed by Stephen in *A Portrait of the Artist* when he thinks of himself as "a priest of the eternal imagination, transmuting the daily bread of experience into the radiant body of everlasting life" (p. 221).

In the sentence just quoted, and in several other places, we find the word *imagination*, a word Joyce uses in two related but distinguishable ways: to indicate the imaginative faculty of an individual person (see, for example, *Portrait*, pp. 63, 181), or to indicate the principle of the Imagination, the "eternal imagination" of the passage just quoted. This individual imagination is the artist's creative faculty, and is his personal type of the Imagination, a creative principle which precedes any individual artist and stems from God.[12] Shortly before this passage, in his discussion with Lynch, Stephen has said, "This supreme quality the *whatness* of a thing is felt by the artist when the esthetic image is first conceived in his imagination. The mind in that mysterious instant Shelley likened beautifully to a fading coal" (p. 213).[13] A few moments later he tells Lynch: "The esthetic image in dramatic form is life purified in and reprojected from the human imagination. The mystery of esthetic like that of material creation is accomplished. The artist, like the God of the creation, remains within or behind or beyond or above his handiwork, invisible, refined out of existence, indifferent, paring his fingernails" (p. 215).[14] These passages suggest that the Imagination is the agent of aesthetic creation, a point which Stephen is even more explicit about when he says, "O! In the virgin womb of the imagination the word was made flesh" (p. 217); they also explicitly tell us that the artist is the "priest" of this imagination. Another analogy that Stephen suggests in these passages is that between the artist and God. This analogy is again suggested in *Ulysses* when Stephen refers to God as "the playwright who wrote the folio of this world" and when he quotes Dumas' dictum that "After God Shakespeare has created most."[15]

These two analogies, priest/artist and God/artist, and this view of the Imagination, sporadically and incompletely presented as they are, deserve closer consideration, for they clarify and enlarge the power of the Word implicit in the naming power of language, and they suggest a theoretical and metaphysical basis on which Joyce found it

possible to practice his art. Faced with a problem similar to Stephen's
—of finding some ground on which his art could be more than solipsistic
self-indulgence and fancy—Joyce found his answer partly in these
analogies.[16] The following diagrams present their implied correspon-
dences more clearly and systematically.

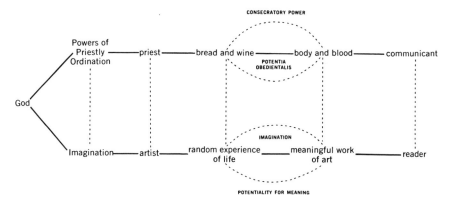

Diagram One: The Priest / Artist Analogy

The upper line of this diagram shows that the priest, drawing on and
embodying (but not creating) the powers of his priesthood, acts via
his more specific consecratory power on the bread and wine to tran-
substantiate them into the body and blood, which are then received
by the communicant. While the priest by his ordination shares or becomes the agent of God's power, it is prior to him and transcends him,
just as the consecratory power by which the transubstantiation occurs
comes through him but is independent of him. The second line shows
that the artist, drawing on and embodying (but not creating) the
power of the Imagination, acts through his individual imagination on
the random experience of life to create a meaningful work of art,
which is then received by the reader. The middle part of the diagram,
representing the transubstantiation and the creation of the art work,
is the most complex and demands fuller explanation. In the upper
line, the priest's consecratory power is his individual type of the power
of God, and it is through this power, through the material substance
of the bread and wine, and through a capacity inherent in these elements that the transubstantiation takes place.[17] In the lower line,
the artist's imagination, his individual type of the eternal Imagination,
is the power within him which, through the medium of language,
evokes the potentiality for meaning in the random experiences of

life and produces the "transubstantiation" into art. In the cases of both priest and artist the end result is a joint product of a power within them (type of some larger power) and a potentiality inherent in the field of experience. Earlier, in the discussion of the naming power of language, I pointed out that every instance of naming involves a blending of an inner power of the namer and an outer potentiality in reality. Here we have a more complex and detailed example of the same principle. The artist who sees his art in this way can regard it as having one foot in the inner, subjective world of the imagination, while the other is planted firmly in the material world, and as being consequently more than mere mechanical reproduction on the one hand or irresponsible fancy on the other.

But this first diagram does not tell the whole story, for it obscures a sense in which the artist's role is analogous not to the priest's but to God's, and it fails to do justice to the activeness of the reader's role in the work of art. For these reasons we must supplement it with a diagram depicting the God/Artist analogy.

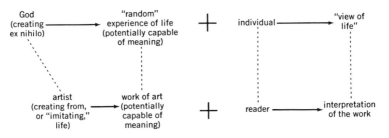

Diagram Two: The God / Artist Analogy

The upper line of this diagram shows that God, creating ex nihilo, produces life, something so varied and complex as to seem purely random, but carrying within it an inherent capacity to be given meaning. The individual, acting through his own imagination and the power of the word, selects and interprets this random but potentially meaningful experience to realize and express his view of life. The major difference between God's creation and the artist's (shown in the lower line) is that the artist's is not ex nihilo, for his begins with the raw material of life, and his creation is thus in one important sense always an imitation.[18] By his act of artistic creation (involving the Imagination and the Word), the artist produces a work of art which, while potentially capable of meaning, has some appearance of multiplicity and randomness about it. This work of art is itself a selection from and interpretation of life, but further selection and interpretation must occur if the work is to be understood, if its potentiality for meaning is to be realized. The role of the reader is to act on this multifaceted work of art and form his own interpretation, a role which, especially in modern art, is itself active and creative.

The role of the reader or interpreter, while not a necessary part of our topic, does bear some interesting relationships to the roles of the artist or of the individual developing a view of life, for the idea of interpretation implied by this diagram presents us again with a joining of capacities in the observer and in the observed. The observer brings his powers of interpretation to bear on a field of experience (life, or a work of art) which is by nature susceptible of interpretation, and his resultant interpretation realizes some, though never all, of the potentialities inherent in it. Not that all observers will have equally valid interpretations; there are indeed wrong interpretations, since the observed field of experience includes certain possibilities and excludes others. The person who concludes that he can fly like a bird by flapping his arms, wrongly interprets the natural world and will wind up, like Hamlet's famous ape, breaking his neck. In literary criticism it is hard to show that any interpretation is this drastically incorrect, but there are wrong interpretations. This is not to say that there is only one right interpretation—this approach to the problem precludes that—but it does allow for interpretations of varying scope and validity, depending on how fully or how correctly the observer realizes the potentialities inherent in the field of experience. This view of interpretation, then, leaves us somewhere between the traditional objectivist view which sees the meaning of life or of an art work as objectively present and only passively observed by the viewer, and those versions of the modern, subjectivist theory which hold that meaning is purely a product of the observer, and that whatever meaning any observer posits is a valid meaning.

The common element found in both of these diagrams and in the naming power of language is the idea of the word, the art work, the interpretation of life or of art, as a joint product of observer and observed, of subjective and objective. These analogies should enable us to see how a work of art or a view of life can be at once individual and objective, and they may offer some hope to those plagued by solipsism, whether aspiring writer or puzzled reader. For Joyce, as I have suggested, these analogies seem to have provided some basis for the practice of art. One hopes they will do the same for Stephen. When Stephen says of Shakespeare that "He found in the world without as actual what was in his world within as possible" *(Ulysses,* p. 213), he is expressing his own hope and need as an artist—that his experiences, while individual, are not idiosyncratic, and that the works of art he may create are not merely solipsistic, but have some objective relevance. The analogies we have examined suggest that his hope is not spurious, and that through the agency of the Imagination and the power of the Word, the artist's quest is not futile but has a substantial goal.

Notes

1. See, for example, Archibald Hill's review of *Finnegans Wake* ("A Philologist Looks at *Finnegans Wake,*" *Virginia Quarterly Review,* xv, 1939, 650-656), or Hugh Kenner's *Dublin's Joyce* (London, 1955). Hill says that Joyce's whole canon reveals "a preoccupation with the form of language divorced from its meaning" (p. 651) and that Joyce denies the "arbitrary and social nature of language" (p. 653). Kenner says that Joyce's "subject was language" (p. 17); and his negative, ironic reading of *Ulysses* seems to me to stem largely from his over-emphasizing and distorting the importance of language per se in that novel.

2. Here and throughout this essay, "reality" is seen as having two dimensions— a material or substantive dimension and a dimension of potentiality. Language influences reality mainly through the latter.

3. *A Portrait of the Artist as a Young Man* (New York: Viking Press, 1964), p. 7. All quotations are from this "definitive" text; subsequent page references will be given parenthetically.

4. It might be argued that Stephen's judgment is directed not at the medium per se, but at some content previously associated with these words. This is partly true, but it misses my point. Had Cantwell's thought been put in different language, Stephen's judgment about it would have been different, probably diametrically different. His value judgment, then, was diverted from the content of the statement to its medium.

5. The phrase in Miller's book is "a day of dappled, breeze-borne clouds." For details, see Don Gifford, *Notes for Joyce* (New York, 1967), p. 144.

6. One of Joyce's most important revisions between *Stephen Hero* and *A Portrait* is his deletion of the death of Stephen's sister Isabel (based on the death of Joyce's brother George). This makes it possible for Stephen to formulate the falsely optimistic view of life he has in *A Portrait* insulated from the shattering fact of death, and makes his later encounter with it more traumatic.

7. In *Stephen Hero* Joyce says of the romantic attitude, "The romantic temper, so often and so grievously misinterpreted and not more often by others than by its own, is an insecure, unsatisfied, impatient temper which sees no fit abode here for its ideals and chooses therefore to behold them under insensible figures. As a result

of this choice it comes to disregard certain limitations. Its figures are blown to wild adventures, lacking the gravity of solid bodies, and the mind that has conceived them ends by disowning them" (rev. ed.; London: Jonathan Cape, 1956, p. 83).

8. That Stephen's artistic creation in *Ulysses* is the naturalistic Parable of the Plums instead of another romantic villanelle shows his shift from an inner to an outer orientation. But just as Joyce's early romantic poems *(Chamber Music)* and naturalistic stories *(Dubliners)* were temporary way stations on the path to his later more balanced performances, so, one hopes, are Stephen's. And the title he gives his story indicates that he does see it as more than mere naturalism.

9. *Letters of James Joyce,* ed. Stuart Gilbert (New York, 1966), I, 55.

10. Richard Ellmann, *James Joyce* (New York, 1959), p. 169. The idea of a petition that the Holy Ghost transform the bread and wine into the Body and Blood of Christ is only one of the possible meanings of *epiclesis,* but it is most probably the one Joyce had in mind. Western liturgists still debate whether the *epiclesis* is or is not present in the Roman Mass. Most seem to feel that no specific *epiclesis* is required and that some other part of the Mass fulfills that function. See the *New Catholic Encyclopedia* (1967), v, 464–466.

11. Stanislaus Joyce, *My Brother's Keeper,* ed. Richard Ellmann (New York, 1958), pp. 103–104.

12. Henceforth I will use Imagination to indicate the principle; imagination, to indicate the individual artist's creative power.

13. In his early essay on James, Clarence Mangan Joyce makes a similar but fuller statement about the Imagination: "But the best of what he has written makes its appeal surely, because it was conceived by the imagination which he called, I think, the mother of things, whose dream we are, who imageth us to herself, and to ourselves, and imageth herself in us—the power before whose breath the mind in creation is (to use Shelley's image) as a fading coal" *(Critical Writings,* p. 78).

14. Stephen's language owes something to Flaubert. See *Critical Writings,* p. 141, where Mason and Ellmann quote a letter from Flaubert to Mlle. Leroyer de Chantepie.

15. *Ulysses* (New York: Random House, 1961), pp. 213, 212.

16. If Joyce found it here, why has not Stephen, who expresses some of these ideas himself? The answer lies partly in the complexity of the relationship between Joyce and Stephen, partly in the gap between theoretical knowledge and actual practice. Joyce himself doubtless wrestled with this problem, but for dramatic purposes Stephen's encounter with it is heightened and expanded. Also the validity of this answer must appear more clearly to us than it does to Stephen, for whom it is one tenuous possibility among a forest of them, and who does not yet have the faith in it to base his actions on it.

17. The scholastic term for this potency is *potentia obedientiae*—"the aptitude of material things to be made efficacious instruments of divine grace in the Sacraments" *(New Catholic Encyclopedia,* XI, 634). Technically the potentiality of language to embody meaning is an example of *potentia passiva* rather than *potentia obedientiae.* For fuller discussion see the *New Catholic Encyclopedia,* XI, 633–635.

18. The left side of the diagram is skewed to suggest that God is prior to the artist, who is himself a part of God's creation.

Fantasia and the Psychodynamics of *Women in Love*

HOWARD M. HARPER JR.

In his third novel, *Sons and Lovers* (1913), D. H. Lawrence began to explore directly and courageously the meanings of his own personal experience. Its central concern—the search for psychic wholeness—became the major theme of Lawrence's emerging art. In discovering his real theme, he produced his first great book, which remains a landmark in the modern tradition of realistic, autobiographical fiction cf adolescence and initiation.

As soon as *Sons and Lovers* was in the hands of his publishers, Lawrence became intensely involved in a new work tentatively entitled *The Sisters,* which finally appeared as two novels, *The Rainbow* (1915) and *Women in Love* (completed in 1916 but, because of legal difficulties with *The Rainbow,* not published until 1920). *The Rainbow* begins as a chronicle of the Brangwen family, and reaches its ultimate focus in Ursula Brangwen, the thoroughly modern woman who emerges from this heritage. At the beginning Lawrence places the Brangwens within the contexts of nature (as they move to the rhythms of their farm and its seasons) and history (as they respond to, and profit from, the first intrusions of industrialization into their natural world). Though these contexts remain important, they are gradually revealed as part of the more vital and significant context of human relationships —and especially sexual relationships. Each generation of Brangwens lives in a more complex world, in which natural fulfillment becomes constantly harder to achieve.

In the third generation the search of Ursula, which constitutes more than half the book, takes her through a variety of emotional and sexual experiences. At the end, recovering from a fever and the miscarriage of her lover's child, she realizes that even her lover has been an illusion: "It was not for her to create, but to recognize a man created by God. The man should come from the Infinite and she should hail him. . . . She was glad that this lay within the scope of that vaster power in which she rested at last. The man would come out of Eternity to which she herself belonged."[1]

Trying to watch Eternity for a sign of this regeneration, Ursula is distracted by the peripheral horrors of the here-and-now: "the expression of corruption triumphant and unopposed," the cancerous flowering of industrial civilization. But at last, shining above the corruption, she sees the transcendent rainbow:

> And the rainbow stood on the earth. She knew that the sordid people who crept hard-scaled and separate on the face of the world's corruption were living still, that the rainbow was arched in their blood and would quiver to life in their spirit, that they would cast off their horny covering of disintegration, that new, clean, naked bodies would issue to a new germination, to a new growth, rising to the light and the wind and the clean rain of heaven. She saw in the rainbow the earth's new architecture, the old, brittle corruption of houses and factories swept away, the world built up in a living fabric of Truth, fitting to the over-arching heaven.[2]

Several eminent critics of Lawrence have found this famous passage unconvincing,[3] an inappropriate conclusion for Ursula's story, which seems to consist of one disaster after another. Yet Ursula has faced each crisis bravely, openly, and honestly, and her incorrigible hopefulness here is not really too surprising.

Necessary and inevitable in the book itself, Ursula's vision of the rainbow also has its place in the larger story of which this book is only a part—the great myth which emerges from Lawrence's work as a whole. Ursula herself, under various names, is a major figure in this larger myth, in which *The Rainbow* is an intermediate stage. She will reappear in *Women in Love,* where her man will come from the Infinite and she will hail him. But there too their story is "inconclusive." Its real ending is in *Lady Chatterley's Lover* and *The Man Who Died*— where it turns out also to be a beginning.

Women in Love represents the most complex stage in the development of this final myth. Whether or not the novel is Lawrence's masterpiece, there can be no doubt that it is his most deep, complex, and comprehensive fiction. Lawrence himself has said that "A book only lives while it has power to move us, and move us *differently;* so long as we find it *different* every time we read it. . . . The real joy of a book lies in reading it over and over again, and always finding it different, coming upon another meaning, another level of meaning." [4] *Women in Love* offers this kind of challenge.

The novel enacts the movement of four major characters through "allotropic states" of being [5] in their search for fulfillment, and for wholeness. Ursula and Birkin approach these goals through their permanent commitment to each other; Gerald and Gudrun never do. But wholeness requires more than the sexual commitment of male and female; it must also include the commitment of female to female and of male to male. By virtue of their blood relation, Ursula and Gudrun are irrevocably committed to each other when the book begins. Birkin and Gerald move toward such a commitment, and almost reach blood brotherhood in Chapter xx, "Gladiatorial," but never fully achieve it. The rest of the book illustrates the consequences of this failure.

Women in Love is organic, and it moves with the stark power and economy of a morality play. This may seem a strange judgment to some readers who have endured the book for the first time—bewildered, annoyed, embarrassed, or simply tired and bored. It may seem to lack the power and immediacy of the more obviously autobiographical and conventional *Sons and Lovers,* or of *The Rainbow,* or of some of the brilliant short stories, or even of the rather blatantly argumentative *Lady Chatterley's Lover.* But *Women in Love* can become a powerful experience—once we learn its language.

In order to tell this unique story Lawrence had to invent a language. Like every true original he found himself at last in an artistic region without maps, a region illuminated only by an evanescent rainbow. Like James Joyce (to use the most conspicuous example), he had to discover a new language—not because he couldn't handle the one he inherited, nor because he wished to mystify us, but because he had something to say which could not be said in any other way. None of our given languages was adequate to convey the illumination of the rainbow, to communicate the unique qualities of his insights. So Lawrence's new, prophetic tongue, like Joyce's, is necessarily unique and difficult. We cannot learn it by reading other novelists.

Women in Love marks the full emergence of Lawrence as prophet of the apocalypse, calling out his warning to a civilization which he saw entering its death agony. Its fatal illness, according to his diagnosis, was a rampant obsession with will and reason. Its symptoms were the atrophy of sensual awareness and psychic openness. "I think; therefore I am" was, in Lawrence's view, a monstrous misconception of human nature and an unpardonable sin against the sacred mystery of human existence.

Despite all the condescending criticism aimed at Lawrence, the painful fact is that he was right. The history of our time has vindicated the scope of his vision and the truth of his insights. The crisis of modern culture, he recognized, arose from an increasingly rigid, idealistic, and rationalistic conception of man's nature and of man's role in society. Western culture, the culmination of many centuries of Platonic and Judeo-Christian tradition, had grown more and more blind to the sensual and the nonrational dimensions of human experience. This problem is at the heart of Lawrence's violent objections to Freud. As Phillip Rieff has pointed out in his excellent introduction to Lawrence's two long essays on the "unconscious," those objections were uninformed and unfair because "Lawrence failed to understand how undogmatic was his chosen rationalist opponent."[6] But as Rieff also acknowledges, Lawrence's rather shrill attack on "the fundamentalists of rationalism" was entirely justified. This is a major reason why his work remains so fascinating and relevant today.

Lawrence's most explicit attempt to "explain" human nature is the long essay *Fantasia of the Unconscious* (1922). Seen from a rigorously scientific, physiological point of view, *Fantasia*, with its talk of planes and plexuses, is nonsense. But seen symbolically, as a complex metaphor for the expression of psychological insight, it is profound. And since its symbology is almost identical with that of *Women in Love*, the essay provides a very useful, though far from exhaustive, key to the novel. Lawrence had long been interested in the symbologies of primitive cultures,[7] and his own mode of thought was now becoming increasingly symbolic—as we can see in *The Rainbow*, which begins almost in the manner of the traditional Victorian family chronicle but ends as a modern psychological novel. *Fantasia*, begun five years after *Women in Love* was finished, should not be regarded as a rationale for the novel, but rather as a gloss for it. As Lawrence himself says in the Foreword to *Fantasia,*

> This pseudo-philosophy of mine—"pollyanalytics," as one of my respected critics might say—is deduced from the novels and poems, not the reverse. The novels and poems come unwatched out of one's pen. And then the absolute need which one has for some sort of satisfactory mental attitude towards oneself and things in general makes one try to abstract some definite conclusions from one's experiences as a writer and as a man. The novels and poems are pure passionate experience. These "pollyanalytics" are inferences made afterwards, from the experience.[8]

The "pollyanalytics" are expository; they attempt to tell what Lawrence's art tries to show. *Fantasia* is an attempt at a metaphysics which will illuminate human life in a perspective far beyond the reach of a strictly objective, mechanistic physics. *Fantasia* begins as an answer to the savage criticism of his earlier essay, *Psychoanalysis and the Unconscious* (1921), in which he had set forth his basic conception of "the nature of the true, pristine unconscious" (p. 9), which cannot be known scientifically, but only experientially. Freud's argument for the sexual basis of all human activity, Lawrence felt, was too reductive. For Lawrence "the essentially religious or creative motive is the first motive for all human activity. The sexual motive comes second" (p. 60). Beginning with this assumption, and with his belief in the unity and coherence of all natural life, Lawrence goes on in *Fantasia* to elaborate his metaphysics of that life—from the human being's role within his family to his relationship with the sun and moon. *Fantasia* deals not only with abstractions but also with practical problems (e.g., education); it deals with both "unconscious" and "conscious," at many levels: its subject is, in the largest sense, human awareness.

The beginning of all awareness, Lawrence says, is in the great "sympathetic" center of the solar plexus. It is here that man feels the deep awareness that "I am I, the vital centre of all things. . . . All is one with me. It is the great identity" (p. 75). This is not an intellectual but a sensual awareness. Also sensual, but "voluntary" or "volitional"[9] rather than sympathetic, is the awareness, centered in the "lumbar ganglion," that "I am I, in distinction from a whole universe, which is not as I am" (p. 75). This is the feeling of identity, separateness, independence, and mastery which balances the sympathetic feeling of oneness with all of creation. Together these two kinds of awareness constitute what Lawrence usually calls the "lower" or "sensual" "plane."

The "upper" or "spiritual" plane develops somewhat later. Here there is also a polarity between the sympathetic and volitional modes of awareness. The sympathetic, centered in the "cardiac plexus," is the instinct to seek "the revelation of the unknown"; "here there is no more of self. Here I am not. . . . Now I look with wonder, with tenderness, with joyful yearning towards that which is outside me, beyond me, not me. . . . The other being is now the great positive reality, I myself am as nothing" (pp. 77–78). And opposed to this awareness is that of the "thoracic ganglion," the volitional center of intellectual individuality and analytical capacity.

Together these four kinds of awareness constitute the first "field" of consciousness. Of the second "field," which develops at puberty, Lawrence says rather little. The distinctions between the two fields are not very important here, since the modes of awareness in each seem almost identical. The notion of two fields, however, is another interesting illustration of Lawrence's obsessively dualistic view of reality.

Throughout both *Fantasia* and *Women in Love* it is implied that the volitional modes of awareness are naturally somewhat stronger in males, the sympathetic in females; the spiritual in males, the sensual in females. Furthermore, the spiritual is stronger in the northern races, the sensual in the southern.

Lawrence's well-known obsession with the sensual, with "blood consciousness," does not mean that he advocates sensuality at the expense of spirituality. Instead, he advocates "polarity," a dynamic balance between the spiritual and sensual and between the sympathetic and the volitional. He advocates wholeness and a constant, dynamic enlargement of our awareness of ourselves and our world. To move toward wholeness and fulfillment, the individual must seek and develop polarized relationships which open to him other modes of awareness. In *Women in Love* Gerald revitalizes his sensual awareness in his relationship with the Pussum, and his sympathetic awareness in his relationship with Birkin. Eventually, however, his "circuits" are weakened and finally broken, so that he drifts further into northern, willful isolation: he must freeze to death in the Alpine cold rather than make the revitalizing journey south into Italy with Birkin and

Ursula. Gerald's fate is inevitable because, as Lawrence says in *Psychoanalysis,* "the individual is never purely a thing-by-himself. He cannot exist save in polarized relation to the external universe, a relation both functional and psychic-dynamic" (p. 44).

Thus in *Women in Love* the characters must always be seen in the context of their dynamic relationships. Although each is predisposed toward one of the four primary modes of awareness, the possibilities of the other modes are always open to him through dynamic relationships. The total number of such relationships is, of course, infinite, and the existence of each individual within his world is infinitely complex. But a few vital "circuits" (Lawrence constantly uses electrical terminology to describe the dynamics of these relationships) define the instantaneous essence of the individual.

In the Foreword to *Women in Love* Lawrence says "that every natural crisis in emotion or passion or understanding comes from this pulsing, frictional to-and-fro which works up to culmination."[10] The sexual implications of this statement are obvious enough. Less apparent are its implications for the dynamics of the story itself. Each chapter embodies this same principle: each begins with its characters in certain allotropic states of being, from which they move, through their interactions with each other, to culmination in new allotropic states. This culmination is always the most important part of the chapter, since it contains the meaning of everything which has led up to it and made it necessary. And the same principle holds for *Women in Love* as a whole: the final culmination is necessitated by everything which has gone before—and in that sense, contains the meaning of the entire book.[11]

Lawrence says frankly in the Foreword that "This novel pretends only to be a record of the writer's own desires, aspirations, struggles; in a word, a record of the profoundest experiences in the self" (p. x). Birkin, Lawrence's self-portrait, is clearly the central figure of the book, and its central relationships are those between him and Ursula and between him and Gerald. Wholeness requires that he enter into polarity with a man as well as with a woman. The polarization with Ursula is successful, but the circuit with Gerald is broken, and the book ends with Birkin telling Ursula that she is not enough for him:

> "Having you, I can live all my life without anybody else, any other sheer intimacy. But to make it complete, really happy, I wanted eternal union with a man too: another kind of love," he said.

"I don't believe it," she said. "It's an obstinacy, a theory, a perversity."

"Well—" he said.

"You can't have two kinds of love. Why should you!"

"It seems as if I can't," he said. "Yet I wanted it."

"You can't have it, because it's false, impossible," she said.

"I don't believe that," he answered. (p. 548)

In failing to establish the blood brotherhood which he had proposed in the central chapter (xvi), he has failed Gerald and helped to condemn him to death. Birkin's wish for "another kind of love" is not so much an implied desire for a homosexual relationship with Gerald as an oblique admission of his own inadequacy. The book ends not with Gerald's death, but with Birkin's contemplation of that death and with his realization that his own quest for wholeness has failed.

This is the final crisis toward which the entire novel moves. Its full significance, of course, can be seen only in the perspective of the story as a whole, which traces the movement of Birkin and the others through the necessary allotropic states of being. The actions of *Women in Love* are complex, but they are governed by the same laws of psychodynamics which Lawrence defines most explicitly in *Fantasia* and which he illustrates throughout his art. A full analysis of the psychodynamics of this novel is out of the question here, but we can at least look at the essential elements of Birkin's story—its beginning, its middle, and once more its all-important end.

Chapter i, "Sisters," establishes the initial psychodynamic orientation of the characters. Opening with an "objective" narrative point of view, it modulates into the consciousnesses of the sisters. Gudrun thinks that "one needs the *experience* of being married," while Ursula sees it as "the end of experience" (p. 7): Gudrun tends to transform life into abstract intellectual experience, while Ursula is more able to accept it phenomenologically, as it is. In the terms of *Fantasia,* Gudrun, with her "diffidence" (p. 8), exists primarily in the volitional mode of awareness, while Ursula, with her "sensitive expectancy," is sympathetic. Glowing with "that strange brightness of an essential flame that was caught, meshed, contravened" (p. 10), Ursula has a greater potential for spontaneous sensual action and a greater range of latent awareness. When their conversation is ended, "Gudrun's cheek was flushed with repressed emotion. She resented its having been called into being" (p. 11). She is destined always to maintain this willful isolation and repression. As they walk through the colliery region toward the church, she tells Ursula that "Everything is a ghoulish replica of the real world" (p. 12), and she wishes to avoid it and its inhabitants. But Ursula herself has accepted this "dark, uncreated, hostile world" (p. 13) as real.

At the church we meet the two major male characters. They are offstage as the drama opens; their entrances are prepared for thematically in the initial conversation between the sisters; they are first seen through the consciousnesses of the sisters—all this underscores their dominant roles in the drama to follow. Gerald, who is second in importance, appears first. He is "a fair, sun-tanned type"[12] and has a "strange, guarded look" (p. 15). To Gudrun "There was something northern about him that magnetised her. In his clear northern flesh and his fair hair was a glisten like sunshine refracted through crystals of ice . . . pure as an arctic thing." She is suddenly aware that "His totem is the wolf" (p. 16).[13] All this places him clearly in the spiritual-volitional realm of consciousness, and foreshadows his final end.

Birkin's supreme importance is emphasized in still another way: he is introduced through a long interior monologue by Hermione, who abruptly appears in the book now for just this reason, apparently. Willful, spiritual, and rich, she represents a grotesque inversion of the natural sympathetic-sensual femininity described in *Fantasia*. In her sensual atrophy she moves with "a peculiar fixity of the hips," and is "impressive" but "macabre" and "repulsive" (p. 16). She and Birkin "had been lovers now, for years" (p. 20), and she recalls in anguish her long struggle to bring him under her domination, and his desperate resistance. We are told that he trails one foot (a mark of sensual disability[14]) and that "His nature was clever and separate. . . . Yet he subordinated himself to the common idea, travestied himself" (p. 22). Ursula recognizes this as a defense mechanism: "There was a certain hostility, a hidden ultimate reserve in him, cold and inaccessible" (p. 23).[15] The chapter ends with Birkin, as seen by Ursula, "neutralized" by Hermione, "possessed by her as if it were his fate, without question" (p. 24). In contrast, Gerald, as seen by Gudrun, appears "erect and complete"; he has "changed the whole temper of her blood."

It is significant that the first chapter ends with this implied comparison, for it is this relationship with which the novel will be finally concerned. In this initial definition and differentiation of the allotropic

states of the various characters, the women—Ursula, Gudrun, Hermione
—are seen directly, immediately, even definitively; Lawrence tells us
what they are thinking and feeling. The men—Birkin and Gerald—
are seen indirectly and more mysteriously, through the consciousnesses
of the women. Of the three women only Ursula seems potentially capable
of wholeness; both Gudrun and Hermione seem imprisoned by their
own intellectuality and willfulness. All this, however, is immediately
apparent only in the context of *Fantasia* rather than of the novel itself,
where the psychodynamics emerge in an artful, rather than an expository manner. And Ursula, at least, turns out to be anything but a flat
or transparent character; she is, in fact, the most multi-dimensional
character in the book, and more fully human than Birkin himself.
Her judgment, we come to realize, is to be trusted, and her perception
of Birkin as "neutralized" by Hermione—i.e., his individuality and force
have been drained by Hermione's will—is brilliant as well as accurate.
Gudrun's judgment of Gerald is much less reliable.

In this "neutralized" state at the beginning of the novel, Birkin
is pedantic and misanthropic. Although he preaches an abstract love
for humanity, he feels contempt for most individual human beings,
as we see in his lectures to the Criches (in Chapter ii), to Ursula and
Hermione (iii), and to Gerald (on London as a living hell in v, and
on the Pussum as the African totem in vii). This state is shattered,
however, by Hermione's paperweight of lapis lazuli, which brings Birkin
into naked, sensual communion with "the vegetation" (viii). Though the
pain of intellectual consciousness returns, the estrangement from Hermione is permanent, and Birkin is free to come "in contact" with Ursula
(xi). Accepting Ursula's challenge (xiii), Birkin responds (typically)
on the theoretical level, explaining his notion of polarity: "an equilibrium, a pure balance of two single beings:—as the stars balance each
other" (p. 168). After each interprets the Mino's treatment of the
stray female, Birkin wearily submits to Ursula's demand that he declare his love.

In the complex "Water Party" chapter the four main characters
are swept into the "dark river of dissolution" (p. 196). The body of
Diana Crich is found with her arms locked around the neck of her
rescuer-lover—the inevitable fate of the goddess of the moon (in *Fantasia* the moon, symbolic of volition and death, is polarized with the
sun, source of warmth and life). The chapter ends with Birkin "lapsed
into the old fire of burning passion" (p. 213) and Ursula, drowning

in her own passion for him, "capable of nothing" (p. 216). In xv she lapses toward death and a hatred of Birkin.

In xvi, "Man to Man," the middle chapter of the book, Birkin too is "in pure opposition to everything," drifting toward death. Full of "almost insane fury" against what he feels is Ursula's assumption of the role of "Magna Mater" (p. 227), which of course inhibits "the perfection of the polarised sex-circuit" (pp. 228–229), he falls psychosomatically ill. But Gerald moves to the rescue, and his visit to Birkin's sickbed is described with the overtones of a seduction scene. Birkin proposes *Blutbruderschaft* and Gerald refuses, yet Birkin senses the other man's "unadmitted love" (p. 239), and both gain a feeling of peace. Birkin's descent toward death is over, and Gerald's is in remission as the second half of *Women in Love* begins. The love and gratitude which Birkin now feels—despite Gerald's inability to pledge blood brotherhood—make his own later failure much more painful; owing his own life to Gerald, Birkin fails to care enough in the Tyrol.

Thus the middle chapter takes us to the psychodynamic and thematic center of *Women in Love*. The second half of the book begins with a new explicitly historical perspective. The history of the Crich family is also the history of the Industrial Revolution, and Gerald's immersion in the dark, cold river of dissolution is also the fate of Industrial Man. This implies a determinism which shifts still more of the moral responsibility to Birkin: perhaps Gerald does not enter into *Blutbruderschaft* because, as Industrial Man, he cannot—and Birkin himself has failed to open the possibilities of the relationship far enough.

Unable to enter into the holy mysteries, Gerald enters into the obscene mysteries instead in Chapter xviii, which is followed by its polar opposite, "Moony" (xix), in which Birkin tries to destroy the specter of the moon on Willey Water, where Diana had drowned. Foreseeing the terrifying African and Nordic (sensual and spiritual) forms of ultimate destruction, and even a vision of Gerald's death (p. 290), Birkin seizes with relief the intuition of a third alternative which leads to life, sanity, and wholeness—"the way of freedom." Setting off to find Ursula, he encounters her father instead,[16] and Birkin leaves with his proposal unanswered and everyone furious.

Instinctively, it seems, Birkin turns once more to Gerald, whom he finds "suspended motionless, in an agony of inertia, like a machine that is without power" (p. 303). But the naked wrestling energizes Gerald, who at last confesses his love: "I don't believe I've ever felt as much *love* for a woman, as I have for you—not *love*" (p. 314). And in the conversation which follows, it is Birkin who withdraws (interestingly, Lawrence does not directly acknowledge this). It is now Gerald who talks of "love" and of "something abiding, something that can't change," while Birkin is unwilling to enter fully into *Blutbruderschaft.*

Ursula, energized by the encounter with Hermione (xxii), returns to Birkin again in "Excurse" (xxiii). He gives her rings, they quarrel, and she denounces him violently but returns to worship at his "loins," and their relationship enters at last its full consummation—spiritual and sensual, sympathetic, and volitional—which is given its full ironic illumination by the consummation of Gerald and Gudrun in "Death and Love" (xxiv). Gerald sees the way to his own salvation—"to accept Rupert's offer of alliance, to enter into the bond of pure trust and love with the other man, and then subsequently with the woman" (p. 404)—but he must reject the crucial commitment which Birkin had rejected earlier (xx), and which confronts Birkin once more at the end of xxvi: "*Do* I want a real, ultimate relationship with Gerald? Do I want a final, almost extra-human relationship with him—a relationship in the ultimate of me and him—or don't I?" (p. 416).[17] This ultimate question is forgotten, however, as Ursula and Birkin are married and enter into "a new, paradisal unit regained from the duality" (p. 423).

In the complex drama of "Continental" (xxix), the longest chapter in the book, there are five major players. Birkin and Ursula provide the norms against which the psychic deformities of the others are measured. Gudrun's "strange rapture" (p. 457) at the altar of the frozen world recalls Ursula's earlier worship of Birkin in "Excurse," but with the ghastly difference that Gudrun is worshipping, narcissistically, the very source of death, while Ursula's reverence had been for the source of life. And while Gudrun is in her trance, Gerald, her demonic lover, "strong as winter," takes her again, in an increasingly horrible re-enactment of "Death and Love." She now feels estranged from nature, "divorced, debarred, a soul shut out" (p. 459)—and, almost at once (as if in response to an incantation) the inhuman Loerke makes his entrance. Gerald becomes more and more the mechanical man, a dynamo running down. Gudrun, now fully initiated into the icy mysteries, reaches beyond him to the ultimate horror—the mechanical artist, Loerke, with his belief that man's fulfillment is "serving a machine, or enjoying the motion of a machine—motion that is all"

(p. 484). He even more than his earlier female counterpart, Hermione, is "pure, unconnected will, stoical and momentaneous" (p. 486).

As Gudrun moves into affinity with this creature, she too becomes increasingly inhuman, until even her sister—who alone has effectively answered his dehumanizing theories of art—is repelled. At last Ursula tells Birkin that she must leave the icy, "unnatural" world of the Tyrol, and he agrees that "We'll go tomorrow to Verona, and be Romeo and Juliet" (p. 495). Then comes the final departure from Gerald, whose last words imply that Birkin has failed him:

> "I've loved you, as well as Gudrun, don't forget," said Birkin bitterly. Gerald looked at him strangely, abstractedly.
> "Have you?" he said, with icy scepticism. "Or do you think you have?" He was hardly responsible for what he said.
> The sledge came. Gudrun dismounted and they all made their farewells. . . . Something froze Birkin's heart, seeing them standing there in the isolation of the snow, growing smaller and more isolated. (p. 502)

Gerald's last words to Birkin are haunting, and Birkin's later anguish is not merely self-indulgent. He knows that he has failed Gerald and himself. His view of Gerald and Gudrun standing in the snow is also a perception of the shrinking dimensions of the worlds of awareness which they inhabit. And he knows that by abandoning those worlds he has constricted them still more, so that his last view of Gerald and Gudrun is a vision of death itself.

With Birkin and Ursula gone, that vision is not long in being realized. "Snowed Up" (xxx) is a confirmation of the frozen isolation which Birkin had foreseen, and Gerald is left to re-enact his father's death. His entire will expressed through his hands (as *Fantasia* suggests), he tries to kill Gudrun—as Hermione had tried to kill Birkin—but he realizes that not even that matters anymore, and he wanders wearily higher and higher into the mountains, to his icy *Götterdammerung*.

The aftermath of all this in the final chapter, "Exeunt" (xxxi), is profoundly pessimistic. The fate of Gudrun is even more terrible than Gerald's. He has found "sleep," but she is condemned to a living death. After Gerald's death "Her one motive was to avoid actual contact with events" (p. 541), and in Lawrence's last descriptions of her words like "cold," "pale," "impassive," "barren" predominate. She finally vanishes in two chilling sentences: "Gudrun went to Dresden. She wrote no particulars of herself" (p. 548). Loerke, we recall, had invited her to Dresden. And there is no longer a self to write of.

One of the most damning comments on Gudrun and Loerke is that "they never talked of the future" (p. 517), for in Lawrence's view, life itself is a commitment to the future. Birkin and Ursula, throughout the second half of the story—until they return to the Tyrol to claim Gerald's corpse—constantly look to the future. And in a sense, Birkin's famous epiphany on the "timeless creative mystery" (pp. 545–546) represents a commitment to the future. But its mystic affirmation is undercut by the reality of Gerald's corpse, "Dead, dead and cold! . . . Strange, congealed, icy substance—no more" (p. 546). Ursula, seeing him "convulsively shaken" with grief, "recoiled aghast from him" and "could not but think of the Kaiser's *'Ich habe es nicht gewollt.'* She looked almost with horror on Birkin" (p. 546).

This insight, as brilliant as it is unexpected, brings the real tragedy of *Women in Love* into much sharper focus. Birkin did not "will" Gerald's personal apocalypse any more than the pitiful Kaiser willed the Great War. Rather, the tragedy of both—and the irony of the Kaiser's statement—arises from a failure of will,[18] and the consequent failure to achieve a dynamic and balanced relationship with the real world of people and events.

Gerald's failure is overwhelmingly obvious, and is taken by most critics to be the point of the book as a whole. But Birkin's failure, though more subtle, is equally important. Some readers, expecting him to be the "hero," are disappointed or even angry that he turns out often to be a bore, a snob, too detached and ineffectual, sometimes even cruel. They resent the seemingly inconclusive conclusion—they don't like to wade through those hundreds of incomprehensible pages only to be left with the echo of Birkin's whining.

But this too is part of the profound truth of *Women in Love*. Birkin's search for wholeness fails because he does not dare enough. He can't face the "ultimate" in Gerald, any more than the Kaiser could face the ultimate realities of an emerging industrial Germany. Birkin and Gerald are the poles of the modern split personality, each trapped in a sector of awareness which is far too limited—Birkin in the "spiritual-sympathetic," losing his sense of self in an obsessive grasping for mystical unity with the cosmos, Gerald in the "spiritual-volitional," losing his sense of cosmic unity in his narcissistic will to power. Trying to become supermen, they both become less than human.

Lawrence's own view of reality is something else. It must not be confused with Birkin's; it includes Birkin's, but is vastly larger than that. This is not to deny that the book is autobiographical—it is profoundly autobiographical—but to insist that Lawrence's awareness of the implications of his story is much larger than most of us have realized. It is true that Birkin's failure is Lawrence's own—the failure of the Christ-like prophet who is increasingly isolated and finally martyred by his own insatiable idealism. But it is also true that Lawrence himself recognized that failure (as Chapter xx, "In the Pompadour," for example, makes clear). Together with the failure of Gerald, increasingly isolated too and finally frozen in his narcissistic willfulness, the failure of Birkin defines the failure—and the fate—of western man and his civilization.

The impasse which Lawrence reached at the end of *Women in Love* was never fully resolved. His failure was not a failure of courage or of effort: the "leadership" novels which followed—*Aaron's Rod* (1922), *Kangaroo* (1923), and especially *The Plumed Serpent* (1926)—are the record of his effort to find a way out. For the real ending of the story we must turn to his last work—to the *Last Poems* and especially, in the present context, to the last fiction: *Lady Chatterley's Lover* (1928) and *The Man Who Died* (1931).

The last novel closes with Mellors' letter to Connie: "We fucked a flame into being," he says, and now it is time to be chaste, until it is time once more to "fuck the little flame brilliant and yellow, brilliant!"[19] Their chastity now is not mere barrenness: Connie, whose husband Sir Clifford has had his sex "smashed" by the war and his spirit made monstrous by his own fascination with industrial power, now carries Mellors' child. The shorter but equally brilliant *The Man Who Died* ends in the same way. The risen Christ, now made whole by the priestess of Isis, leaves her temple and their unborn child, to drift with the current along the shore of darkness. But "I shall come again, sure as Spring," he promises her.[20]

Lawrence himself is both Clifford and Mellors, both the crucified and the risen Christ. As his wife Frieda wrote, "The terrible thing about *Lady C.* is that L. identified himself with both Clifford and Mellors, that took courage, that made me shiver, when I read it as he wrote it."[21] Like his earlier fiction these last books have been attacked for their inconclusive endings. But Lawrence told the truth about life as he saw it, and he saw that even though each life has its ending, most are inconclusive. Yet in the last fiction the inconclusiveness is optimistic: Mellors and Connie, the risen Christ and the fulfilled priestess of Isis, are seen in a new perspective—the perspective of a great cyclic myth in which human life and hope, like the legendary phoenix which Lawrence adopted as his own personal symbol, are eternally reborn from their own ashes. For Lawrence himself, now mortally ill, there was no doubt an element of wish fulfillment in all of this. But that does not invalidate the myth itself, which is the coherent and convincing culmination of his work as a whole.

Notes

1. *The Rainbow,* Compass Books ed. (New York: Viking, 1961), p. 493.

2. Ibid., p. 495.

3. F. R. Leavis calls it "a note wholly unprepared and unsupported, defying the preceeding pages. . . . The Lawrence of *Women in Love* could not have written that paragraph" *(D. H. Lawrence: Novelist,* Clarion Books ed., New York, 1969, pp. 142–143). Lawrence, Leavis argues, had already moved far beyond the abandoned conception which gives the book its title.

Graham Hough says that the conclusion "is quite insufficiently based, nothing in the book up to now has led up to it. Regenerations are not achieved by mere rejection. . . . All that the end of *The Rainbow* ultimately expresses is a vague hope and the need to end somehow" *(The Dark Sun: A Study of D. H. Lawrence,* Capricorn Books ed., New York, 1959, pp. 71–72).

For a full review of critical opinion on the ending of *The Rainbow,* see Edward Engelberg, "Escape from the Circles of Experience: D. H. Lawrence's *The Rainbow* as a Modern *Bildungsroman,*" *PMLA,* LXXVIII (1963), 103–113. Engelberg believes that the ending is appropriate.

4. *Apocalypse,* Compass ed. (New York, 1966), pp. 5–6.

5. Lawrence used this term in a famous letter to Edward Garnett, June 5, 1914:

You musn't look in my novel for the old stable *ego* of the character. There is another *ego,* according to whose action the individual is unrecognisable, and passes through, as it were, allotropic states which it needs a deeper sense than any we've been used to exercise, to discover are states of the same single radically unchanged element. (Like as diamond and coal are the same pure single element of carbon. The ordinary novel would trace the history of the diamond—but I say, 'Diamond, what! This is carbon.' And my diamond might be coal or soot, and my theme is carbon.) . . . Again I say, don't look for the development of the novel to follow the lines of certain characters: the characters fall into the form of some other rhythmic form, as when one draws a fiddle-bow across a fine tray delicately sanded, the sand takes lines unknown.

See *The Selected Letters of D. H. Lawrence,* ed. Diana Trilling, Anchor Books ed. (New York, 1961), p. 80.

6. *Psychoanalysis and the Unconscious and Fantasia of the Unconscious,* Compass Books ed. (New York, 1960), p. x.

7. Lawrence wrote *Women in Love* under the influence of Jane Harrison's *Ancient Art and Ritual,* Frazer's *The Golden Bough* and *Totemism and Exogamy,* and especially E. B. Tylor's *Primitive Culture,* according to Darrow Ransdell Johnson, "Myth and Ritual in *Women in Love,*" M.A. thesis, University of North Carolina at Chapel Hill, 1966.

8. *Psychoanalysis and the Unconscious and Fantasia of the Unconscious,* p. 57. Page references to these two essays in the subsequent discussion are shown parenthetically in the text.

9. Lawrence uses these two terms interchangeably, but uses "voluntary" much more often than "volitional." The latter term, however, now seems less ambiguous and more clearly associated with the "will."

10. *Women in Love,* Modern Library ed. (New York: Random House, n.d.), p.x. Page references in the subsequent discussion are indicated in the text.

11. All great novels, of course, have this quality of inevitability, which arises from the truth, integrity, and coherence of their creative vision. But *Women in Love* is more schematic than most because Lawrence's growing messianic obsessions at this time led him into increasingly schematic perceptions of reality, and the expression of these perceptions in his art grew more schematic too—in a language which ever fewer of the uninitiated would take the trouble to learn.

12. Lawrence disapproves of suntans consciously acquired. In *Apocalypse* he says that "all these modern sunbathers . . . become disintegrated by the very sun that bronzes them" because the sun is opposed to "the nervous and personal consciousness in us" (p. 43), which is polarized with the moon. *Apocalypse,* Lawrence's interpretation of the Book of Revelation, is his last piece of "pollyanalytics" and the final expression of his philosophy. Like *Fantasia* it is a valuable gloss for his fiction.

13. In *Fantasia* we learn that cats, wolves, tigers, and hawks live chiefly from the volitional centers (p. 102). But cows, bulls, and birds are associated with the upper sympathetic center, and horses with the solar plexus. *Women in Love,* like much of Lawrence's other fiction, is full of scenes in which animals are used to reflect and symbolize human states of consciousness.

14. Throughout *Fantasia* Lawrence maintains that the upper part of the body reflects the health of the spiritual centers, the lower the sensual. Masturbation, for example, is the sick intrusion of the spiritual or intellectual nature into the sensual domain. Hermione's attempt to kill Birkin with the paperweight is an expression not of her sensuality, but of her obsessive will.

Facial and sensory characteristics, however, are something else again. The eyes, for example, may express either sympathy (when they are full, soft, and dark) or volition (when they are hard and cold) (pp. 100–102). The teeth are instruments of the sensual will (pp. 98–99). And the nose is also expressive of Lawrence's four humors: cardiac (short), thoracic (long), solar (thick and squat), or lumbar (high and arched). *Fantasia* is a handbook of physiognomy.

15. As the Foreword to the novel implies, this is also Lawrence's own judgment of himself at the corresponding stage of his own development. Throughout his work he portrays himself as a Christ figure, most explicitly, perhaps, in his painting *Resurrection* (1927), in which the resurrected Christ is very clearly D. H. Lawrence himself. The inevitable fate of the Christ figure is to move further and further into sympathetic spirituality, away from the center of wholeness. In the terms of *Fantasia,* "Any excess in the sympathetic mode from the upper centres tends to burn the lungs with oxygen, weaken them with stress, and cause consumption. So it is just criminal to make a child too loving. No child should be induced to love too much. It means derangement and death at last (p. 97)." Thus Lawrence prophesies his own death from tuberculosis.

16. Their conversation, which begins with remarks about the weather and the moon, re-enacts Birkin's earlier attempts to shatter the moon's image on the water: Brangwen now is also willful and deathly—of his daughters he says "I would rather bury them, than see them getting into a lot of loose ways such as you see everywhere nowadays. I'd rather bury them—" (p. 294). Ursula, intruding here as she had earlier, moves into a state of "pure opposition," but Gudrun disparages Birkin so violently that Ursula turns "in spirit towards Birkin again" (p. 302).

17. Ursula "looked at him for a long time, with strange bright eyes, but she did not answer" (p. 416). Her eyes signal her awareness of the sensual mysteries, and her reluctance to answer may indicate that she can't face the implications of Birkin's feeling for Gerald. At any rate, both Chapters xxv and xxvi end with the failure of the two men to enter into an "ultimate" relationship—a failure which somehow dooms Gerald's relationship with Gudrun and which prevents that of Birkin and Ursula from ever reaching perfect wholeness.

18. In the symbology of *Fantasia* the Kaiser's withered arm would be associated with a failure of will.

19. *Lady Chatterley's Lover*, Signet ed. (New York, n.d.), p. 282.

20. *St. Mawr and The Man Who Died*, Vintage Books ed. (New York, n.d.), p. 210. *The Man Who Died* was originally published as *The Escaped Cock* (1929).

21. Letter to Harry T. Moore, January 14, 1955, quoted in his Afterword to *Lady Chatterley's Lover*, Signet ed., p. 296.

Mrs. Woolf
and Mrs. Dalloway

HOWARD M. HARPER JR.

It took Virginia Woolf almost twenty years to finish the story of the Dalloways. In her first novel, *The Voyage Out* (1915), begun as early as 1906 or 1907, Richard and Clarissa Dalloway appear in Chapter III, dominate the action for three chapters, then vanish as suddenly as they came. They appear also in the background of four short stories in *A Haunted House.*[1] But their definitive portrait is, of course, *Mrs. Dalloway* (1925), the first of Mrs. Woolf's indisputably major novels. And the reasons for her emergence into greatness are intimately related to her discovery of the real meanings of the Dalloways' story.

As she implies in her Introduction to the Modern Library edition, this discovery centers around Septimus Warren Smith. In the "first version" of the novel Clarissa's "double" did not exist, and "Mrs. Dalloway was originally to kill herself, or perhaps merely to die at the end of the party."[2] This first version was probably only a very tentative plan; there is no mention of Clarissa's death or suicide in the published extracts from Virginia Woolf's diary. Significantly, Septimus first appears in the entry which reveals that *"Mrs. Dalloway* has branched into a book."

The accepted view of Septimus by literary critics has been that

Septimus Warren Smith, whose experience in the war has led him to a state of mind in which he cannot respond at all to the reality of the existence of other people, is driven mad by the meaningless

[220]

isolation of the self, and his madness is exacerbated into suicide by the hearty doctors who insist that all he has to do is imitate the public gestures of society . . . and he will become an integrated character again.[3]

Septimus is undoubtedly a victim of the war and of his doctors, and this view of him is unquestionably sympathetic. But Virginia Woolf's own view of Septimus is the whole truth, much less sentimental and much more satisfying. It holds Septimus himself morally responsible for his madness and death. It is directly, unambiguously, and rather emphatically stated in the novel itself. The reasons for it arose from Virginia Woolf's own experience, and are reflected in her development of the Dalloways.

I

In early 1913, less than a year after her marriage, Mrs. Woolf was finishing her first novel and, to her husband's alarm, showing increasing signs of mental strain and instability. By the summer she had crossed the threshold of insanity; publication of the book was postponed, and Leonard Woolf was devoting almost all his time to her care. According to him the major cause of this breakdown seemed to be anxiety over the book (and subsequent experiences would show that the time of publication would always be traumatic for her). In the summer of 1914 she began to recover slightly, but in January 1915 suffered a relapse: one morning, Leonard says, "she was having breakfast in bed and I was talking to her when without warning she became violently excited and distressed. She thought her mother was in the room and began to talk to her. It was the beginning of the terrifying second stage of her mental breakdown"[4] which lasted until the following winter.

The Woolfs learned to recognize the warning signs of her recurring insanity and, through trial and error, to alleviate them, so that she was able to lead a relatively long and very productive, if somewhat restricted, life. Neither they nor the many doctors they consulted over the years really understood her illness, and even if much more information were available today, an adequate "explanation" would be very difficult. But since her own experience is at the heart of her unique vision of the self and the world, the major symptoms are worth noting.

In the depressive phase of her insanity she was fully aware of the reality around her, but violently hostile toward her nurses and herself; she had to be protected constantly against her suicidal impulses. She blamed herself for her mental state and for the burdens it placed upon Leonard. He was the only person who could communicate with her or persuade her to eat. In the manic phase, however, she was so violently hostile toward him that he could not enter her room, but she was fairly docile with her nurses, and "in a state of violent excitement and wild euphoria, talking incessantly for long periods of time."[5] She was unable to accept, or often even to recognize, outward reality: she heard the sparrows outside her window chattering in Greek, she spoke with her mother (who had died many years before), and so on.

Thus the deep polarities implicit in her novels seem to be reflected also in her insanity. In her depressive phase she seems to have been submitting herself to the authority of her father (identified now to some extent with Leonard) and to the ideals which he would always represent for her. Never capable of living up to these ideals, she became suicidally depressed. In her manic phase, however, she seems to have been closer to her mother, whose personality was open, vital, instinctive, pragmatic. As Virginia Woolf saw it, the essentially male impulse was toward abstraction and death, the female toward sensuality and life,[6] and during her insanity she was unable to reconcile or synthesize them, but instead swung violently from one to the other.

Mrs. Woolf was also aware that there was considerable self-indulgence in her mental illness. In her diary for August 8, 1921, she speaks of

> all the horrors of the dark cupboard of illness once more displayed for my diversion. Let me make a vow that this shall never, never happen again; and *then* confess that there are some compensations. To be tired and authorized to lie in bed is pleasant . . . merely to receive without . . . giving out is salutary. I feel that I can take stock of things in a leisurely way. Then the dark underworld has its fascinations as well as its terrors; and then sometimes I compare the fundamental security of my life . . . with its old fearfully random condition. Later I had my visitors, one every day, so that I saw more people than normally even. Perhaps, in the future I shall adopt this method more than I have done. . . . Lytton [Strachey], I note, is more than ever affectionate. One must say to one's old friends 'Ah my celebrity is nothing—nothing—compared with this.'[7]

In several places the tone of this confession is unmistakably ironic. But the fact remains that Virginia Woolf recognizes her illness as an escape from responsibility, an opportunity to be lazy, to gain attention and affection and sympathy, to be pampered. It is a method for dominating her husband and friends. Her "vow that this shall never, never happen again" implies some control over its happening again—and in fact, the Woolfs did learn that by taking certain common sense precautions they could prevent, or at least greatly dampen the fluctuations in her mental stability.

II

The novel which helped to precipitate Virginia Woolf's breakdown in 1913 is the story of Rachel Vinrace's initiation into social and intellectual sophistication, into love and—very nearly—sex. Although *The Voyage Out* is a very pale shadow of Virginia Woolf's major work, it is interesting as a document in her literary history, and as a projection of her own anxieties. Her major anxiety, perhaps, is expressed in the death of her heroine at the end, a death which seems—like the deaths of Mrs. Woolf's own mother, her half-sister Stella, and her brother Thoby—unnecessary, untimely, and unfair.[8]

The perspectives in which the Dalloways are seen here are quite different from those of the later *Mrs. Dalloway*. Richard is a bore and a stuffed shirt. "Pompous and sentimental," Rachel's aunt calls him, invoking two of the most derogatory adjectives in Mrs. Woolf's lexicon. She, an ardent feminist, has him loudly oppose women's rights. Her idol, Jane Austen, puts him to sleep. But to Rachel his stupidities and platitudes don't matter; she hears only his "rich, deliberate voice." Accidentally meeting on deck during a storm, they take refuge in her cabin. The ship lurches, they are thrown together, and he kisses her "passionately." Overwhelmed, she collapses in her chair, "with tremendous beats of the heart, each of which sent black waves across her eyes." He recoils and holds his head in his hands. " 'You tempt me,' he said. The tone of his voice was terrifying." On deck once again Rachel regains her calm, yet is filled with a "strange exultation" and the feeling that "something wonderful had happened." But Richard is distant thereafter, and when the Dalloways debark, he manages to look at Rachel only "very stiffly for a second before he followed his wife down the ship's side."

At first, Clarissa too is seen rather satirically. She dresses pretentiously, talks in clichés, and writes condescendingly about the other passengers. But her effect on Rachel is more profound than Richard's. She communicates to the girl something of her own vitality and enthusiasm, and draws her out as no one else has ever done. The two become very close, and Rachel is left with the feeling that life "was infinitely wonderful, and too good to be true."

Although the early Mr. Dalloway is not an intellectual, in other respects he resembles Mr. Ramsay of *To the Lighthouse:* egocentric, attractive to women, outwardly strong and overbearing, inwardly weak and frightened—and therefore demanding absolute attention and affection. Though Rachel is impressed by his social position and his seeming assurance, at the deepest level she is aware only of his voice and his body, his overwhelming sexuality. She responds to him as women do to Mr. Ramsay, but more extremely: her heart pounds, and her consciousness drowns in black waves. And her view of Clarissa is like Lily's of Mrs. Ramsay—awe for the woman who can face the threat of that overwhelming masculinity and even "triumph" over it.

Thus the Dalloway chapters of *The Voyage Out* seem to be a very tentative, possibly unintentional, exploration and expression of Virginia Woolf's feelings toward her father and mother, feelings which would find their definitive statement in *To the Lighthouse.* The first novel is not that story, but the story of the young girl who must die without fulfillment of the sensuality which the older man awakens in her. And in her voyage out the Dalloways (like the Stephens) must vanish suddenly at an unnamed port of call which, symbolically, may be Rachel's destination too.

Mrs. Woolf returned to Mrs. Dalloway in 1922 as she was finishing *Jacob's Room.* At first she planned only a short story, which was published in the *Dial* in July 1923 as "Mrs. Dalloway in Bond Street."[9] Its events and motifs correspond to those of the opening section of the novel: "Big Ben struck the tenth; struck the eleventh stroke. The leaden circles dissolved in the air." Clarissa's consciousness of the present is constantly shaped by her memories of the past, and her journey through Bond Street is an evocation of English, as well as family, history. She is proud of her heritage, but aware that death is implicit in it.

She meets her old friend Hugh Whitbread, who tells her, in his indirect way, that his wife is "out of sorts" in menopause. And thinking that Mrs. Whitbread "is about my age," Clarissa remembers when Hugh would come over from Oxford years ago and she or her sister could not ride because of the menstrual period. Tears rise to her eyes when she sees her idol, Lady Bexborough, sitting like a queen in her carriage, with her quiet dignity, suffering, and determination to "go on." This perception, culminating in the words "there she is," foreshadows Peter's perception of Clarissa herself in the final words of the later *Mrs. Dalloway*, "For there she was."

Entering the shop, Clarissa notices at once that the shop-girl "looked quite old. . . . If it's the girl I remember she's twenty years older." Reluctant to put her to any trouble, "perhaps the one day in the month . . . when it's an agony to stand," Clarissa is on the verge of asking her to spend her holiday at the Dalloways' country home, but remembers the "lesson" of her honeymoon—of "the folly of giving impulsively." And her inhibition depresses her. Another customer enters and orders white gloves in an authoritative voice. Clarissa's thoughts return to mortality; she decides that if Richard were to die tomorrow, she herself, like Lady Bexborough, "would go on." The new customer is "gray-headed" and "elderly," and Clarissa wonders where she has seen her. The modulations of consciousness suggest, however, that she knows well enough: she thinks again of the dirge from *Cymbeline* which had been haunting her, "Fear no more the heat o' the sun," and of the war, "Thousands of young men had died that things might go on."

Then, as in *Mrs. Dalloway*, there is a loud explosion in the street. The shop-women cower, but Clarissa, "sitting very upright, smiled at the other lady. 'Miss Anstruther!' she exclaimed." The elderly spinster embodies the denial of openness, considerateness, sexuality, life itself— all which Clarissa represents. The explosion, reverberating with the full significance of the earlier allusions to war and death in the story, frightens the shop-girls. But Clarissa, in the deepening twilight of her life, despite the death of her God, her young man, and of thousands of young men, will choose, like Lady Bexborough, to go on.[10]

This choice, the unconscious and inarticulate, but nevertheless full expression of her character, is what the story is finally about. It is an argument for what Mrs. Woolf so often called "life itself." The references to menstruation and menopause suggest the nature as well as the limitations of the life force. And opposed to this is the authoritative masculine force represented by Big Ben ("nothing but steel rods consumed by rust if not for the care of H. M.'s Office of Works," Clarissa thinks) and by the war ("Thousands of young men had died . . .").

In this story Richard is a mere shadow; we see him only through Clarissa's consciousness, which has now become the center of Virginia Woolf's interest. Clarissa seems to feel that his sense of identity is far more certain than her own; he knows nothing of Shakespeare; and on their honeymoon he had taught her "the folly of giving impulsively." None of this is conclusive evidence as to Richard's character—which in any case is not very important in the Bond Street story—nor does it convey any very strong feeling about him. But the three oblique comments on Richard do seem to emphasize his masculinity: they could apply equally well to the most towering male in Mrs. Woolf's fiction, Mr. Ramsay of *To the Lighthouse*. His feeling about "the folly of giving impulsively" is the most telling of these three comments, for as Virginia Woolf now saw it, impulsive giving is at the heart of the feminine, instinctive acceptance of life—the everlasting yes which woman murmurs, muffling the thunder of man's everlasting no.

This had been Julia Stephen's secret, and her daughter was just now beginning to realize that it was Clarissa Dalloway's too. Although the Bond Street story is an interesting and successful vignette, Virginia Woolf new saw that her own fascination with Clarissa demanded much more than that. In her *Diary* for August 16, 1922, she wrote that Mrs. Dalloway "ushers in a host of others, I begin to perceive." It was not until Mrs. Woolf discovered who these others were and why they were necessary that she could learn why she was so fascinated with this seemingly shallow society woman. *Mrs. Dalloway* is the record of that discovery.

III

In its final form *Mrs. Dalloway* is a pattern of symbolic action in which the character of Clarissa is gradually revealed. In a sense the pattern ends where it began, with a view of Clarissa in her social role. At the climactic moment of the novel she moves away from her guests to the window to experience vicariously the young man's death and to contemplate her own. But Clarissa need not die tonight. She leaves the window and the little room of her isolated consciousness and, once more the perfect hostess, returns to her guests. Our final view of Clarissa is once more a social view, but it is now a much more satisfying view than our glimpse of her in Bond Street. Having seen her from many perspectives, we now know enough to share Peter's final perception of her wholeness: "For there she was."

The meaning of her story resides not so much in its specific ideas and insights, profound as they sometimes are, as in the way in which it is told. Most of it is "shown" (rather than "told") through interior monologue. The author enters the minds of more than two dozen characters, and describes their thoughts and actions in the third person. There is no stream-of-consciousness recording everything which passes through their minds, but selections and summaries in which the characters reveal themselves—and, indirectly, Clarissa. There is almost no direct interpretation or evaluation of this material by the author herself. Although the attitudes and thought patterns of the characters are differentiated, the language itself is not—in keeping with the assumption that, despite individual differences, human nature and experience are, in the largest sense, universal. But some of the narrative (perhaps ten percent) is not filtered through the consciousness of the characters, but told directly—though in the same style as that of the "subjective" passages.

Because the shifts in the narrative point of view are not always clearly "tagged," because they are sometimes very frequent and abrupt, and because the depth of penetration into the characters constantly changes, the reader is kept off balance in trying to identify the precise point of view and to evaluate the information being given. Confusing as such shifts often are, they are essential to the success of the narrative strategy, the revelation of Clarissa: "For there she was." It is essential that we do not understand her too soon, but that we learn about her as we should in real life—from many perspectives and from fragmentary and sometimes even contradictory evidence.

IV

The meaning of *Mrs. Dalloway* is evoked also through the configuration of the characters, through their relationships to Clarissa and to each other. The meaning of Clarissa's life and even of her personality, Mrs. Woolf discovered, lay in her feeling for other people. And this is why, in returning to the story for the last time, she saw that Clarissa "ushers in a host of others." The first and most crucial of these "others" is

Septimus. Appropriately, he first appears in her *Diary* for October 14, 1922, in the entry which records that *"Mrs. Dalloway* has branched into a book; and I adumbrate here a study of insanity and suicide; the world seen by the sane and the insane side by side. . . ."

In the opening panoramic view of Bond Street, we first see him as "pale-faced, beak-nosed" (a subliminal hint of his affinity with Clarissa, whose pallor is noticed by her old friends and who is often described with bird imagery). In the next paragraph we are drawn into his consciousness and into the terrors of his paranoia. He is the first of the major characters whose consciousness is revealed to us. In her Introduction to the Modern Library edition Virginia Woolf calls him Clarissa's "double." Like Clarissa, he has great sensitivity, insight, intelligence. But the direction of all of this is inward, so that he eventually becomes imprisoned within his own subjectivity, unable to relate his psychotic insights to the real world around him. Finally, the only way that he can preserve the purity of his "secret" (as Clarissa, with her own extraordinary insight, calls it) is through his own death. His world has become so small that all he can think to do when Dr. Holmes intrudes upon it is to jump out the window.

To those who take a sentimental view of Septimus, this may seem a heartless description of his suicide. But as the dark alter ego of Clarissa herself, he is at the heart of what the book is about, and it is important that we see his act as Virginia Woolf herself saw it. An "explanation" of his insanity and suicide was apparently necessary to the sanity and survival not only of the heroine, but of the author as well. The "tunnel" [11] which she excavates for Septimus is described directly rather than through the revelations of the other characters, as the other tunnels are constructed.

Septimus's history reveals a constantly increasing egocentricity and withdrawal from the real world—all of which ends, as it must, in death. He sees himself as the archetypal martyr, as Prometheus, as Christ, as "the most exalted of mankind," who must proclaim to the world an apocalyptic vision: "The supreme secret must be told to the Cabinet; first that trees are alive; next there is no crime; next love, universal love. . . ." [12] These and other insane pronouncements contain much truth, which is sometimes shocking in its impact, as when he recognizes Peter Walsh as a dead man (Peter had just awakened from his dream of death in Regent's Park), or when he recognizes his own inability to feel. Missing from these insights, however, is their essential human context. As his "tunnel" shows, Septimus has never been able to feel —in the sense of perceiving and responding to the real emotions of other people. His grotesque relationships with Miss Isabel Pole and especially with Lucrezia reveal this. He had asked Lucrezia to marry him "one evening when the panic was on him—that he could not feel" (p. 131).

Returning to London after the war, he neglects his work and immerses himself in his books once again. He discovers that Shakespeare "loathed humanity" and especially sex: "Love between man and woman was repulsive to Shakespeare. The business of copulation was filth to him before the end" (p. 134). So he turns away from Lucrezia, who now wants children, and descends further into misanthropy. The crisis comes when his wife, lonely and unhappy, weeps for the first time since their marriage. He hears her sobbing, but feels nothing, and

> At last, with a *melodramatic gesture* which he *assumed mechanically* and *with complete consciousness of its insincerity,* he dropped his head on his hands. Now *he had surrendered;* now other people must help him. People must be sent for. *He gave in.* (italics mine; p. 136)

The terror which human nature, "the brute with red nostrils," inspires in Septimus is entirely real and deserves our pity. But Virginia Woolf was careful to show that he is wrong, and to show how and why. "Shell shock" is Sir William Bradshaw's instant diagnosis, not hers. In her view Septimus, with complete consciousness of his insincerity, gave in. His despair and misanthropy, his visions and voices (complete with birds chattering in Greek), his terrifying inability to feel, his horror of sex and his decision not to have children—all this is Virginia Woolf's too. And she saw in Septimus's insanity, as in her own, a large measure of self-indulgence, and the fatal consequences of giving in to it.

V

The other characters are less important in their relationships to Clarissa than Septimus is, but each has a necessary role. Lucrezia, who is a reflector for Septimus, is also, symbolically, the fulfillment of Clarissa's relationship with Peter. Lucrezia submits completely to a man who demands everything, who inflicts himself upon her totally, without regard for the sanctity of her own individuality. He cannot relate her feelings to anything which seems real to him (i.e., to anything within the walls of his own subjectivity).

Seeing Peter at her party, standing in his corner, disapproving and aloof, Clarissa is angered: "But why had he come, then, merely to criticise? Why always take, never give? Why not risk one's little point of view?" (p. 255). He lacks, she feels, "the ghost of a notion of what any one else was feeling" (p. 69). Early in their relationship, she discovered that "with Peter everything had to be shared, everything gone into. And it was intolerable . . . she had to break with him or they would have been destroyed, both of them ruined, she was convinced . . ." (p. 10).

Richard does not force her to respond to him in any stereotyped way, does not try to "convert" her or to inflict his own values or personality upon her. He allows her to be herself. Bringing her roses at three in the afternoon, he can't tell her "in so many words" that he loves her. But the roses tell her; his gentle solicitude tells her. Peter, of course, would have told her in so many words; to him, experience must be abstract, verbal, to become meaningful. But Richard is much larger than that. His love for Clarissa goes far beyond the purely "masculine" pride, abstraction, and fascination with power which Clarissa knows are ultimately destructive. In this sense Richard now fulfills a strangely prophetic remark of Clarissa's in *The Voyage Out:* "He is man and woman as well." Mrs. Woolf had discovered that Clarissa's survival, like her own, depended upon a love which was at once sacred and profane, public and private, personal and impersonal, unlimited and undemanding. The Richard Dalloway of *The Voyage Out* was inconsistent with this new knowledge, and had to be transfigured.[13]

If Clarissa had married Peter, her fate could have been Lucrezia's; if she had not married, her fate could have been Miss Kilman's. Doris Kilman represents Clarissa's sexual inhibitions carried to a grotesque extreme. She is also the female counterpart of Septimus, for her denial of the flesh is, like his, a denial of life itself.

In Elizabeth Dalloway, Clarissa's heritage is personified. Torn between the forms of salvation offered by Clarissa and Miss Kilman, Elizabeth instinctively chooses life, much as Clarissa had reacted against the overwhelming demands of Peter. Elizabeth's pilgrimage through the Strand symbolically re-enacts Clarissa's journey on the omnibus years before (when she had revealed her theory of immortality to Peter) and is a similar commitment to the "divine vitality" of life.

Another form of salvation, secular and specious, is offered by Sir William Bradshaw, the smug and greedy psychiatrist whose insensitivity to Septimus's suffering is, in effect, a death warrant. Bradshaw is the guardian of the complacent and comfortable, who pay him to "shut people up," to declare, authoritatively, that to be radically different is to be insane and to deserve imprisonment. In some ways his world is as narrow as that of Septimus. But his views are sanctioned by society. The long, direct, and withering criticism of Bradshaw (the passage is quite out of proportion to its importance in the novel) also seems to be an expression of Mrs. Woolf's personal contempt for a kind of doctor she herself apparently encountered too often.[14]

VI

The themes implicit in this configuration of characters are also expressed in a coherent pattern of imagery which grows increasingly powerful and meaningful as the story unfolds. It ranges from the rather specific (the airplane, Peter's knife, Clarissa's dress, Miss Kilman's mackintosh), to the more generalized (flowers, trees, threads, colors), to the highly complex (the figures of the old grey nurse or the ancient street singer, the interplay of sun and waves, the concept of time). Daring, frequent, and consistent, it is seldom merely mechanical, but is convincing proof of the novel's depth and passion, its spontaneity and poetic intensity.

The dominant image, as in Virginia Woolf's other great novels, is the wave, symbolic of her view of life as powerful, mysterious, tumultuous, thrilling, threatening, fluctuating, finally breaking. Throughout *Mrs. Dalloway* the water imagery not only expresses this view of life, but also delineates and differentiates the characters.

Clarissa is a "mermaid" who rides the crest of the wave. The morning, she feels as the novel opens, is "fresh as if issued to children on a beach. . . . What a plunge!" and the air, reminding her of the early mornings at Bourton, when she was eighteen, is "like the flap of a wave; the kiss of a wave" (p. 3). She often feels, at the threshold of her drawing room, like a diver hesitating before his plunge. She is responsive to everything the wave represents, to the fullness of every moment. And sometimes she feels

a sudden revelation, a tinge like a blush which one tried to check

> and then, as it spread, one yielded to its expansion, and rushed to
> the farthest verge and there quivered and felt the world come closer,
> swollen with some astonishing significance, some pressure of rapture,
> which split its thin skin and gushed and poured with an extraordi-
> nary alleviation over the cracks and sores! Then, for that moment,
> she had seen an illumination . . . an inner meaning almost ex-
> pressed. (p. 47)

Here the sexual aspect of the wave imagery is evident; the moment of
illumination seems almost a moment of sexual climax. Though Clarissa
reproaches herself for her reserve, her coldness and impenetrability
(and Peter reproaches her too), this passage and others reveal, as Peter
finally realizes at her party, that she is not cold.

Approaching her house in Westminster and seeing the fashionable
guests arriving, Peter perceives the scene in terms appropriate to
Clarissa's role: "it seemed as if the whole of London were embarking
in little boats moored to the bank, tossing on the waters, as if the whole
place were floating off in carnival" (p. 249). The party itself is described
in a rather subdued way, without much use of the rich imagery we
have come to expect. But this is only to prepare us for the moments of
revelation to come, and increases our anticipation and appreciation of
them. At last Peter sees Clarissa escorting her prime minister into the
room:

> She wore . . . a silver-green mermaid's dress. Lolloping on the
> waves and braiding her tresses she seemed, having that gift still; to
> be; to exist; to sum it all up in the moment as she passed . . . all
> with the most perfect ease and air of a creature floating in its
> element. But age had brushed her; even as a mermaid might behold
> in her glass the setting sun on some very clear evening over the
> waves. There was a breath of tenderness; her severity, her prudery,
> her woodenness were all warmed through now. . . . (p. 264)

The dress, of course, is the one which Peter, thoroughly annoyed,
had watched her mend that morning. Though faded by the heat of the
sun, it is radiant still in the evening of her life.

Septimus, obsessed with martyrdom, sees himself as a drowned
sailor: "I went under the sea. I have been dead, and yet am now
alive, but let me rest still . . . as, before waking . . . the sleeper feels
himself drawing to the shores of life, so he felt himself drawing towards
life, the sun growing hotter . . ." (p. 104). Evident here is the contrast

between the motif of drowning and that of "the heat o' the sun," life, which Septimus must finally deny. Less evident, but also important, is the association with Clarissa's own fear of drowning: "far out to sea and alone, she always had the feeling that it was very, very dangerous to live even for one day" (p. 11).

Sitting beside the grey nurse on the bench in Regent's Park, Peter Walsh "sank into the plumes and feathers of sleep, sank, and was muffled over" (p. 85). As his consciousness drowns in sleep, he begins to dream—of death, which he sees as a woman "risen from the troubled sea . . . sucked up out of the waves to shower down from her magnificent hands compassion, comprehension, absolution" (p. 86). The imagery of waves and drowning suggests Peter's fear of, and preoccupation with, death, and subliminally links him with Clarissa and Septimus. Unlike Septimus, Peter can remain open to the same divine vitality which Clarissa loves. Though he cannot ride the crest of the wave, still he can perceive her as a mermaid.

Lucrezia, more fully "feminine" than Clarissa herself, is vital, open, responsive, committed. As she sews, Septimus is aware of her "bubbling, murmuring," and in his ears "her sentence bubbled away drip, drip, drip, like a contented tap left running" (p. 218). After his death she is left with her memories ("most were happy"), "the caress of the sea, as it seemed to her, hollowing them in its arched shell and murmuring to her laid on shore, strewn she felt, like flying flowers over some tomb" (p. 228). In other words, the sea of divine vitality hallows her memories and gently returns them to the shores of life.

Miss Kilman denies this divine vitality. The sound of St. Margaret's, Clarissa's clock, "seemed to break, like the spray of an exhausted wave, upon the body of Miss Kilman standing still in the street for a moment to mutter 'It is the flesh' " (p. 194). Though Clarissa herself is afraid of sex, afraid of life, she can still, like a mermaid, ride the crest of that divine vitality. But Miss Kilman can only deny the vitality and wrap her grotesque virginity in her ugly, water-repellent mackintosh, which is also her shroud.

VII

The sounds of St. Margaret's and of Big Ben associate the water imagery with the theme of time. As Mrs. Woolf had recognized in her tentative title for this novel, *The Hours,* time is a necessary and inevitable theme of Clarissa's story. And like the wave imagery the motif of time serves to define individual characters, as well as a world view.

Throughout *Mrs. Dalloway* Big Ben announces the time: "First a warning, musical, then the hour irrevocable. The leaden circles dissolved in the air." The warning is musical, an anticipation of the hours, a perception of time as future, as promise. It is this promise that Clarissa is in love with: she feels "a particular hush or solemnity; an indescribable pause; a suspense (but that might be her heart, affected, they said, by influenza) before Big Ben strikes" (pp. 4–5). But the promise is also a warning. It is followed by the hour, irrevocable. The moment is solemn because it contains its own negation, and Clarissa's feeling of solemnity is also an awareness of her mortality: "the pause . . . might be her heart." First promising more moments, Big Ben finally announces the loss of moments, in an irrevocable confirmation of death. But this too has its negation: the narrow prison of death dissolves in the air, in the ambience of life itself, which is timeless.

Clarissa has a "transcendental theory" which contravenes Big Ben's warning. Peter remembers how, many years before, in their enchanted voyage on the omnibus through the Strand, she had told him that

> to know her, or any one, one must seek out the people who completed them; even the places. Odd affinities she had with people she had never spoken to. . . . It ended in a transcendental theory which, with her horror of death, allowed her to believe, or say that she believed (for all her scepticism), that since our apparitions, the part of us which appears, are so momentary compared with the other, the unseen part of us, which spreads wide, the unseen might survive, be recovered somehow attached to this person or that, or even haunting certain places after death . . . perhaps—perhaps. (pp. 231–232)

Placed in the scene following Septimus's suicide, Clarissa's "theory" brings his death into perspective.

But it is far more than theory, and it is not merely transcendental. It is a very concrete, practical approach to life. For Clarissa recognizes what Septimus never can—that the essence of one's personality and experience is not separate and unique, but only fulfilled and completed in other people. (Even Septimus will survive—in Lucrezia's memories, of which "most were happy.") So Clarissa is identified not with Big Ben, though the strokes of those irrevocable hours haunt her, but with St. Margaret's, which always strikes two minutes late:

> Ah, said St. Margaret's, like a hostess who comes into her drawing-room on the very stroke of the hour and finds her guests there already. I am not late. No, it is precisely half-past eleven, she says. Yet, though she is perfectly right, her voice, being the voice of the hostess, is reluctant to inflict its individuality. Some grief for the past holds it back, some concern for the present. . . . And the sound of St. Margaret's glides into the recesses of the heart and buries itself in ring after ring of sound, like something alive which wants to confide itself, to disperse itself, to be, with a tremor of delight, at rest—like Clarissa herself, thought Peter Walsh . . . with a deep emotion, and an extraordinarily clear, yet puzzling, recollection of her, as if this bell had come into the room years ago, where they sat at some moment of great intimacy, and had gone from one to the other and had left, like a bee with honey, laden with the moment. (pp. 74–75)

Inevitably, the voice of St. Margaret's breaks like an exhausted wave upon the body of Miss Kilman. And for Septimus, time is only a dead, dry word which splits its husk. He composes "an immortal ode to Time" (p. 105), to the dead, but cannot bear to look upon time or death as they really are. Septimus, "smiling mysteriously," announces "I will tell you the time" (p. 106). In closing himself to the ambience of life, he has become the leaden, authoritative voice of Big Ben. But Clarissa creates a warm, living celebration of the moment, which she loves. As the lovely voice of St. Margaret's, with her feminine "lap full of odds and ends," she is fully aware of death, but denies that it is mighty, just, or eloquent, and moves instead into the recesses of the heart, to create "every moment afresh."

There is one other voice of time in *Mrs. Dalloway:* "the clocks of Harley Street nibbled at the June day, counselled submission, upheld authority, and pointed out in chorus the supreme advantages of a sense of proportion . . ." (pp. 154–155). Associated with the despicable Bradshaw, these clocks are the voice of the Establishment. Significantly, they introduce the smug "ruminations" of Hugh Whitbread, who, like Bradshaw, is a cautious, complacent, pompous parasite. Just as Septimus exemplifies the darkest psychic forces within

Clarissa, so Bradshaw and Whitbread represent the most decadent forces
within her social class.

VIII

In this final version of the Dalloway story, Clarissa and Richard exemplify the best qualities of their society. Their transfiguration from
The Voyage Out through the Bond Street story to *Mrs. Dalloway*—from
caricatures to characters, from satirical examples to serious ex-
emplars—is interesting not only in itself but as an index to the growth
of Virginia Woolf's art and attitudes. She confessed to her *Diary* that
she never overcame her original dislike of Mrs. Dalloway,[15] and it is
true that even in the final version of the story there is some disdain
for the trivia of Clarissa's everyday life. But there is also the conviction
that, in the largest sense, her life is anything but trivial. On the surface, her parties are frivolous, but they bring people together, expand
their awareness. They are truly, as Clarissa somehow knows, "an
offering" (p. 184), a sacrament to life itself. Clarissa's gift reaches its
full ironic definition in Septimus's final offering: " 'I'll give it you!'
he cried, and flung himself vigorously, violently down on to Mrs.
Filmer's area railings" (p. 226). Clarissa's feeling for family, social,
and national traditions may sometimes be too sentimental, but the
fact remains that these traditions deserve to be taken seriously. The
crowd in Bond Street is distracted from the prime minister's car by
the airplane, herald of the new era, writing its meaningless message
in the wind;[16] but Clarissa is not distracted, and she is right.

Mrs. Dalloway's secret, which Virginia Woolf worked so long and
so passionately to discover, is very close to the recent theories of psy-
chotherapy which have been based upon existential phenomenology.[17]
For Clarissa existence is not merely an abstraction (despite her abstract "theory" about it), but primarily tangible and concrete. All
phenomena that appear to her are regarded as real, and are granted
admission to her awareness. Throughout her life she has enlarged the
dimensions of that awareness; she allows people and things to dis-
close themselves to her fully and as they really are. She resents Bradshaw and Miss Kilman and their absolutes, the rigid categories into
which they force experience: "Had she ever tried to convert anyone
herself? Did she not wish everybody merely to be themselves?" (p. 191).
And she remains open to her own possibilities: "she would not say

of herself, I am this, I am that" (p. 11). So her nature is dynamic, always emerging, growing, as she discovers new dimensions in her existence, new possibilities for relating to and caring for its unfolding phenomena. And as these possibilities increase, she gains increasing freedom.

Because Septimus narrows down and closes off the possibilities of his existence, he is condemned to death. Like Melville's Bartleby, Septimus replies to life with "I prefer not to." Clarissa, with her great empathy, shares even the physical sensations of this young man's death. It opens an abyss for her and thus places her own commitment in a larger perspective. In throwing his life away, he has somehow made her feel the dimensions and mystery of her own.

That mystery, which may be explored and even partially illuminated, but never finally explained, is what Virginia Woolf's greatest books are about. The unique, almost incredible awareness which enabled her to write them also made it very difficult and dangerous for her, like Mrs. Dalloway, to live for even one day. At last, with her London and her civilization in the throes of Hitler's apocalypse, and with her inner existence also narrowed and threatened by the returning voices of her insanity, Virginia Woolf "gave in": the fate she had discovered for Clarissa's darker self became at last her own. But the secret she discovered in Clarissa's story had helped to forestall that fate, and from these new regions of Virginia Woolf's awareness there emerged some of our very greatest fiction. Like the voice of St. Margaret's, reluctant to inflict its individuality, with some grief for the past, some concern for the present, it moves into the recesses of the heart— there, in miraculous proof of Clarissa's "transcendental theory," to reverberate forever.

Notes

1. "The New Dress," "The Man Who Loved His Kind," "Together and Apart," and "A Summing Up." The first story was published originally in *Forum* (New York, May 1927), LXXVII, 704–711. The others appeared for the first time in the posthumous collection (1944).

2. *Mrs. Dalloway,* Modern Library ed. (New York, 1928), p. vi.

3. David Daiches, *The Novel and the Modern World* (Chicago, 1965), p. 10.

4. Leonard Woolf, *Beginning Again* (New York: Harcourt, 1964), p. 172. The five volumes of Leonard Woolf's autobiography are *Sowing: An Autobiography of the Years 1880–1904* (1960), *Growing . . . 1904–1911* (1962), *Beginning Again . . . 1911 to 1918* (1964), *Downhill All the Way . . . 1919 to 1939* (1967), and *The Journey Not the Arrival Matters . . . 1939–1969* (1970), all published by Harcourt and, in England, by the Hogarth Press. This autobiography and Virginia Woolf's *A Writer's Diary* are the basic sources available to date for the facts of Mrs. Woolf's life. For an excellent bibliography of her work, see the Soho Bibliography by B. J. Kirkpatrick, *A Bibliography of Virginia Woolf* (rev. ed.; London, 1967).

5. *Beginning Again,* p. 161.

6. For a discussion and full bibliography of Mrs. Woolf's notions of masculine and feminine traits and their ideal synthesis in "the androgynous mind," see Herbert Marder, *Feminism and Art: A Study of Virginia Woolf* (Chicago, 1968). An adequate description of her very complex and ambivalent attitudes toward her parents is beyond the scope of this essay; the fullest and most accurate expression of these feelings is her novel *To the Lighthouse,* in which her parents are Mr. and Mrs. Ramsay.

7. *Downhill All the Way,* p. 50. This entry had not been included by Mr. Woolf in his edition of *A Writer's Diary.*

8. Julia Stephen died when her daughter Virginia was thirteen. At first Virginia felt nothing; then she collapsed and attempted suicide. She also experienced breakdowns when Stella Duckworth died in pregnancy a year later and when Thoby died in 1906. These three appear as Mrs. Ramsay, Prue, and Andrew in *To the Lighthouse.*

9. *The Dial,* LXXV (July 1923), 20–27.

10. The young man's name in the story is Jack Stewart; he may be a prototype for Peter Walsh. Clarissa thinks how he would have made fun of her for quoting Shelley in Picadilly. The Bond Street story is much fuller and more specific in its references to people and places than the corresponding section of *Mrs. Dalloway.*

11. Apparently in August 1923 Mrs. Woolf found her technical "key" to the story: "what I call my tunnelling process, by which I tell the past by installments, as I have need of it" *(A Writer's Diary: Being Extracts from the Diary of Virginia Woolf,* ed. Leonard Woolf, New York, 1954, p. 60, October 15, 1923).

12. *Mrs. Dalloway,* Harvest Books ed. (New York: Harcourt, 1953), p. 102. Page numbers to this edition are subsequently given parenthetically in my text.

13. The later Mr. Dalloway is a tribute to Leonard Woolf, the man who in real life embodied these same vital qualities. His autobiography, though consciously understated and remarkably objective, reveals the great dimensions of the Woolfs' love for each other.

14. *Downhill All the Way* describes an encounter with a Harley Street physician who seems very like Sir William Bradshaw. In their odyssey through the offices of various specialists and pathologists, the Woolfs encountered at least three distinguished doctors, each of whom found

> that Virginia was suffering from the disease in which he specialized. He was wrong; we ignored his diagnosis and decided to forget about it and Harley Street. She not only recovered from the three fatal and incurable diseases; the disquieting symptoms gradually disappeared.
>
> At our last interview with the last famous Harley Street specialist to whom we paid our three guineas, the great Dr. Saintsbury, as he shook Virginia's hand, said to her: "Equanimity—equanimity—practise equanimity, Mrs. Woolf." It was, no doubt, excellent advice and worth the three guineas, but, as the door closed behind us, I felt he might just as usefully have said: "A normal temperature—ninety-eight point four—practise a normal temperature, Mrs. Woolf." (p. 50)

"Equanimity" is only another name for "Proportion, divine proportion, Sir William's goddess" (p. 150). The Woolfs' response seems considerably more realistic than the advice itself.

15. *A Writer's Diary*, pp. 77–78 (June 18, 1925).

16. The airplane, as it turns out, is advertising toffee. Various people in the crowd interpret the skywriting variously, but Clarissa, significantly, does not notice it: " 'What are they looking at?' said Clarissa Dalloway to the maid who opened her door" (p. 42). But to Septimus it is a revelation of "unimaginable beauty" (p. 31), a prophetic vision which will divorce him increasingly from real phenomena and finally from life itself. The response of the crowd, whose eyes are turned from the institutions of the past toward the instruments of the future, is also ominous: the new reality, written in the wind, has no meaning other than the subjective responses to it.

17. Medard Boss's *Psychoanalysis and Daseinsanalysis* (trans. Ludwig B. Lefebre; New York, 1963) is a powerful and fascinating application of existential phenomenology in psychoanalysis. The terms in which Clarissa's personality are described here are adapted largely from Dr. Boss's book.

Mrs. Woolf herself was undoubtedly well acquainted with early psychoanalytical theory. Her husband says, in *Downhill All the Way* that

> In the decade before 1924 in the so-called Bloomsbury circle there was great interest in Freud and psycho-analysis, and the interest was extremely serious. Adrian Stephen, Virginia's brother . . . with his wife Karin, became a qualified doctor and professional psycho-analyst. James Strachey, Lytton's youngest brother, and his wife also became professional psycho-analysts. James went to Vienna and was analysed by Freud, and he played an active part in the Institute of Psycho-Analysis, which . . . had been founded in London. . . . (p. 164)

In 1924 the Woolfs' Hogarth Press became Freud's English publisher and the publisher of the International Psycho-Analytical Library. Mrs. Woolf did not meet Freud himself until 1939, after he escaped to London from the Nazis. Mr. Woolf says that Freud, in great pain now from the cancer which was to kill him eight months later, "was extraordinarily courteous in a formal, old-fashioned way—for instance, almost ceremoniously he presented Virginia with a flower" (pp. 168–169).